CASS SERIES: STUDIES IN INTELLIGENCE
(Series Editors: Christopher Andrew and Richard J. Aldrich)

OUR MAN IN YUGOSLAVIA
The story of a Secret Service Operative

D1547986

Also in the Intelligence Series

British Military Intelligence in the Palestine Campaign 1914–1918 by Yigal Sheffy
British Military Intelligence in the Crimean War, 1854–1856 by Stephen M. Harris
Signals Intelligence in World War II edited by David Alvarez
Knowing Your Friends: Intelligence Inside Alliances and Coalitions from 1914 to the Cold War edited by Martin S. Alexander
Eternal Vigilance: 50 Years of the CIA edited by Rhodri Jeffreys-Jones and Christopher Andrew
Nothing Sacred: Nazi Espionage against the Vatican, 1939–1945 by David Alvarez and Revd. Robert A. Graham
Intelligence Investigations: How Ultra Changed History by Ralph Bennett
Intelligence Analysis and Assessment edited by David Charters, A. Stuart Farson and Glenn P. Hastedt
TET 1968: Understanding the Surprise by Ronnie E. Ford
Intelligence and Imperial Defence: British Intelligence and the Defence of the Indian Empire 1904–1924 by Richard J. Popplewell
Espionage: Past, Present, Future? edited by Wesley K. Wark
The Australian Security Intelligence Organization: An Unofficial History by Frank Cain
Policing Politics: Security Intelligence and the Liberal Democratic State by Peter Gill
From Information to Intrigue: Studies in Secret Service Based on the Swedish Experience 1939–45 by C. G. McKay
Dieppe Revisited: A Documentary Investigation by John Campbell
More Instructions from the Centre by Andrew Gordievsky
Controlling Intelligence edited by Glenn P. Hastedt
Spy Fiction, Spy Films and Real Intelligence edited by Wesley K. Wark
Security and Intelligence in a Changing World: New Perspectives for the 1990s edited by A. Stuart Farson, David Stafford and Wesley K. Wark
A Don at War by Sir David Hunt K.C.M.G., O.B.E. (reprint)
Intelligence and Military Operations edited by Michael I. Handel
Leaders and Intelligence edited by Michael I. Handel
War, Strategy and Intelligence by Michael I. Handel
Strategic and Operational Deception in the Second World War edited by Michael I. Handel
Codebreaker in the Far East by Alan Stripp
Intelligence for Peace edited by Hesi Carmel
Intelligence Services in the Information Age by Michael Herman
Espionage and the Roots of the Cold War: The Conspiratorial Heritage by David McKnight
Swedish Signal Intelligence 1900–1945 by C.G. McKay and Bengt Beckman
The Norwegian Intelligence Service 1945–1970 by Olav Riste
Secret Intelligence in the Twentieth Century edited by Heike Bungert, Jan G. Heitmann and Michael Wala
The CIA, the British Left and the Cold War: Calling the Tune? by Hugh Wilford

OUR MAN IN YUGOSLAVIA
The story of a
Secret Service Operative

SEBASTIAN RITCHIE

FRANK CASS
LONDON • PORTLAND, OR

First published in 2004 in Great Britain by
FRANK CASS PUBLISHERS
2 Park Square, Milton Park,
Abingdon, Oxon OX14 4RN

and in the United States of America by
FRANK CASS PUBLISHERS
270 Madison Ave,
New York, NY 10016

Transferred to Digital Printing 2005

Website: www.tandf.co.uk

Ritchie, Sebastian, 1963
  Our man in Yugoslavia: the story of a secret service operative
  1. Reed, Owen 2. Great Britain. MI6 3. Intelligence officers – Great Britain –
  Biography 4. World War, 1939–1945 – Campaigns – Yugoslavia 5. World War,
  1939–1945 – Secret Service – Great Britain
  I. Title
  940.5'48641'092

ISBN 0 7146 5559 7 (cloth)
ISBN 0 7146 8441 4 (paper)
ISSN: 1368–9916

Library of Congress Cataloging-in-Publication Data

Ritchie, Sebastian, 1963 –
  Our man in Yugoslavia: the story of a Secret Service Operative/Sebastian Ritchie.
    p. cm
  Includes bibliographical references and index.
  ISBN 0-7146-5559-7 – ISBN 0-7146-8441-4 (pbk.)
  1. Reed, Owen, d. 1997 2. Great Britain. MI6 – History. 3. World War,
  1939–1945 – Secret Service – Great Britain 4. World War, 1939–1945 –
  Underground movements – Yugoslavia. 5. Yugoslavia – History – Axis
  occupation, 1941–1945. 6. Spies – Great Britain – Biography. I. Title.

D810.S8R357 2004
940.54'8641'09497–dc22

2003069763

Typeset in 10/12pt Sabon by FiSH Books, London WC1

To All Good Folks round Wallow Barrow Crag

Contents

List of Photographs and Maps

Abbreviations

AFHQ	Air Forces Headquarters
BLO	British liaison officer
CIGS	Chief of the Imperial General Staff
CSA	Committee for Secret Activities
ESB	Egyptian State Broadcasting
Force 133	SOE Middle East (1941–43)
Force 266	SOE/British Military Mission to Yugoslavia, Bari (1943–44)
Force 399	British Military Mission to Central Europe (1944–45)
GHQ	General Headquarters
GSH	Glavni Stab Hrvatska (Partisan General Staff Croatia)
HSS	Hrvatska Seljacka Stranka (Croatian Peasants Party)
ISLD	Inter-Services Liaison Department (SIS in the Middle East)
JANL	Yugoslav Army of National Liberation
JOS	Joint Operations Staff
LO	Liaison Officer
LRDG	Long Range Desert Group
MAAF	Mediterranean Allied Air Force
MAC	Mediterranean Air Command
MEBU	Middle East Broadcasting Unit
MI9	British escape and evasion organization in the Second World War
NAAFI	Navy, Army and Air Force Institutes
OCTU	Officer Cadet Training Unit
OKW	Oberkommando des Wehrmacht (German Army High Command)
OSS	Office of Strategic Services
OZNA	Odsek-odeljenje zastite naroda (Department for People Protection)
PWE	Political Warfare Executive
RAC	Royal Armoured Corps

RNVR	Royal Navy Volunteer Reserve
RTR	Royal Tank Regiment
SACMED	Supreme Allied Commander Mediterranean
SAS	Special Air Service
SASO	Senior Air Staff Officer
SBS	Special Boat Service
SIME	Security Intelligence Middle East
SIS	Secret Intelligence Service (also known as MI6 and 'C')
SOE	Special Operations Executive
1 I(U) Section	SIS's operations section in Bari
UNRRA	United Nations Relief and Rehabilitation Administration
USAAF	United States Army Air Force
ZAVNOH	Zemaljsko Anti-fasisticko Vijece Narodnog Oslobodjenja Hrvatska (Partisan government of Croatia)

FILES HELD BY THE NATIONAL ARCHIVES CITED IN THE NOTES

AIR	Files of the Air Ministry and the Royal Air Force
BW	Files of the British Council
CAB	Files of the Cabinet Office
FO	Files of the Foreign and Commonwealth Office
HS	Files of the Special Operations Executive
HW	Files of the Government Communications Headquarters
PREM	Files of the Prime Minister
WO	Files of the War Office and the Army

OTHER ARCHIVAL SOURCES

AHB	Air Historical Branch
BBC	British Broadcasting Corporation archive
RP	Private papers of Owen Reed

Acknowledgements

This book was an entirely private and personal project researched and written in my spare time. It is not a product of my work as an official historian at the Air Historical Branch (RAF). It is largely based on records held by the family of Owen Reed, and on documents available to the public at the National Archives in London, and I have neither sought nor received any privileged access to documents of any kind on the basis of my official position.

The research on which it is based began as long ago as 1989, when I had no expectation of finding sufficient material to produce a manuscript of this length. I conducted a short interview with Reed, and he gave me his wartime diaries and the few papers he had kept on his time in Yugoslavia. I then built up a day-to-day log of his activities there, using such records as I could find in the National Archives – largely those in the War Office classes. But it was only after his death, when his wartime correspondence and other relevant papers became available, that I realized a book might be possible. It seemed to me that such a study would be eminently worthwhile given the near-total absence of documented work on the Secret Intelligence Service – a gaping hole in the history of British intelligence in the Second World War. A more detailed understanding of their role might fundamentally change current interpretations of wartime events, in the same way that the history of the War was substantially revised after the disclosure of the so-called 'Ultra secret' in the 1970s.

Invaluable help has come from quarters far too numerous to acknowledge comprehensively here. But I would particularly like to thank the Reed family for access to Owen Reed's wartime papers, photographs, correspondence and record of service. I am also indebted to Michael Foot and Ann Lane for assistance and encouragement and for reading and commenting on the manuscript, and to Mark Wheeler for some valuable research leads. At the Air Historical Branch I benefited immeasurably from Clive Richards' encyclopaedic knowledge of the sources in the National

Archives, while Mary Hudson was extremely helpful with photographs, and Sebastian Cox's interest and enthusiasm spurred me on. Similar encouragement came from Richard Overy at King's College, London. The symposium on intelligence and special operations held at the Royal Military College, Canada, in 2002, proved hugely valuable in suggesting some broader lessons that might be drawn from Reed's story and I am deeply grateful to Brian McKercher both for organizing the symposium and for inviting me to present a paper.

Otherwise, it is a fact that this book could never have been written without the assistance of Owen Reed himself. Sadly, however, he did not live to read it. He alone might have been able to correct such errors and omissions as have undoubtedly found their way into its pages but which nevertheless remain entirely my responsibility.

Introduction

This book is not so much a biography as an operational history. Its subject, Owen Reed, was a successful BBC broadcaster, who eventually rose to become head of Children's Television and later of Staff Training. His legacy to the world of broadcasting included such enormously popular British children's programmes as *Play School* and *Blue Peter* – still running after more than 40 years. However, Reed was never prominent in public or business life, and his full life story would make interesting but not especially remarkable reading. Yet his record during the Second World War is a very different matter, for it was during the War that he found his way through convoluted channels into the employment of the British Secret Intelligence Service (SIS – also known as MI6), who parachuted him into German-occupied Yugoslavia. There he worked as an intelligence officer with the communist resistance forces, or Partisans, supplying information to SIS on enemy activities and on the Partisan movement itself. The story of his time with SIS is the central focus of the following narrative: it is, to the author's knowledge, the first documented history of a British Secret Service field operative.

Reed's SIS assignments to Yugoslavia involved close collaboration with the Special Operations Executive (SOE) – the organization responsible for sabotage and subversion in enemy-held territory; during the first half of 1944 he effectively worked for both SIS and SOE simultaneously. But whereas SOE's wartime role in Yugoslavia has been the subject of an enormous literature over the past two decades, SIS's operations there have received hardly any attention from historians. This omission results not from any lack of interest but from the fact that the vast majority of SIS records remain classified and therefore cannot be employed for historical research without official sanction.[1] Fortunately, though, Reed's close proximity to SOE resulted in the opening of many documents relating to his wartime exploits, including signal logs, reports and a small file of SIS papers relating to his assignment to Istria in 1944, which was somehow overlooked by the weeders. He also kept brief diaries and a number of papers, and gave interviews both to the BBC and to the author before his death in 1997. Numerous private letters were then also located and made available to the author. These sources, together with a variety of published memoirs by SOE officers, permitted the reconstruction of Owen Reed's war, from his enlistment into the Army to his service as a liaison officer at El Alamein, from the illness that stranded him in Cairo to his recruitment into SIS, and from his first parachute drop into Yugoslavia in October 1943 to his final evacuation in July 1945.

If the result is a very personal account, Reed's story nevertheless sheds important new light on the wartime history of SIS – one of the world's most secretive organizations. Academic research on the development of British policy towards Yugoslavia in the Second World War has largely concentrated on the period between the spring of 1941 and the winter of 1943, and on the protracted debates surrounding Churchill's decision to reorient British support away from the so-called 'Chetnik' royalist guerrillas headed by Draza Mihailovic and towards Tito's Partisans. Scholars have located little evidence to suggest significant SIS involvement in Yugoslavia in this period.[2] The multi-volume official history, *British Intelligence in the Second World War*, records that 'the SIS played little part in developments in Yugoslavia'. The activities of their Yugoslav section are said to have been 'frustrated by the competing demands of the SOE for the limited transport available' and by the difficulty of recruiting 'agents who were independent of the resistance organizations'. Intelligence reports from agents inside Yugoslavia allegedly came from 'SOE liaison missions' with the Partisans rather than from SIS operatives.[3]

Memoirs written by former members of SOE and its successor in Yugoslavia, the British Military Mission, have presented only a slightly more informative picture. Fitzroy Maclean, Churchill's personal envoy to Tito, who headed the Military Mission, makes absolutely no mention of SIS in his famous account, *Eastern Approaches*, presumably for security reasons.[4] Sir William Deakin, who participated in a joint SOE-SIS mission to the Partisans in May 1943, similarly avoided any reference to SIS in his memoirs, describing SIS operatives as 'military intelligence officers', and referring to SIS as the 'War Office'.[5] Others, such as Michael Lees, have acknowledged the presence of an SIS operation in Yugoslavia only to sustain their criticism of British policy there, arguing that key SIS staff were communist sympathizers who slanted their reports in order to secure British support for the Partisan cause.[6] More recent works by Sir Peter Wilkinson and Franklin Lindsay offer only fleeting references to SIS, but dwell on their bungled attempt to infiltrate two agents into Austria through Slovenia, on the subsequent capture of one of them, and on his treachery in divulging the location of nearby Partisan and Allied units to the Germans. Wilkinson was far more complimentary about Reed himself, but failed to identify him as an SIS officer.[7]

No academic studies have focused specifically on the history of SIS in the Second World War. From beyond the academic community, a number of authors have surveyed the lives and careers of well-known SIS personalities, such as Sir Stewart Menzies and Kim Philby, relying heavily on interviews and on secondary sources to compensate for the prevailing shortage of SIS documents, with varying degrees of success. Inevitably the results tell us more about the specific individuals concerned than the operations they conducted.[8] Nigel West's more general history of SIS is both interesting and authoritative, but sadly it is not documented. Moreover, as a survey of the period 1909–45, West's study inevitably lacks detailed coverage of many SIS operations during the wartime period. Where Yugoslavia is concerned, for example, he referred only to the infiltration of two agents into Tito's headquarters in Montenegro in 1943, one of whom was killed shortly after his arrival.[9]

By unlocking a chain of documentary evidence on SIS activity in Yugoslavia extending from the early months of the Second World War to the conclusion of hostilities in 1945, Reed's story strongly suggested a need to revise these fleeting and often negative judgements. The public availability of such documentation alone indicated that a more thorough investigation of SIS's wartime role in Yugoslavia was long overdue. But while it was always to be expected that such an exercise might allow some of the existing verdicts on the Service to be reappraised, there is far more to Reed's story than this. Indeed, it represents a much-needed case study illustrating how one British officer found his way into SIS, the means by which the Service's field operatives were recruited and trained, their objectives in Yugoslavia, the problems they encountered in working there and the extent to which they fulfilled their missions. A central theme throughout is the changing relationship between SIS and the Partisans – their initial solidarity, founded on the common objective of defeating fascism, and the later deterioration, as the Second World War ended and the Cold War began. As this relationship altered, so too did SIS's intelligence priorities. The implications of Reed's experiences for our more general understanding of SIS's wartime history in this theatre are considered in the final chapter.

In what is primarily a work of military history rather than biography it would not be appropriate to dwell on Reed's private life in any detail, but one fundamental truth should be emphasized. Throughout his life he was above all else a family man, who loved nothing more than the company of those nearest and dearest to him. During the War he encountered many hardships and dangers between the Egyptian desert and the mountains of Yugoslavia. He was exposed to enemy fire, bombing and strafing; he witnessed the death or injury of many of his comrades at El Alamein; and he was parachuted into a completely unknown foreign country, occupied by the Germans, where for a time he worked in near-total isolation from other Allied personnel. Fear, loneliness and demoralization – the inevitable human reactions to such experiences – had periodically to be confronted and conquered. Yet throughout this story not one of these trials and tribulations weighed so heavily upon him as the challenge of enduring years of enforced separation from his wife and children.

NOTES

1. This does not mean that there are no SIS records to be found in the National Archives. The most rewarding classes are the War Office (WO) series and Special Operations Executive (SOE) (HS) series; some War Office files contain unadulterated SIS material, apparently because the reviewers did not realize that the Inter-Services Liaison Department (ISLD) was a cover name for SIS. Official policy concerning SIS documents has changed in recent years. Most wartime SIS papers were routinely removed from the Foreign Office files before their despatch to the National Archives in the 1970s in accordance with Section 3(4) of the Public Records Act of 1958. This states that 'any records may be retained after the said period [30 years] if, in the opinion of the person who is responsible for them, they are required for administrative purposes or ought to be retained for any other special reason'. But the SOE files opened in the 1990s contain photocopies of SIS minutes and memoranda from which the signatures have been removed. The infiltration of SIS agents into enemy-occupied territory is recorded in considerable detail in the RAF (Air Ministry and the Royal Air Force – AIR) classes at the National Archives. Both the WO and AIR classes reveal names that have been painstakingly concealed in the HS series. The British Council (BW) papers held by the National Archives also shed some interesting light on SIS activities in Yugoslavia prior to the German occupation in 1941.
2. M.C. Wheeler, *Britain and the War for Yugoslavia, 1940–1943* (Boulder, CO: East European Monographs distributed by New York: Columbia University Press, 1980), p. 164; S. Trew, *Britain, Mihailovic and the Chetniks, 1941–42* (London: Macmillan, 1998), pp. 130–1. See also M. Deroc, *British Special Operations Explored: Yugoslavia in Turmoil 1941-1943 and the British Response* (Boulder, CO: East European Monographs/distributed by New York: Columbia University Press, 1988).
3. F.H. Hinsley with E.E. Thomas, C.F.G. Ransom and R.C. Knight, *British Intelligence in the Second World War*, vol. 1 (London: HMSO, 1979), pp. 369–70, 371; *ibid.*, vol. 3, pt 1 (London: HMSO, 1985), p. 144.
4. F. Maclean, *Eastern Approaches* (London: Reprint Society, 1949). Written so soon after the War, Maclean's book would probably have been subject to particularly rigorous vetting procedures.
5. F.W.D. Deakin, *The Embattled Mountain* (Oxford: Oxford University Press, 1971), pp. 108, 181.
6. M. Lees, *The Rape of Serbia: The British Role in Tito's Grab for Power 1943–1944* (San Diego/New York/London: Harcourt Brace Jovanovich, 1990), p. 37; a very similar critique is presented in D. Martin, *The Web of*

Disinformation: Churchill's Yugoslav Blunder (San Diego/New York/London: Harcourt Brace Jovanovich, 1990). Both of these studies are polemics that exaggerate Britain's influence on Yugoslavia's internal politics during the Second World War and largely ignore the strategic considerations that persuaded the Western Allies to support the Partisans.

7. F. Lindsay, *Beacons in the Night: With the OSS and Tito's Partisans in Wartime Yugoslavia* (Stanford, CA: Stanford University Press, 1993), pp. 158–9; P. Wilkinson, *Foreign Fields: The Story of an SOE Operative* (London: I.B. Taurus, 1997), pp. 149, 151, 180–2, 198. Wilkinson described Reed as a British liaison officer, the term normally used to describe officers from SOE, and later from the Military Mission.

8. See, for example, A. Cave Brown, *'C': The Secret Life of Sir Stewart Menzies, Spymaster to Winston Churchill* (New York: Macmillan, 1987). There is unlikely ever to be a more comprehensive account of Menzies' life, but the limitations of Cave Brown's study are amply demonstrated by his near-total neglect of SIS's Middle East operation, which he wrongly claims to have been launched in Algiers in the summer of 1943. Of the various accounts of Philby's treacherous career the author found A. Boyle's *The Fourth Man* (New York: Dial Press, 1979) particularly impressive.

9. N. West, *MI6: British Secret Intelligence Service Operations, 1909–1945* (London: Grafton, 1985), p. 383. While West succeeded in locating and interviewing many former SIS officers and staff, his research in the National Archives was apparently confined to the Foreign Office classes. He therefore overlooked many references to SIS in the War Office and AIR files, and in some of the official Second World War narratives.

1

The Life and Death of the 24th Armoured Brigade

Owen Reed was born in Putney, London, on 13 September 1910. He was youngest of the four children of Arthur Reed, a professor of English at King's College, London, and of Esther Reed, née Casson, a younger sister of the actor Sir Lewis Casson. Reed was educated at King's College School, Wimbledon, and read Classics at Christ Church, Oxford. Although his childhood was overshadowed by the First World War, in which he lost two uncles, he grew up very happily in a close-knit and supportive middle-class family. His parents were devoted to their children's educational advancement but also strongly encouraged more active outdoor pursuits, such as walking and motorcycling: Reed early developed a life-long enthusiasm for motorized transport, and taught his own father how to drive. But perhaps the most profound influence on his early life was the unusually close relationship that he developed with his uncle Lewis and aunt, Sybil Thorndike. He was devoted to them, and they in turn treated him as a son. As his father was additionally an expert in Tudor drama, it is hardly surprising that by the time Reed went up to Christ Church he was already passionately interested in the theatre.

As a freshman Reed threw himself into the Oxford University Dramatic Society, and acted in a number of plays. He also learnt to fly in the University Air Squadron. But this extra-curricula activity inevitably began to impinge on his academic performance and he had finally to choose between his studies and the theatrical career that he was, by this time, determined to pursue. The offer of a part from a repertory company, the Little Theatre, in Hull, proved decisive. He chose the theatre and left Oxford in 1931 without a degree. For the next two years he acted in provincial repertory theatre. He was a good actor and was fortunate enough to work with some of the most famous members of an outstanding generation of thespians, Gielgud included. But he missed the lucky breaks that so often make the difference between success and failure on the stage, and his parts were thus interspersed with periods of 'rest', when he undertook a variety of odd jobs to make a living of sorts. When he married Dorothy Louise Goscombe (always known as 'Paddy') in 1934 he realized he could not hope to support a family on such an unreliable income. Having obtained a few small acting parts on BBC radio programmes, Reed decided to apply to the Corporation – then rapidly expanding – for a permanent post as a radio announcer. Although unsuccessful, he was recommended for a producer's position in Birmingham, which he accepted. There he first worked on outside broadcasts before becoming a producer of radio features and drama. He soon showed himself to be an exceptionally capable and innovative programme maker, but he found the radio medium too restrictive and yearned for a return to the stage, a move strongly discouraged by the BBC's Midland Regional Director. Eventually a compromise was reached whereby Reed worked as a radio actor for the Corporation's Schools Department and for the Midland Region while simultaneously undertaking refreshment training at the Embassy School of Acting. In 1939 he became a member of the Old Vic Company, which was then led by his uncle Lewis, and embarked with them onboard the liner *Alcantara* on a tour of the Mediterranean, which included performances in Italy, Greece and Egypt. War broke out shortly after his return to Britain.[1]

Reed was an intensely kind and human character. Although he never maintained a large social circle, he loved company and made friends wherever he went: his personal warmth and charm were instantly captivating. Through his chosen career he nurtured a truly remarkable linguistic talent, adoring his mother tongue and championing the cause of plain and correct English usage throughout his life. He excelled in conversation, storytelling and public speaking, and wrote in a style that was at once lively and vivid but also sharp and concise. He was also an avid reader, and he loved classical music. But while he always followed current affairs closely, he was not a political man. Like so many of his contemporaries he flirted with socialism and pacifism at Oxford, but he was too much of a realist to be seduced by utopian ideologies. His outlook on the world was calm, tolerant and philosophical, and he had a shrewd understanding of human weaknesses, not least his own.

At root such political beliefs as he harboured in the 1930s were liberal and democratic. He watched the rise of national socialism in Germany and its subsequent expansion in Europe with a terrible sense of inevitability founded on popular British perceptions of the First World War. Once again, Germany was emerging as a menace to freedom and civilization, and to the way of life he cherished for himself and for his family. In September 1939 he saw military service as a duty not only to his country but also to his kin.[2] But when he duly sought to enlist for an aircrew post in the Royal Air Force (RAF) he was to his surprise rejected on health grounds (he had fallen seriously ill with rheumatic fever during his period as an outside broadcaster). So he returned to the BBC's Schools Department as a producer and an announcer, before joining the Army in October 1940, at the age of 30, and receiving an A1 medical rating. It was the obvious alternative, for he had served for five years in the Officer Training Corps at school; and it was entirely in keeping with his fascination for all motorized vehicles that he should have sought a commission in the Royal Armoured Corps (RAC).[3]

Two months later Reed was attached to the 52nd Heavy Training Regiment of the RAC at Bovington, Dorset. He was trained as a Driver Mechanic and completed the recruits' gunnery course at Lulworth, before being recommended for an Officer Cadet Training Unit (OCTU) in March 1941.[4] He received his Corps training at the 102nd OCTU at Blackdown, Wiltshire. His reports predictably record his strongest performance in the Driving and Maintenance Wing, where he was described as 'a very keen student of a good type'. His theoretical and practical knowledge was said to be 'quite good and his driving of all vehicles exceptionally good'. In gunnery he was also rated 'above average'. He had more difficulty with the radio course, 'but soon gained in confidence and made steady progress', eventually gaining an 'average' grade. His Company Commander's overall assessment described him as 'hard working and keen with plenty of personality and a sound knowledge'. The OCTU's Commanding Officer fully supported this assessment, noting that Reed had produced good results throughout. 'He possesses the qualities of a leader and will make a good reliable officer.'[5]

On 3 January 1942 Reed received his Commission as a 2nd Lieutenant and was shortly afterwards posted to the 47th Battalion, Royal Tank Regiment (RTR), at Shoreham-by-Sea in Sussex.[6] Equipped with Valentine infantry tanks, the 47th was one of the three component battalions (the others being the 45th and 41st) of the newly formed 24th Armoured Brigade, commanded by Brigadier Arthur Kenchington.[7] Each battalion was divided into squadrons, B Squadron in Reed's case, and each squadron into troops of three or four tanks. Reed became a troop commander, a post typically assigned to subalterns, and soon learnt that the brigade was to be despatched to Egypt. After less than three months of further training and exercises they swapped their Shoreham base for a former transatlantic liner, the hub of a large convoy of ships which set sail from Liverpool for the Middle East on 7 May.[8]

Before his departure from Britain Owen Reed's wartime record was entirely unremarkable. Like so many others he joined up as soon as the Army's recruitment machinery allowed. After proving his suitability for officer training he followed the standard programme of instruction given to all officers of the RAC. His overall performance was above average, but by no means exceptional. On embarkation there was no reason for him to expect that his war would be very different from that of any other subaltern in the

1. Owen Reed, before his embarkation for Egypt, 1942.

24th Armoured Brigade. And yet his first significant divergence from conventional military service occurred almost as soon as the convoy had put to sea.

The voyage began like a peacetime trip: the chaos in the cabin until the inmates shook down, the first meal selected from a printed menu, and the curious feeling of being suspended in mid-air, not quite ashore, but not quite at sea. Officers were provided with the usual peacetime cruise facilities – lounge, bar, hairdressers – and were fed on dishes that had been unobtainable in Britain since the beginning of the War. Reed was given a comfortable berth with cabin-mates whom he knew and liked. Everything seemed as lively and attractive as in pre-war times, lending an air of unreality, as if the ship were embarking on a cruise to Madeira and the 24th Armoured Brigade had all wandered on board by mistake.[9]

Of course, military discipline soon reimposed itself, quickly dispelling any temptation to look on the journey as a holiday. Reed was given responsibility for some 60 rank-and-file troops, a duty that was broadly in keeping with the variety of routine assignments allotted to other junior officers. But there the similarity ended, for Reed was then separated from his fellow subalterns by his selection for a very important and unusual task, which was determined solely by his peacetime occupation. Shortly after embarkation Brigadier Kenchington revealed himself to be a passionate broadcasting devotee, and announced his intention of organizing a comprehensive news service using the on-board loudspeaker system. One of his staff immediately remembered Reed's BBC background and he was duly summoned to Kenchington's cabin and appointed ship's newsreader.[10] He found himself on the air four times daily, addressing the brigade from a little chart room on the bridge. A fairly efficient news sheet, produced twice a day by the wireless room, was augmented by material gathered from the BBC's overseas broadcasts. Reed also organized a ten-minute topical talk, and doubled up as disc jockey with a motley collection of gramophone records benevolently supplied by the ship's officers.

And so his life quickly reverted to something much nearer the BBC broadcaster's than the army officer's. After breakfast each morning he would visit the officers' ward room and hastily attempt to make sense of the typescript for the morning news bulletin, which was very small, very uneven and heavily abbreviated ('Hull, US Secretary State reported have announced Mexico to be given every aid resist aggression Axis Powers'). Added confusion arose because each news item was committed to paper directly from the airwaves, regardless of context. The bulletins might start with two lines on Libya, switch to the death of a Grand National favourite, or to the latest Hollywood gossip, and then continue with cataclysmic war news from Russia. Reed's news-reading credentials were thus taxed to the very limit. From the ward room he would make his way to the bridge and the chart room, which housed the PA system, a bizarre contraption which emitted green sparks and made a peculiar whining noise. The bulletins went out at 9 am, midday, half-past four, and 7 pm, before blackout. When they were over Reed discovered that he could take advantage of his presence on the bridge by hiding in a secluded nook at one end of the captain's private promenade deck, where there was always a great wind blowing and a magnificent view over the bows of the ship.[11]

The job was accompanied by many other privileges, too. 'In no time', he recorded:

> I was being treated by the ship's staff, and even by some of the Army, with the same religious respect that used to be accorded to heralds in the days of the Trojan War. On that ship the sacred right of the herald was a direct route to all the comforts available.

He was excused from tedious duties like guard officer or orderly officer, and allowed to use the ship's ward room as a 'studio' – in fact a perfect haven and place of refuge. As a familiar face on the bridge he was soon *persona grata* with the ship's officers, whom he found a hospitable crowd, and lunchtime drinks invitations from one or another of them became a daily occurrence. He was even befriended by the ship's captain.[12]

And then there was Brigadier Kenchington. Reed's first impression was that he was 'not only a brilliant man but a kind, discriminating and human one...A gloriously exhilarating character with radical views, great dramatic talent, and a lightening brain.' He found Kenchington's theatricality particularly appealing. The brigadier could, he felt, have been a great bishop, farmer or innkeeper. But 'he *was* a great actor. War and the art of war were to him a production of a work of drama.' Reed's admiration was evidently reciprocated, for he soon found himself attached to Kenchington's staff, an appointment that would in time irrevocably alter his destiny. He had no training in staff work and was at first intimidated by the calibre of the other officers, but he persevered and his efforts clearly met with their approval.[13]

The troops managed by Reed varied from cooks to orderly room clerks. Preparing a timetable of their daily activities proved a simple enough task, and censoring their mail was monotonous but occasionally entertaining. More problematic was the challenge of training them for three hours a day in a corner of a claustrophobic men's mess deck five levels down, with artificial light and no port-holes. During the first week he lectured them *en masse*, succeeding only through some of the most spectacular and far-fetched improvisations of his career. But he soon exhausted every subject he knew anything about. The class-work eventually resolved itself into a tutorial system during which he took each man, one by one, through the same series of questions on elementary map reading and direction finding. In one letter he marvelled 'at the naked audacity of a military system which sent such woefully untrained men into battle'. Many of his soldiers literally did not know the difference between north and south. But he found them all remarkably patient and polite, qualities all the more impressive given the cramped and squalid conditions in which they were accommodated – conditions that contrasted sharply with the relative luxury of the officers' quarters.[14]

Reed's most enduring recollection of the voyage was of its monotony. The sea was calm throughout. There were no alarms other than practices and although, occasionally, rumours of submarine activity would circulate from deck to deck, they gave little justifiable cause for concern. Sometimes the escorting destroyers would vanish into the Atlantic haze, leaving all on board the troop ship to speculate on their whereabouts and on the reason for their departure.[15] But the escorts invariably returned to their normal stations before long. From his privileged position on the bridge the vision of the convoy was at first, in his words, 'an unrecorded wonder of the world'. But even that dramatic spectacle quickly lost its effect by exactly repeating itself every time he witnessed it.[16] Although the convoy's precise location soon became a mystery, its southerly heading was confirmed by the stars and by the steadily rising temperatures, which became particularly uncomfortable after nightfall and blackout. He eventually made himself a bed on deck and 'slept gloriously in a whirl of air and roaring of sea'.[17]

The uncertainty over their location ended when the convoy made a fleeting call at Freetown.[18] Thereafter it progressed south down the African coast to reach Cape Town in early June; there, at last, the brigade was allowed ashore. 'Our arrival was fraught with emotion and spectacular beyond description', Reed wrote:

> Coast line, sunrise, whales spouting, porpoises leaping, naval pageantry and every effect imaginable produced for our benefit . . . An arrival by liner at a place you've known about and read about and have a mental picture of, which is dramatically replaced and transcended, at a steady 14 knots, by a reality far exceeding your expectations. On top of that came the rising pressure of emotion – mass emotion in our case – at the mere making of a landfall after those endless days of sea-loneliness.[19]

The brigadier decided that all the troops would be sent to a camp up country, leaving a skeleton staff on board, Reed among them. He had ample opportunity to explore the city and to sample the abundant and overwhelming hospitality offered by its inhabitants. But he spent most of his time walking alone in the surrounding hills and mountains. Unable to mention Table Mountain by name, he nevertheless recorded in one letter hiking under a colossal sunset along the side of 'a large mountain that throws out a series of spectacular headlands into the sea'. Finally he found himself peering, with some trepidation, over the edge of a great precipice and watching the smoke rolling up from the harbour thousands of feet below.[20] After Cape Town the convoy called at Port Elizabeth, where the inhabitants were less accustomed to troops, so that their hospitality had a much more intimate and personal quality. Emerging for the first time from the docks Reed was beckoned over to a large Chevrolet. The car door swung open to reveal an entire family, who welcomed him as if he were a long-lost son coming home. In no time he was sinking into leather upholstery and heading for a quiet suburb, where a mountainous dinner had been prepared. The same pattern was repeated every evening for a week, 'a rare experience indeed to encounter friendship at first sight from every quarter'.[21]

The convoy crossed the equator again in early July – the very hottest time of the year. In another letter home, Reed described the sea as 'a featureless pool of platinum', while the sun, 'instead of being a single bright friendly face' was in his words 'a huge concentration of glare in a sky which is already an even white heat all over...a murderous colourless leprous miasma...With one accord and with deliberate, grim concentration, every hand and every gadget on board is devoted to keeping itself cool.'[22] His letter continued:

> We have a phosphorescent wake behind us like a great carpet of curdled milk...The luminosity is so great that the whole ship is lit up. It must be an amazing sight from a distance, and I begin to realize where some of the ghost ship yarns come from. Lines of wild geese, black against the waves, convoy us through the night and weird creatures heave sluggish fins out of the water and flounder away again...We pass insubstantial little islands which seem to float above the sea...We passed a boat yesterday – our first for ten days – but it was quite unreal. If we'd steered for it I'm sure we'd have found there was nothing there.[23]

They finally reached Egypt on 9 July.[24]

The 24th Armoured Brigade encamped in evenly spaced tents in an immense area of desert profusely watered with showers and taps. On one boundary lay an airstrip – a couple of bomber squadrons; on another, a canal conveyed an almost continuous procession of Egyptian barges on a dead straight course from east to west. The camp's exit was marked by the beginning of an equally straight asphalt road, which drew a shimmering line across the desert before finally dissolving into a mirage. Reed found himself sharing a spacious tent with a Roman Catholic padre, one John Jeffreys, whom he knew well from the voyage, and liked. Among the array of possessions that had somehow accompanied Jeffreys from England were a gramophone and some records, which they played *ad infinitum* in the following weeks, so that years later Reed was reminded of his Egyptian adventures by such unlikely compositions as Dvorak's *Songs My Mother Taught Me*. He was also fortunate enough to be allocated a half-share of Jeffreys' batman, Wallace, an utterly dependable north-easterner.[25] The camp lay so far behind the front line that they encountered little evidence of overt hostilities and saw nothing of the enemy. But they could not discount the possibility of air attack. They spent their first weekend in the desert 'digging-in' their tent so that it was ultimately pitched about three feet below ground level, and was surrounded by another three feet of displaced sand and rock.[26]

On his arrival in Egypt Reed was obliged to relinquish his position on the brigadier's staff and to return to the 47th Battalion as a troop leader. But this proved to be only a temporary resumption of normal military service. In little more than a week Kenchington sent for him again and appointed him liaison officer (LO) – effectively a combination of messenger and scout – attached to brigade headquarters. In this capacity he travelled around between units in his own scout car.[27]

The 24th Armoured Brigade's three battalions each had a theoretical strength of about 50 tanks. But during their first month in the desert they possessed nothing like that number, their operational status being entirely dependent on the arrival of reinforcements in the form of British Crusaders and American Shermans. Opportunities for exercises and manoeuvres were thus limited throughout July and early August, and occasional forays into the desert were interspersed with periods of mundane camp duty. The intense heat was a strong disincentive to energetic activity and Reed spent some time struggling to find any motivation. But in time he made himself one of the most popular officers in the brigade by establishing a canteen for the troops – a mess tent and a makeshift bar selling beer, soft drinks, snacks and toiletries procured from a nearby NAAFI depot.[28]

For officers the focal institution of brigade life became the brigade officers' mess tent. There, for a weekly fee, Reed found he could obtain a range of dishes – lamb, roast potato, fresh fruit – far superior to the standard fare provided by the 47th. The mess became a regular evening haunt, offering, as it did, the company of fellow subalterns, a radio just capable of relaying home broadcasts, and what was then a new discovery, American canned beer, albeit at extortionate prices. The other regular social gathering was a twice-weekly jaunt to the nearby lakeside resort of Ismalia.[29] After about two weeks Reed obtained permission to venture into Cairo, chancing on a party of four other subalterns from the brigadier's staff with similar ambitions. He took them to lunch at the Gezira Sporting Club, which he had visited during his tour with the Old Vic before the War. After wandering around the neighbourhood of the bazaar in the afternoon he returned to the Gezira Club, bathed and showered, ate tea, watched a cricket match and then wrote his letters home. In the evening he rejoined his party for dinner. In his correspondence Reed admitted to some feelings of shame at the manner in which Egypt had been swamped under the British war machine, and recognized that Cairo, in particular, had been overwhelmed by the influx of British and Commonwealth soldiers. Nevertheless, his sympathies were not limitless. Like so many other Westerners he found Cairo's combination of heat, dirt and overcrowding difficult to endure. In a moment of particular frustration he described the city as 'a scurvy, lousy, bug-ridden, poverty-stricken dump inhabited by a rabble of disease-ridden degenerates'. So the Gezira Club was a blessed oasis, and he became a regular visitor.[30]

In his capacity as an LO Reed was obliged to abandon the camp routine for periods of two or three days to become a desert nomad, only joining the brigade in the evening to draw rations, water and petrol, otherwise cooking meals out in the desert on a portable stove. He thrived on those desert journeys, relishing the challenge of plotting courses to unknown destinations with no landmarks for assistance.[31] The brigadier was delightful to work for and as always theatrical; the LOs' tasks were invariably assigned in the most unorthodox fashion:

> Reed-O! Job for you! Go and find Tomlinson and the 17th and find what bearing he has to march on to get his artillery back on the centre line. Oh, and tell the General if you see him that we're here and there's some beer on ice for him. Oh, and Reed-O! For God's sake have some yourself. Jenkins! Beer for Mr Reed![32]

His staff at brigade headquarters were equally agreeable. Those Reed did not know from the voyage were of a familiar type and they accepted him without demur.[33] There were several other LOs: his closest colleagues were Savile Greenwood, Irish Sam Marshall and John Welton. Welton became his inseparable companion in the following year. A source of far less satisfaction was his driver, Trooper Richmond, a morose Liverpudlian. 'Richmond's walk, voice, face, manner and fashion of driving betray a discontent with life so ingrained that it assumes the proportions of a permanent grievance', Reed observed. 'Rude but reliable is all I can say of him.' He clearly resented driving officers around the desert and was scrupulous in his avoidance of the normal military courtesies. On more than one occasion Reed considered upbraiding him, but he had no desire to incur the personal animosity of a man he was fated to spend so much time with. So together they took a negative position and sat in total silence for hours on end while their scout car roared and idled through the sand dunes.[34]

On 8 August, back at the base camp, Reed walked into the brigade mess tent and found to his astonishment all the officers assembled with Winston Churchill, Averill Harriman and the Chief of the Imperial General Staff

(CIGS), General Sir Alan Brooke, seated before them. Churchill had decided to visit Cairo to appoint a new Commander-in-Chief of the Eighth Army and had used the opportunity to inspect several armoured brigades, including the 24th.[35] 'He looked like a great bleached white toad', Reed recorded:

> He sat absolutely still while we all crept in and slipped into our chairs, and then he began to talk. I always imagined him to have an electrifying presence: he has – utterly compelling. He talked very quietly and convincingly and we hardly breathed.[36]

Churchill began with his own powerful war analysis and then announced that the President of the United States had given him Sherman tanks and that the Navy was bringing them as fast as possible; in a few weeks the British Army would be able to field the most powerful and best equipped armoured force of its size in the world.[37] The CIGS spoke next, but he was merely friendly. Then came Harriman. Reed described him as the most encouraging sight he had seen since the War began:

> Harriman has charm and freshness and a certain boy-like gravity. He leant over us, very tall and shy and self-effacing, and quietly promised us all the help of the American continent as if he was a rather timid young doctor assuring a nervous relative that he would do his best for a difficult case. I felt that if Hitler could have seen that quiet sombre young man he would have called his adventure off and asked for terms.[38]

At the end, walking out of the tent, Churchill turned straight to Reed and Jeffreys as they stood nervously fingering their berets, smiled and said 'Good luck – and God bless you', before stumping off into the blazing sun, a broad grin on his face and two fingers stuck in the air. For Reed it was a profoundly moving experience: first the gigantic surprise of discovering that the brigade, in its dusty seclusion at the end of nowhere, could be considered so important in London and Washington, and then the subsequent silence. There was no parade and no cheering and yet the tension was overpowering. Churchill seemed very frank, matter-of-fact, reassuring and determined. 'There was no tub-thumping or oratory', Reed wrote. 'Just a reminder that he had not forgotten us and a promise that he would not do so.'[39]

When the Shermans finally arrived they were a revelation. Not that American tanks were entirely new to the British Army. The Stuart light tank had been in service in north Africa since 1941. It was fast, manoeuvrable and reliable, but it did not represent a significant improvement over British models in armament or armour. The heavier Grant had arrived in limited numbers earlier in the summer but although faster and better armed than British infantry tanks it was poorly laid out, the all-important 75 mm gun being mounted in the hull instead of the turret, so that it could only fire forwards in a limited arc. The Sherman was superior to both, let alone to the existing inventory of British machines. Compared with infantry tanks like the Matilda II, it was very fast and manoeuvrable, more reliable and easier to maintain. Its frontal armour was only slightly thinner and it boasted a turret-mounted 75 mm gun whereas the Matilda was only equipped with a two-pounder. Compared with lighter tanks like the Crusader it enjoyed similar advantages in reliability and maintainability and was better armed and armoured. Ergonomically it was superior to all British tanks. In battle it was certainly a match for the Panzer III and for the early Mk IVs, if not the later ones. In short, the Sherman at last provided the British Army with a fast and reliable standard battle tank that was both well armed and armoured. It was, however, very far from invulnerable.

Space for crew, equipment, ammunition and, most of all, its bulky radial engine was created by raising the Sherman's hull well above the top of its caterpillar tracks, so that it had a noticeably higher silhouette than equivalent British machines such as the Crusader. It therefore presented an easier target in restricted battle areas, where advantages in speed and agility were impossible to exploit. Moreover, the Sherman's speed was derived from an engine designed to run on high-octane gasoline, similar to aeroplane fuel and equally combustible. Almost any penetration of its defensive armour would cause the Sherman to explode, fuel and ammunition erupting in a spectacular but deadly combination. Although adequately equipped with escape hatches, which must have saved many a life, exploding Shermans often sent their entire five-man complement to the heavens. Within the German Army the Sherman notoriously retained the macabre nick-name 'Tommy-Boiler' for the duration of the war.[40]

The immediate consequence of the Sherman's arrival was that the 24th Armoured Brigade finally reached its full establishment. Early in September, after a short period of acclimatization, the brigade abandoned its sedentary base-camp life and began a series of protracted and convoluted exercises in the desert – preparation for an eventuality that was still unknown. Before their departure Reed spent hours sorting out all his camp equipment, and sent much of it into store. Then, with some experience of the desert to his credit, he so ordered his remaining possessions that they would fit in their entirety in the back of the scout car. A frenzied expedition to a salvage dump in Cairo and some thoroughly ruthless scrounging yielded several additional items of outdoor equipment, including an American four-gallon water container, which gave a large reserve on board.[41]

Reed periodically joined the rest of the brigade in various makeshift and spartan desert encampments but usually his job as LO kept him on the move. The distances involved were often considerable and the terrain

invariably limited the scout car's speed, so journeys could only be
accomplished in stages and he was often compelled to camp out on his own
in an army bivvy – a small tent that took five minutes to erect. It was an
enjoyable enough life in its essentials: he loved the air, space and sun, and
the freedom from having to think about any time but the present. It was
only company that he missed and which Richmond would not, or could
not, but certainly never did provide. The feeling of loneliness and hostility
was sometimes acute, especially at night.[42]

As an LO he continued to have direct contact with Kenchington, who
remained a lively and witty commentator on the absurdities of their daily
life, and frequently amazed his subordinates with his boundless energy and
eccentricity. He once halted his scout car and several accompanying
vehicles so he could climb a tree in search of dates![43] Reed was often used
as a pioneer and a pathfinder for the brigade on its wanderings, but he also
became accustomed to engaging the high and mighty and to conducting the
brigadier's arguments for him. On one occasion he delivered a furious letter
from Kenchington to GHQ, Cairo, and – with that poker-faced detachment
LOs have to cultivate – carried utter consternation up through higher and
higher strata of the General Staff hierarchy until a certain major-general
was sending out priority calls all over the Middle East. Reed never lost his
fondness for Kenchington but as the forthcoming offensive drew nearer
there were signs that the brigadier was out of his depth, for he began to
display a marked propensity for despatching his LOs on futile errands over
long distances with messages that were promptly cancelled. 'Nine out of
every ten of my hot and dusty desert missions are null and void by the time
they are finished', Reed complained.[44]

In the middle of September Kenchington disappeared.[45] Reed at first
thought he had been promoted and posted elsewhere, but he returned to
the brigade in due course. He had in reality been briefed on Montgomery's
plans for the El Alamein offensive in October. During the ensuing weeks
select groups of officers were appraised of the plan, and Reed's position as
an LO ensured that he was among them, despite his junior rank. In the
days immediately preceding the battle, as they were moving towards the
front, he found himself 'wandering round the desert with a map showing
the location of every British minefield and unit and a notebook containing
Monty's plans for the two corps which carried out the attack'. He hardly
dared to sleep.[46]

The battle of El Alamein started on 23 October 1942 with a colossal
artillery barrage and an infantry offensive through the minefields to clear
two corridors for the armour which was theoretically to smash through the
Axis lines. That night the 24th Armoured Brigade left its assembly area and
slowly advanced along three mine-free tracks – code-named 'Boat', 'Bottle'
and 'Hat' – which led to the 10th Armoured Division's corridor (see Map

1).[47] Reed moved with the 47th Battalion along Boat. The tracks were indicated by little signs fixed to pylons, supported by heaps of stones. The signs were constructed by placing lamps inside petrol tins punched with holes in a picture of each sign, so that the battalion's huge crocodile of tanks nosed its way along for miles through the dark following a series of twinkling golden boats. 'Then we found we had gone as far as the boats went', Reed wrote later, 'and that's where Jerry was and that's how it all began'.[48] All the tanks and support vehicles were refuelled in the early hours of the following morning and deployed for the impending advance. The close proximity of enemy minefields left little room for manoeuvre and the

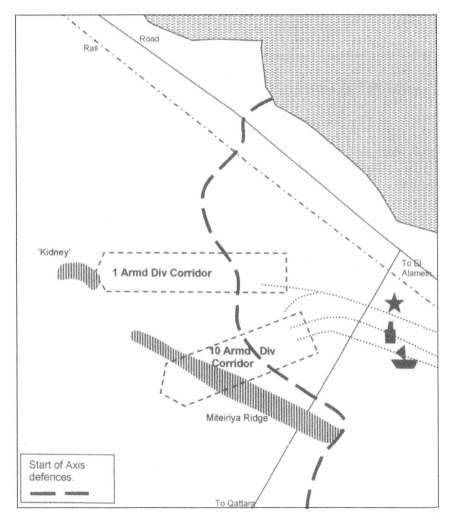

Map 1. The opening phase of the Battle of El Alamein.

brigade might have offered some easy targets to the Axis guns. But fortunately their attention was focused on Miteiriya Ridge, which lay to the west of the British armoured formations.

The attack began along the track codenamed Bottle from an intersection with the Qattara Road at 8 am on the 24th and almost immediately ran into difficulty: the minefield remained largely intact, and the only breach was covered by German anti-tank artillery. Kenchington hurriedly convened a conference of senior officers and it was decided that further mine clearance would have to take place under cover of darkness before an attempt was made to cross the ridge. That evening the sappers bravely went to work but progress was slow, and the brigade's true vulnerability was in the meantime exposed by an air attack, which left 18 lorries and several tanks in flames. Kenchington had no option but to order dispersal, a complex task given the close proximity of enemy mines and of other British and Commonwealth units.

By the following morning only one lane over Miteiriya Ridge had been cleared. Along it moved two of the brigade's three battalions while the third, the 45th, was deployed in hull-down positions to provide covering fire. The objective was to engage enemy tanks from the 15th Panzer Division. A fierce fire-fight ensued with the German forces beyond the ridge, but the two advancing battalions successfully reached their objective, which was open ground exposed to enemy view. They were then compelled to maintain this position all day under both tank and long-range artillery fire, pending the arrival of other formations on their northern flank. The limited mine-free territory offered little opportunity for the gleaming new Shermans to demonstrate their speed or manoeuvrability, while dust storms and clouds of smoke so reduced visibility east of the ridge that it was almost impossible for the 45th Battalion to give accurate supporting fire. Fortunately, of course, enemy gunners were confronted by precisely the same problem. Both sides emerged from this opening engagement with only moderate casualties.

Late in the afternoon Kenchington was ordered to send his forces north to the 1st Armoured Division corridor to assist another armoured brigade. As the proposed route ran through a minefield to the east of the ridge, well within range of the enemy's artillery, he decided that the territory would have to be fully reconnoitred before any general move could be sanctioned, and entrusted this unenviable task to his LOs. Together they advanced out into the desert, their scout cars weighed down under sandbags, but the constant threat posed by enemy mines and artillery soon brought them to a halt. The official record states baldly that 'the reconnaissance reported that a move along that route would not be possible'. The brigadier was left with no alternative but to order a withdrawal to the original starting line on the Qattara Road; the proposed move would have to be accomplished along another marked track to the north-east, codenamed 'Star', which was clear of mines and beyond the range of the enemy guns. Having withdrawn, the brigade duly negotiated Star on the 26th and deployed for battle on a ridge to the east of the topographical feature known as 'Kidney'. The following day they were to protect the left flank of the 7th Motor Brigade, advancing further to the north.

From a purely tactical perspective the plan was entirely justified. As expected, enemy forces attacked the 7th Motor Brigade, only to be repelled by Kenchington's tanks; they lost several Panzer Mk IIIs and IVs and 200 supporting infantry were taken prisoner. But the cost for the 24th Armoured Brigade was appalling. After the Germans had withdrawn the British tanks were again left on open ground, some on a west-facing slope, with their thin top armour exposed to the enemy artillery only a short distance away on the opposite ridge. No fewer than 26 were destroyed or damaged; the 47th Battalion lost its commanding officer, its acting commanding officer, an adjutant, two squadron commanders and several troop leaders. In a later engagement involving the 45th Battalion the casualties were at least more evenly divided.

Running frantic and perilous missions between brigade headquarters and the forward units Reed encountered scenes of indescribable carnage. From the valley to the east of Kidney the sky was completely obscured; there was only a dense, red mist – impenetrable clouds of smoke and sand filtering out the sun and reflecting simultaneously the grim light of incinerated vehicles. The air smelled of cordite and burning petrol; all around him guns fired, shells burst, tanks exploded, the wounded screamed and officers shouted orders and counter-orders to anyone who cared to listen.[49] Sheltering in a slit trench with a group of infantrymen he found himself pondering his uncle, Lewis Casson, and other men who had fought through the Great War; he knew them now far more intimately than before.[50]

That night any serviceable tanks from the three battalions were allocated to the 45th in preparation for another deployment in support of the 133rd Infantry Brigade, which had captured an objective some 2,000 yards forward of the British lines. Kenchington's orders were to protect their left flank by advancing yet again on to open ground, which was exposed to both frontal and flanking fire from the enemy. His suggestion that the task could be accomplished just as well by firing from protected positions around Kidney was rejected. On the morning of 28 October the battalion duly advanced west until a devastating artillery barrage drove them back; 21 Shermans and Crusaders were knocked out. During the afternoon German forces were engaged from hull-down positions almost continuously for three hours; some of the British tanks were twice replenished with ammunition. Only the arrival of reinforcements and a series of supporting air attacks by the RAF finally forced the enemy to retreat. At 5.30 pm what remained of the brigade struggled back to the Qattara Road and was withdrawn from the line. Any serviceable tanks were transferred to other formations.

Of the various published accounts of El Alamein consulted by the author during the preparation of this book, not one adequately describes the catastrophe that befell the 24th Armoured Brigade. It was a completely new formation composed overwhelmingly of conscripts: before the battle it had never fired a shot in anger, and hardly any of its officers and men had experience of live combat. It was not even fully equipped until the second half of August 1942 and was left with barely two months in which to train for Montgomery's offensive, for which it was predominantly dependent on unfamiliar foreign tanks that had only recently been introduced into the British Army. Nevertheless, the brigade was assigned the task of a frontal assault on the opening day of the battle. Five days later it had effectively ceased to exist. The 24th Armoured Brigade went into battle on 23 October with 95 Sherman tanks and 58 Crusaders. No fewer than 77 Shermans and 48 Crusaders were damaged or destroyed during the ensuing battle and some 250 officers and men were killed or wounded, or could not be accounted for at the time of the withdrawal. Of Reed's small gang from Shoreham he was virtually the only one left: B Squadron was wiped out.[51] Although he did not yet know it, his time as a tank man was at an end.

On 4 November the brigadier sent Reed, John Welton and Sam Marshall (the other LO, Savile Greenwood, had been wounded in the battle) into Alexandria for a bath and change of scenery, and from the moment they stepped into their car the day was a predestined success. They all happened to motor at the same speed, eat at the same price, and drink proportionately, and they were all perfectly content to remain silent. They browsed around shops, sipped morning chocolate, and lunched and swum at a hotel on the coast before making their way to the officer's club, where they bathed and placed themselves unreservedly in the hands of an expert team of Egyptian barbers. Then, after an hour in the library writing letters, they solemnly visited the bar to lay a foundation for the evening ahead. It was in fact Reed's first serious break from teetotalism since the brigade's withdrawal from the front line; it was the first opportunity to celebrate, and it had been his rule never to drink merely for the sake of drinking, or from the fear of remaining sober. But that night they celebrated their return, unscathed, from the 'Valley of the Shadow of Death' – or, more precisely, from its ridge.[52]

Over dinner they fell silent and withdrew into private thoughts of the battle still raging 80 miles to the west. Reed had no idea whether his personal experience of war was better or worse than for most men, but he admitted to himself that it had demanded more courage than he would ever possess and the memory left him little to feel proud of. Throughout he had been, on his own admission, 'horribly frightened' and disgusted at the inordinate offensiveness of the scenes he had witnessed. 'It seemed such a fearful crime against human dignity', he wrote. He was left with a deep admiration for what he described as 'the native courage and goodness of the ordinary Englishman' but also 'with an overpowering sense of despair and abhorrence'.[53] His erstwhile reverence for the brigadier was almost totally exhausted. The futility of so many of his liaison missions had been exasperating enough even before the battle; executed in conditions of extreme personal risk, they encouraged cynicism, wariness and disrespect.[54]

Emerging later from the dining room, he turned to Sam Marshall and said, 'It's no good, we shan't enjoy an evening again till we know we've won it.' On the opposite side of the hall stood a Reuters ticker-tape machine. They ambled over to it and looked on with amazement as it typed out a special war communiqué from General Montgomery. 'The enemy is in full retreat. Our victory is complete.'[55]

NOTES

1. RP, Reed interviewed by J. Lane, 'Oral History of the BBC', undated transcript; Reed's obituary in *The Independent*, by L. Miall.
2. Personal knowledge.
3. RP, Reed interviewed by J. Lane, 'Oral History of the BBC', Reed's record of service.
4. Reed's record of service.
5. *Ibid.*
6. *Ibid.*
7. Kenchington was educated at Folkestone Grammar School and the University of London. He then joined the Army and served with the Royal East Kent Regiment from 1914 to 1917 before transferring to the Royal Tank Regiment, where he remained until the armistice, and for much of the inter-war period. He emerged from the Great War with a Military Cross and a Croix de Guerre, holding the rank of battalion-major; he was promoted lieutenant-colonel in 1934, colonel in 1939 and brigadier in 1942.
8. RP, Owen Reed to Paddy Reed (afterwards cited as 'OR to PR'), 7 May 1942; undated, mid-May 1942.
9. RP, OR to PR, undated, mid-May 1942.
10. *Ibid.*
11. RP, OR to PR, 30 May 1942.
12. RP, OR to PR, 7 June 1942.
13. *Ibid.*; OR to Geoffrey, 1 June 1942.
14. RP, OR to PR, 16 and 30 May 1942.
15. RP, OR to PR, 16 May 1942.
16. OR to Geoffrey, 1 June 1942.
17. RP, OR to PR, 30 May 1942.
18. RP, OR to PR, 16 May 1942.
19. RP, OR to PR, 7 June 1942.
20. *Ibid.*; RP, OR to PR, 25 June 1942.
21. RP, OR to PR, 25 June 1942; OR to Daisy, 30 June 1942.
22. RP, OR to PR, 7 July 1942.

23. *Ibid.*
24. RP, OR to PR, undated, mid-July 1942.
25. RP, OR to PR, 21 and 26 July 1942; 25 August 1942.
26. RP, OR to PR, undated, mid-July 1942; 9 August 1942.
27. RP, OR to PR, 21 July 1942.
28. RP, OR to PR, 9 August 1942.
29. RP, OR to PR, 21 and 26 July 1942.
30. RP, OR to PR, 18 July 1942.
31. RP, OR to PR, 21 and 26 July 1942; 9 August 1942.
32. RP, OR to PR, 9 August 1942.
33. RP, OR to PR, 26 July 1942.
34. RP, OR to PR, 28 September 1942.
35. M. Gilbert, *Winston S. Churchill*, vol. 7, *Road to Victory, 1941–1945* (London: Heinemann, 1986), pp. 159, 166.
36. RP, OR to PR, 25 August 1942.
37. RP, OR to PR, 7 September 1942; Gilbert, *Churchill*, vol. 7, pp. 167–9.
38. RP, OR to PR, 25 August 1942.
39. RP, OR to PR, 7 September 1942.
40. Interview with Reed, 4 November 1989.
41. RP, OR to PR, 1 October 1942.
42. RP, OR to PR, 7, 21 and 28 September 1942.
43. RP, OR to PR, 7 September 1942.
44. RP, OR to PR, 21 September 1942.
45. RP, OR to PR, 13 September 1942.
46. RP, OR to PR, 18 April 1943.
47. Unless otherwise stated this account of the battle is taken from WO 169/4266, HQ 24th Armoured Brigade War Diary, and from WO 201/545, Brigadier Kenchington's notes on operations, 23–9 October 1942.
48. RP, OR to PR, 25 May 1943.
49. Interview with Reed, 4 November 1989.
50. RP, OR to PR, 4 November 1942.
51. RP, OR to PR, 1 January 1943.
52. RP, OR to PR, 4 November 1942.
53. *Ibid.*
54. RP, OR to PR, 29 November 1942.
55. RP, OR to PR, 4 November 1942; RP, transcript of broadcast, 8 May 1943.

2

Base Wallah

In the aftermath of the battle the shattered remnants of the 24th Armoured Brigade were withdrawn to the dreariest of bases – a scruffy bathing beach on the outskirts of Alexandria – and there they quickly resumed the normal base-camp routine. All their equipment was stripped from them so that they became merely so many tired and disgruntled men, standing around under the dirty palm trees or lounging in their tents waiting to be assigned the most menial of duties. Reed relinquished his role as liaison officer and the scout car was requisitioned for an operational unit. 'The fighting spirit which three weeks before had transformed our gang of Oldham garage hands into a band of dauntless crusaders withered almost overnight', he wrote sadly. 'The only just reward of battle, the excitement of the chase, the gaining of booty and the sight of new lands, has been snatched from us.' The War seemed so remote that it was difficult to believe that the brigade's violent initiation had ever occurred at all. There was nothing whatever to do but swat flies and take aimless walks by the sea, and pour money into the overpriced bars and clubs of Alexandria.[1]

It was there at the base camp that Reed fell ill. The initial diagnosis was sand-fly fever. On waking each morning he felt better, only for the fever to return in the afternoon; he lost his appetite, became afflicted with aches and pains and sank rapidly into a state of severe depression. After a few days he was committed to a pristine new hospital in Alexandria, where it was determined that his malady was jaundice – an unpleasant condition but not a life-threatening one. Within a week his temperature was down and he was being permitted a short walk and a shave and whatever food he could force down his unwilling gullet. Otherwise his illness was left to run its course. John Welton soon located him and brought his kit, and then visited daily to provide comfort and moral support.[2] A change of climate and surroundings was eventually prescribed for his recovery and on 23 November he embarked for Palestine on board a Red Cross hospital ship. At Haifa he and the other patients were hauled down the gangway and loaded on to a train, which took them to a convalescent hospital on the coast near Netanya.[3] On the 28th he was allowed up. He found a deckchair and sat out in a windy spot under a huge acacia tree, and later made his way with three other yellow men to a nearby farm, where they bought as much fruit as they could carry back to the hospital on a stretcher.[4]

Reed's convalescence passed pleasantly enough in glorious weather. He quickly regained his appetite and began tackling basic jobs, such as mail censorship. His conscience duly appeased, he would then relax in the sun and search cynically for the truth behind the headlines of the *Palestine Post*, which he purchased from a small Arab urchin who professed never to have any change until he was threatened. He also began taking regular walks along a nearby cliff and down through sand dunes to the seashore.[5] Gradually his strength returned. On 6 December he chanced on three men from the 47th Battalion and took them to a local café. They were new arrivals at the hospital and brought with them disconcerting news from Egypt, which was confirmed by a letter from Welton two days later. The 24th Armoured Brigade and its component battalions had been disbanded: its staff had evaporated and all personnel, officers and men, had been posted to other units, or else were awaiting reassignment at the RAC base depot near Cairo. On returning to Egypt, Reed too would be stationed there.[6]

A few days later, with his doctor's permission, he embarked on a whistle-stop tour of Jerusalem and Bethlehem, after which he was sent to a transit camp near Haifa. From there he made one further pilgrimage to Nazareth.[7] His train back to Cairo left Haifa at nine o'clock on the morning of 16 December and reached its destination at noon the following day. Reed duly reported to the RAC base depot expecting a dull period of routine garrison duties culminating at length in his posting to an unknown unit in some remote and disagreeable corner of the desert. Instead, on calling at the adjutant's office, he learnt to his surprise that he was to be attached forthwith to the Department of Public Relations at GHQ. 'Something to do with making gramophone records', the adjutant muttered vaguely.[8]

At first Reed suspected Kenchington. But on reporting to GHQ he was redirected to Denis Johnston at the office of the BBC. Reed had discovered Johnston and one of his favourite former recording technicians, Chignall, in Cairo shortly before El Alamein, and had swapped BBC shop talk with them for hours over dinner. From the convalescent hospital in Palestine he had written them a short letter, unwittingly alerting them to the possibility that they might call temporarily on his services. A formal request soon reached the brigadier, who was only too willing to oblige.[9]

Until June 1943 the BBC's Cairo office was located in a third-floor suite at 2 Sharia Gameh Sharkass, a small office block in a terrible slum district. The front door was permanently manned by a Boab (building concierge), 'a great half-shaven fellow in a night-shirt', who was keeper of the keys, and who housed himself and his entire family in a tiny room off the hallway.

The building was served by a single lift, which was rarely functional. Access to the BBC was more usually gained via a dark and slippery staircase, which also conveyed a peculiar assortment of women to the offices of Dr Fonad Ali, whose glass-panelled door proclaimed him to be the director of the Helwan sanatorium. The top floor was occupied by one Madame Fifi, who ran an unlicensed 'hostel for the troops'. Her clients periodically wandered into the BBC by mistake with unfortunate but hilarious results, for they would all make their way to the enquiry desk, behind which sat the redoubtable Mrs Beahan, wife of a colonel at GHQ, and very pukka. Two Egyptian commissionaires stood at the BBC door and sprang madly to attention whenever anyone appeared.[10]

Denis Johnston was a Dubliner, a graduate of both Cambridge and Harvard, who had forsaken a legal career to become director of the Dublin Gate Theatre before joining the BBC in 1936.[11] He was appointed war correspondent in the Middle East in 1942 alongside Godfrey Talbot and a three-man engineering staff – Messrs Arnell, Chignall and Phillips – who had been despatched to the Middle East at the end of 1941. Phillips doubled up as office administrator; Mrs Beahan was the only secretary. This minuscule team was responsible not only for reporting on the progress of the War but also for recording radio programmes for the various home and overseas services. Another broadcaster, Aitken, had made programmes for the Arabic service, but he left the BBC before Reed's arrival, abandoning his duties to the remaining staff.[12] When time permitted, recordings were cut locally and flown back to Britain; more usually they were broadcast back and placed on record in London, often to be re-transmitted the very same day.[13]

Reed found the office completely overwhelmed by war reports, as the Allied advance on Tripoli gathered momentum.[14] At this critical juncture in the north African campaign London had sought a Middle Eastern contribution to their Empire Christmas Party, which it termed 'the emotional climax of the broadcasting year' – a near impossible request given the hopelessly inadequate resources available. The show was to be a platform affair before a live audience, which included General Alexander and his staff. Reed was to deliver a lengthy introduction dwelling on the Allies' 'Victory Christmas', and to extol the virtues of the Eighth Army by dragging to the microphone a troop of Commonwealth soldiers.[15]

According to Reed's account, 'the script read like a series of interviews with nine sanitary inspectors of the London County Council', his own part being the rock bottom of banality – a blend of the hearty, the patronizing and the pretentious. Nevertheless, he recognized that it was the best Johnston could produce in very adverse circumstances. In the recording of the dress rehearsal he was unhappy with his own contribution – 'the very embodiment of self-conscious over-articulation' – but his array of speakers performed admirably. All appeared to be well until, barely an hour before the programme began, a cable arrived from their London controller instructing Johnston to re-write the entire commentary, sack the compere (Reed) and substitute the official BBC observer.[16] So Reed's first job for BBC Cairo ended in abject humiliation and before long he was back at the base depot guarding ten Italian generals, none of whom displayed the slightest inclination to escape.[17]

In truth, though, the Christmas Day débâcle was not of his own making, and he had done more than enough to convince Johnston that his services were indispensable. By 3 January he was working on another broadcast involving (ironically, in the light of subsequent events) three Yugoslav airmen who were to send a New Year greeting to the resistance leader, General Mihailovic. Reed was now formally posted to the BBC until the transmission date, and was afterwards assigned to the forces broadcasting organization, the Middle Eastern Broadcasting Unit (MEBU). 'The inevitable vortex is pulling me back into civilian life', he wrote. 'Why couldn't it have left me there in the first place?'[18]

He did not welcome the prospect unequivocally. He loathed Cairo, and having captured a glimpse of active service he had difficulty reconciling the daring and endurance of the fighting soldier with the comfortable and sedate lifestyle of the British officer corps there, whom he described contemptuously as 'base wallahs'. Not that he harboured any particular illusions about his prowess on the field of battle: he realized that he could probably make a greater contribution by commenting on military actions than by participating in them, and he also saw radio news as an important part of the war machine in itself. Moreover, a broadcasting post seemed infinitely preferable to many of the niches found for convalescing subalterns.[19] The problem was rather that MEBU was a very different proposition to the familiar territory of the BBC. For while Johnston and his colleagues were for the most part diligent and professional, those at MEBU were the very opposite. Reed described them as 'an extravagant inner circle of pimply youths...who hang around the studios of the Egyptian State Broadcasting Company and stink...A set of dilettante war-dodgers who had somehow muscled in on a good thing.' To him it appeared that they did little of any consequence, and few of their staff had any significant broadcasting experience.[20] He found himself missing the desert and his healthy nomadic existence. But most of all he missed the brigade. The world he had inhabited in the months before El Alamein had evaporated almost overnight, together with all its friendships, antipathies, enthusiasms and pet jokes.[21] When he enquired into his prospects of rejoining an operational unit he received a wholly negative response: that he was not yet fit for front-line service; that he had no training on Shermans (he had been appointed LO before they arrived); and that, at 32 years of age, he was too old.[22]

With the Yugoslav show out of the way Reed was free to join MEBU, who wished him to establish a forces broadcasting service in, of all places,

Baghdad. But before he could report for duty he suffered a slight relapse and found himself back in hospital for tests.[23] So it was not until 21 January that he moved his belongings from the base depot to the Junior Officers' Club, before making his way to Garden City and his new employer. The next day he drifted aimlessly around the MEBU offices where four rather pasty youths, ex-actors drawn from several different regiments, spent their time blowing out clouds of smoke, running their fingers through their hair, throwing tantrums and engaging in the kind of conversation in which every adjective was heavily over-emphasized, and every sentence began with 'My dear.' He began to wonder what sort of menagerie he had wandered into.

He was initially received by the second-in-command, Scott:

> 'Good morning', he began. 'I am Reed. I've just got away from hospital and want to know about this Baghdad job.'
>
> 'But *my dear*', came the reply. 'How *too* marvellous! I simply can't tell you how *worried* we've been! But *devastated*! Now come with me and I'll make you a captain *at once*! Must be a captain – gives one authority in the studio.'
>
> The telephone rang.
>
> 'Yes? Oh but Bonzo how *could* you! Oh Bonzo *no*! [To Reed] Do you know Bonzo? No? Oh! [Back to the phone] Lunch? But my *dear*, I have Mr Reed of Baghdad. What, bring him along too? But how *too* sweet of you. Bye-bye!'[24]

Reed described 'Bonzo' Davis, the officer-in-charge of MEBU, as 'a tall lugubrious creature with bleached hair'. Before lunch they went to the Egyptian State Broadcasting (ESB) studios to hear him read the news. From his hospital bed Reed had listened to some of the local news programmes and marvelled that anything could be so bad. But what he heard that morning surpassed his worst nightmares: Davis read for 20 minutes and hardly got one sentence right. That evening Reed returned to the Junior Officers' Club with food for thought.[25]

Between them Scott and Davis somehow settled his captaincy in an instant and he then spent two more days trying to ascertain precisely what they wanted him to do in Baghdad, and observing their operation. Their broadcasts were a mixture of news, dance numbers and base-camp amateur vaudeville employing performers from the Armed Services. Their desks were littered with cigarette butts and illustrated papers. On the walls hung an array of army propaganda posters: 'Tough Tactics make Better Soldiers', 'Lend to Defend', and 'VD Beware! An hour with Venus means two years with Mercury!' There were filing cabinets and typewriters and lists of duties and the usual office clutter. But to Reed it all seemed somehow incongruous:

It looked less like a military outfit than the dressing room of the men's chorus in *Cavalcade* – men wearing battle dress as if they were soldiers but with the wrong faces. At intervals one of them would sigh, gather up a sheaf of papers and disappear next door to the ESB building.[26]

Reed was rescued from their clutches, and from a very uncertain fate in Baghdad, by the arrival of a new BBC war correspondent, Frank Gillard,[27] to relieve Denis Johnston. Gillard, whom Reed knew well from his own work with the Corporation, found a staff of just one engineer, Arnell – Chignall having accompanied Talbot to Libya and Phillips having been committed to hospital with double pneumonia and pleurisy. He was faced with the war news from the front, all the outstanding Arabic programmes, a medley of semi-digested European material and the day-to-day administration of the office. In desperate need of more hands he made enquiries about Reed's possible secondment, only to learn of his obligations to MEBU. Gillard realized that there would be no possibility of his transfer unless the order came directly from London. Somehow he managed to channel a request through the BBC's head office at Portland Place to the War Office, emphasizing his critical need for more personnel, and the War Office duly settled the issue with GHQ in Cairo.[28] And so Reed, to his intense relief, returned to the BBC and spent a frantic day with Gillard sifting through two years' worth of accumulated office paperwork and periodically descending into the maelstrom of newspaper journalists and radio broadcasters who haunted the conference rooms of the Armed Services' information staff. He was there when news of the fall of Tripoli finally came through.[29]

As radio producer-cum-news correspondent Reed found himself holding the office fort or battling through a mad round of press conferences and pursuing other sources of information – official and unofficial. Between them they supplied the news sent home as 'today's dispatch from our observer in Cairo, Frank Gillard'. He found the whirl of official bulletins and embassy pronouncements phoney and wearisome, and difficult to square with his own all-too-brief experience of the front. In the endless struggle between pressmen avid for a story and censors intent on denying the passage of anything newsworthy, truth was often the first victim. When any major news broke, like the Casablanca summit, it was either completely suppressed or released to all the media simultaneously in identical words. In all, about 100 newspapers maintained correspondents and paid their expenses, hotel bills and air passages so that they could each convey the very same news and draw the very same conclusions; hence the daily throng of pressmen and the huge unwieldy Service departments for issuing information to assuage them.[30]

Reed had to be prepared to understudy Gillard if Talbot was away.

'Both Gillard and Talbot have gone out of their way to be helpful', he wrote in a typically modest memorandum to London in the spring of 1943:

> If I have learnt nothing else I have a wholesome respect for the amazing speed and certainty with which they set about their work. I fear several pieces have reached you later than they should because I have yet to learn to think at their pace. But their standards are an inspiration to the amateur, and it has been a pleasure to see how they handle what seems to me a very difficult job.[31]

Otherwise he worked on feature programmes, like a St David's day broadcast for the BBC Home Service, and Arabic material, which was amusing in its way.[32] He might have to decide on a subject – say Churchill – and then request the Arabic music staff at ESB to recruit a poet, a composer and a singer, and prepare a programme. In due course the song was written, the music composed and the singer engaged, and they would all gather in the ESB studios to make the record. Arab music at first sounded to him 'like the wailing of the damned', but he quickly realized that there were subtleties of rhythm and pitch inaudible to the unattuned ear, and he was impressed by the 'tremendous passion in the Egyptians' love of it'. Early in March he briefly resumed his pre-war career as a radio artist by acting in a play and reading some poetry for the ESB. For the Home Service he delivered a travel talk on Cairo by wandering round the bazaar neighbourhood and the back streets and maintaining a running commentary on anything that came along.[33]

Administration normally absorbed far more of his attention than broadcasting. For some considerable time the BBC's Cairo office had been operating in an entirely haphazard and hand-to-mouth fashion. Every month the office accounts were supposed to be submitted to London but Phillips had barely and belatedly started December's when he was struck down. Unable to present him with his masses of assorted figures in hospital, Reed set about trying to coax and cajole, threaten or otherwise extract some clues to the chaos from the office secretary, who had only been recruited in December and knew even less than he did.[34]

As the War moved westward the scramble for news abated; material from correspondents at the front was relayed home through Algiers.[35] Yet, while Cairo remained the Allied headquarters in the Middle East it continued to be the key source of official information in theatre; all the RAF news was, for example, issued from Cairo. Gillard went on toiling away manfully until mid-March, when he moved to the front with Arnell, leaving Reed to handle the news as well as the Arabic broadcasts and office administration. Every day he attended a morning press conference, desperately scribbling notes from the guarded utterances of various spokes-men before rushing back to the office and throwing together a story. Then

began the great struggle with the censor – a series of arguments with the
Army, the RAF and finally the political authorities – after which he would
tear over to the ESB, produce his hard-won clearance stamps to the
engineer on duty and catch the 2.30 radio link to London.[36]

It was hard enough for Reed to balance the news reporting and the Arab
broadcasts with finance and administration at a time when he was still
afflicted by the after-effects of jaundice. But BBC Cairo was on the threshold
of a momentous development which, in the short term at least, signalled still
more work. In mid-February the Corporation announced that it was to
launch a very much larger operation in the Middle East. At its head was to
be one Edward Liveing, a former regional director who had been despatched
to Cairo in 1942 to survey the BBC's activities there. Liveing understandably
drew the conclusion that the Corporation had seriously underestimated
Cairo's importance, that their office was desperately under-resourced and
that an altogether more ambitious strategy was required. 'Broadcasting has
opportunities of playing a more effective role here than it is doing at present',
he declared, recommending the 'extension of BBC activities and interests'
and 'the establishment of a permanent BBC Middle East Office and requisite
staff in Cairo'.[37] Unfortunately, of course, he was two years too late. By the
time his proposals had been approved, the necessary funds released, new
staff appointed and appropriate premises occupied, the war in North Africa
was over.

Reed expected Liveing's appointment to signal the end of his sojourn at
2 Sharia Gameh Sharkass, but he was mistaken. Shortly after his arrival
Liveing asked him to continue handling the Arabic programmes and office
administration until the new staff appeared from Britain. Reed had little
experience of office management or finance, and he was still hoping to
return to the Army when his health improved. 'If I ever get fit enough to
know I shan't be a liability I'll chuck this masquerade and...go back to
tanks', he wrote on 21 February. So he only agreed to Liveing's request with
clear misgivings. The threat of returning to MEBU was undoubtedly an
influential consideration and Cairo, at that time, still seemed close and
relevant to the war effort, acting as it did as a conduit for news from the
front. Perhaps he was also thinking ahead: the BBC had been his employer
before the War, and might very well be afterwards. If the Corporation
imagined he was doing them a favour by consenting to stay, he could well
afford to spend a few weeks enhancing their obligation to him.[38]

He soon recognized his mistake. Liveing was followed by a former
Bristol programme director, Pennethorne Hughes, and a recording engineer,
Martin, and together they set out to show each other how to do business.
The result was a monumental increase in phoning, filing, letter writing and
typing. Together, too, they succeeded in monopolizing all the remaining
facilities required for the real work of the office. Following Gillard's
departure, Reed had been left with responsibility for all the office

management, two news despatches per day, news-reading for ESB, Arabic programme output and the press conferences for the BBC's news articles. Notwithstanding, he was now evicted from his office and deprived of his secretary by this trio of pinstriped gentlemen, who constantly came rushing to him to know why the lift was unserviceable or why he had not yet licensed the new directorial car.[39] It came as an immense relief when, towards the end of March, Godfrey Talbot returned from the front to take over the news bulletins.[40]

Reed spent the next two months struggling desperately to disentangle the office's chaotic financial records, becoming ever more exasperated with Liveing and his associates and demoralized about his prospects of returning to active service.[41] In a typical week he found little time for anything beyond work. But the working day was suspended throughout Cairo during the early afternoon. Sometimes he would take a tram to a reasonably priced NAAFI restaurant for GHQ officers; otherwise he would stroll over the Nile bridge to the Gezira Club to watch rugby, racing or polo, and eat lunch on the terrace by the swimming pool. He kept fit by walking, swimming and playing squash two or three times a week.[42] Occasionally he indulged his passion for music by attending concerts.[43] He also struck up a firm friendship with a Syrian named Fadel Shawa, who was director of Arabic music for ESB and acted as agent for the BBC's propaganda songs. Shawa took him to his first Arabic celebrity concert and later engaged some very exotic performers for his programmes, including an old Sheikh who yodelled the Koran and a Bedouin choir.[44]

A salutary reunion with John Welton left Reed conscious of his blessings. Welton had gone straight into another liaison job after the 24th Armoured Brigade was torn asunder. When he returned to Cairo on leave, late in February, Reed observed that Welton retained the outlook of their desert days, when Cairo was a magical city of baths and drinks and dinners. Welton thought that life there must be the seventh heaven – precisely Reed's view of Welton's position as aide-de-camp to a general by the sea near Benghazi.[45] After a couple of days Welton rejoined his unit and Reed bade him a fond farewell, not knowing whether their paths would cross again. So his surprise may be imagined when, less than a week later, an orderly phoned from the 15th Hospital asking if he could visit Lieutenant Welton. A serious car accident had left him with a fractured skull and a damaged spine, and he had been flown straight back to Cairo. The injuries were less severe than originally supposed but he had still to spend several weeks encased in plaster. Unexpectedly, Welton's misfortune proved to be Reed's salvation. Mindful of Welton's kindness during his own hospitalization in Alexandria, Reed made a daily pilgrimage to the 15th Hospital bringing books, fruit, flowers and anything else he could think of to make his friend's mummified existence more tolerable. However much he succeeded in that endeavour, the visits helped him to reconcile himself to the absurdity

of his own situation: to the two years of officer training that had returned
him to the BBC; to the seeming impossibility of further active service and
to the unearned captain's pip on his shoulder. For Welton, at any rate, he
was doing his bit.[46]

Reed eventually escaped from the Junior Officers' Club to rooms at the
Plaza Hotel. At the same time Welton, although still heavily plastered, was
allowed out of hospital, and Reed began spending afternoons with him at
the Gezira Club. His condition improved rapidly and he was soon able to
take a part-time job at GHQ. Shortly afterwards he joined Reed at the
Plaza. In mid-May they moved to a room on the eighth floor, from where
they enjoyed superb views out across the roof tops to the citadel and the
desert beyond. For the first time since his arrival in Cairo Reed breathed
fresh air and slept with the windows wide open.[47] Apart from Welton, his
closest companions were Godfrey Talbot and Chignall. Together they
increasingly gravitated towards the Gezira Club after lunch to drink iced
coffee and tea and talk about everything under the sun except the BBC,
which was a banned subject.[48] Later they would return to their posts until
dinner, after which there were various options – the cinema or an after-
news talk at the ESB, a party, or dinner at the Anglo-Egyptian Union.[49]

The pressure of work increased again early in May, when Talbot went
on leave and the news despatches were once more added to Reed's extensive
list of duties. His only consolation was that they were well received in
London. They rarely made the home news, which was dominated by Frank
Gillard's latest reports from Tunisia, broadcast from Algiers; but they were
used for Empire and African bulletins, and by the European services. The
task became particularly interesting after Tunis fell on 8 May.[50] In his
broadcast that day he recalled the evening at the Officers' Club in
Alexandria seven months before, when the ticker-tape machine announced
victory at El Alamein, while he and Welton looked on in astonishment:

> This morning in Cairo I had a reminder of that evening. For the past
> week there has been the same feeling of pressure, the same strain of
> waiting, as we have watched and listened for news from Tunisia.
> There isn't the same sense of imminence perhaps, but even over those
> thousands of miles of sand we have felt the reverberations of battle in
> the sweltering Cairo streets. The same sense of pressure, and the same
> guilty feeling at sleeping between sheets, and going to cinemas...
> People haven't discussed the news bulletins much, and when they
> have it's been with that studied nonchalance that we always assume
> when our hopes and thoughts and our worries are a long way away,
> committed hopelessly to things that are too vital to talk about.
> They've gone on with the daily round, telling themselves, though
> seldom each other, that 'something must happen. The tension can't

last.' If any comments were passed they were little more than 'wait and see'.

This morning when I went off to the office where I work, I was close on the heels of the same friend who watched the ticker-tape with me at Alex last November. There was nothing new to see. 'Shoe shine, shoe shine officer, half-acker – no good job, no money', laundries getting busy on street corners. Cars hooting. Garry-horses trotting down the hot tarmac, streets wet and steaming after their early morning hosing. Everyone in a hurry to get to work or to sell something to somebody else. Cigarettes? Fly-swat? Papurr? 'Papurr, officer, papurr Ingleesh. Yes? Papurr captain?' We stopped casually and bought one – more a matter of habit than anything – and read the 3 am announcement.[51]

Later in May the BBC's European Department ordained a huge 'All-African Hook-up' commemorating the North African campaign, which required a trip to Alexandria for naval coverage, an eyewitness report from El Alamein, another (provided by Gillard) from Tripoli and a long emotional blurb about life in Cairo since the outbreak of war. Reed set off for El Alamein with Chignall and his recording equipment. At the railway station they recorded a train 'moving westwards into the setting sun' (only it was going towards Alexandria at 2 pm) and then followed convoluted desert tracks to the erstwhile location of 24th Armoured Brigade headquarters, now occupied by a solitary camel and a lot of empty tins. The old tracks – Sun, Moon, Star, Boat, Bottle and Hat – were still there, but reverting to desert very swiftly. A further half-mile along Boat brought him to the place where, the previous October, he had located all that remained of the 47th Battalion and learnt that B Squadron had been obliterated. He was so moved he could hardly say his piece.[52]

The recording complete – at the fourth attempt – they brewed up tea and munched corned beef and sat in silence surveying the desert, and Reed tried to persuade himself that he once knew no other home. But the battle, the brigade and his nomadic desert life seemed so far away that it was hard to recognize himself as the same person. And yet, he pondered, that life had brought out the best in him that he had ever known. By contrast, Cairo had eroded his imagination and initiative, dulled his senses and left him dejectedly struggling with the drab BBC routine as if he had nothing else to live for. By May 1943 he felt but a pale shadow of the desert warrior of El Alamein.[53] After a mad rush from one end of Egypt to the other he delivered his broadcast to London at the eleventh hour and was, to his amazement, overwhelmed with congratulations from the European programmes' producer. When it came to the dress rehearsal he found that his pieces had been built up to the skies. The programme went out live the next night, with contributions from all over Africa, and Reed afterwards received 'a glowing wire' from London.[54]

2. Reed, broadcasting from El Alamein railway station in May 1943.
The German bomb 'has been disembowelled and has nothing but a
desert sparrow's nest inside'.

3. Reed and Chignall broadcasting from the former headquarters of the
24th Armoured Brigade in May 1943.

By June 1943 the BBC's Cairo office was finally assuming the ambitious proportions envisaged by Liveing in February. A Recorded Programmes Department was established; new engineers and secretaries arrived; Reed off-loaded his 27 different accounts on to a new financial secretary and, with Talbot handling all the news, concentrated on making up four months of arrears in Arabic recordings. Plans were drawn up to appoint a permanent Middle East correspondent (as opposed to war correspondents like Gillard and Talbot) and an entire Arabic staff.[55] To accommodate so many personnel larger premises were needed. Liveing located new offices in the Ministry of Information's building by the river, close to GHQ and sandwiched between the British Embassy and Prime Minister Nahas Pasha's residence. He and Pennethorne Hughes moved there without warning on 24 June. Reed was the last to vacate 2 Sharia Gameh Sharkass, remaining only to guard files, equipment and other paraphernalia, ploughing the lonely furrow of his Arabic recordings while the remarkable Chignall moved the household props from under him and despatched them in relays in an Egyptian donkey cart.[56]

Within a short time Reed's life was completely transformed; indeed it became positively luxurious. The directorial car was sent to fetch him in the morning and took him home again at night and at lunchtime. There were no more noxious fumes from the cafés of downtown Cairo, and he was given a spacious office to himself with pleasant views of lush river scenery.

4. The BBC's augmented Cairo staff in June 1943, including Pennethorne Hughes (far left), Godfrey Talbot (standing fifth from right) and Reed (second from right).

After juggling four different jobs for five months he welcomed the chance to focus on a single task.[57] He might simply have relaxed for a while; he deserved an opportunity to rest and recuperate. But he just could not. He was probably shocked out of his inertia by returning to the El Alamein battlefield at the end of May. It was the unnerving contrast between the alert and robust desert soldier of 1942 and the desk-bound Cairo functionary of 1943, lacking in health and self-respect, that heralded his departure from the BBC. As time went on he became seized with the conviction that he had 'seen enough of the war's soft end'. He had returned to the Corporation in January to assist with an emergency, which had then been artificially perpetuated by Liveing. Yet it seemed that under Liveing's direction one crisis or another would continue indefinitely, especially while Reed was there (at the Army's expense) to shoulder any extra burden of work. In the meantime the War had left him far behind. 'I shall very soon be among the forgotten men', he wrote gloomily in June.[58]

Shortly after the office moved his worst expectations were realized when Liveing's entourage disappeared to Alexandria and programme output drew to a complete standstill for lack of any creative input from the top management. Reed might have leaped heroically to their assistance yet again, but only by accepting a further indefinite tie to the BBC and to Cairo, by committing himself to work for which Liveing would undoubtedly have taken all the credit, and by abandoning altogether any hope of contributing more tangibly to the defeat of the Third Reich. Viewed from this perspective his dilemma resolved itself at last. 'The time has come for me to go', he decided. 'To what I don't know. But I've had all I want of Cairo and after all I didn't leave the [BBC's] School's Dept to be a uniformed exhibit in Liveing's shop window. So I'm looking for another job.'[59]

NOTES

1. RP, OR to PR, 4 and 11 November 1942.
2. RP, OR to PR, 17 and 20 November 1942.
3. RP, OR to PR, 26 November 1942.
4. RP, OR to PR, 29 November 1942.
5. RP, OR to PR, 2 and 7 December 1942.
6. RP, OR to PR, 7 and 8 December 1942.
7. RP, OR to PR, 15 December 1942.
8. RP, OR to PR, 17 December 1942.
9. *Ibid.*
10. RP, OR to PR, 5 January 1943; 12 June 1943.
11. *Who Was Who, 1981–1990.*
12. BBC archive R13/167, minutes of a meeting held on 24 September 1941 in SSE's office; minutes of meeting held on 14 October 1941 at Broadcasting House; extract from JR Morley's report on his visit to Cairo, 21 May 1942.

13. RP, OR to PR, 29 January 1943.
14. RP, OR to PR, 18 December 1942.
15. RP, OR to PR, 26 December 1942.
16. *Ibid.*; RP, OR to PR, 21 December 1942.
17. RP, OR to PR, 30 December 1942.
18. RP, OR to PR, 3 and 5 January 1943.
19. RP, OR to PR, 17 December 1942.
20. RP, OR to PR, 30 December 1942; 23 January 1943.
21. RP, OR to PR, 21 and 22 December 1942.
22. RP, OR to PR, 30 December 1942; 25 May 1943. 'I'm no use to the Army without months of retraining.'
23. RP, OR to PR, 12 and 13 January 1943.
24. RP, OR to PR, 21 January 1943.
25. RP, OR to PR, 21 and 23 January 1943.
26. RP, OR to PR, 23 January 1943.
27. Francis George Gillard was educated at Wellington School, Somerset, and at St Luke's College, Exeter. A former schoolmaster, Gillard worked as a freelance broadcaster in the 1930s before joining the BBC in 1941 and becoming one of their most famous war correspondents. After the War he held a number of senior positions in the BBC until his retirement in 1970.
28. RP, OR to PR, 23 January 1943; RP, undated memo from Reed to A.P. Ryan, Controller News, BBC Head Office; BBC archive R13/166/2, Lieving to Ds.G, 20 January 1943; V.D.K. Craddock (Overseas Liaison) to BBC Cairo, 20 January 1943. 'Gillard we agree your approaching Public Relations Army regarding Owen Reed and to help you have cabled Philpotts through War Office channels.'
29. RP, OR to PR, 23 January 1943.
30. RP, OR to PR, 29 January 1943.
31. RP, undated memo from the BBC's Cairo office to BBC London.
32. RP, OR to PR, 7 February 1943.
33. RP, OR to PR, 2 and 8 March 1943.
34. RP, OR to PR, 16 February 1943.
35. RP, OR to PR, 8 March 1943.
36. RP, OR to PR, 20 March 1943; 4 June 1943; BBC archive R13/166/3, E.G.D. Lieving to OSEO, 27 August 1943.
37. BBC archive R13/167, Lieving to Directors General, 18 September 1942; RP, OR to PR, 21 February 1943.
38. RP, OR to PR, 21 February 1943; 2 March 1943.
39. RP, OR to PR, 20 March 1943; BBC archive R13/166/3, E.G.D. Lieving to OSEO, 27 August 1943; C.J. Pennethorne Hughes to OSEO, 26 August 1943.
40. RP, OR to PR, 31 March 1943.
41. RP, OR to PR, 8 and 11 April 1943; 10 May 1943.
42. RP, OR to PR, undated, postmarked 20 March 1943.
43. RP, OR to PR, 7 February 1943.
44. RP, OR to PR, 8 March 1943; 2 July 1943.
45. RP, OR to PR, 22 February 1943.
46. RP, OR to PR, 14 and 31 March 1943; 8 April 1943.
47. RP, OR to PR, 11 and 25 April 1943; 4 and undated June 1943.

48. RP, OR to PR, 2 July 1943.
49. RP, OR to PR, 7 July 1943.
50. RP, OR to PR, 10 and 16 May 1943.
51. RP, transcript of broadcast, 8 May 1943.
52. RP, OR to PR, 25 May 1943.
53. *Ibid.*; RP, OR to PR, 29 May 1943.
54. RP, OR to PR, 4 June 1943.
55. RP, OR to PR, 6 July 1943.
56. RP, OR to PR, 24 and 29 June 1943. Nahas Pasha was the Prime Minister of Egypt and leader of the Wafd, Egypt's strongest political party.
57. RP, OR to PR, 2 and 7 July 1943.
58. RP, OR to PR, 24 June 1943.
59. RP, OR to PR, 14 July 1943.

3

The Secret Intelligence Service and Yugoslavia, 1939–43

At the beginning of the Second World War SIS maintained their overseas presence through a chain of stations vulnerably co-located with Passport Control Offices, and through a separate network of agents – the 'Z' network – operating under commercial cover. During the 1930s, with very limited resources, they were confronted by the formidable task of gathering intelligence on both the Stalinist Soviet Union and national socialist Germany, and it is generally accepted that their activities were more effectively oriented towards the former than the latter. In the years preceding the outbreak of hostilities SIS incurred mounting criticism from the Armed Services because of their failure to obtain much good-quality information on German military preparations. By the time Germany invaded France and the Low Countries in 1940 most of the Passport Control Offices in western and central Europe had been evacuated, and the 'Z' network had been fatally compromised following the capture of two leading SIS field officers by the German Security Service at Venlo, Holland, in November 1939.[1]

With no contingency plans for the German occupation, SIS's European activities became largely confined to stations on neutral soil, such as Stockholm, Lisbon and Berne, or to more peripheral capitals like Istanbul and Tangiers.[2] SIS otherwise located very few agents in occupied countries and instead relied heavily on networks established by London-based intelligence services-in-exile, such as the Czech, Norwegian, Polish, Dutch and French secret services.[3] They also began the War with only a minimal presence in British-controlled areas of the Middle East: such territories had normally been considered the responsibility of the Security Service (MI5) and its military intelligence colleagues on the local commander-in-chief's staff.[4] In July 1940 SIS lost Section D, a directorate responsible for irregular warfare in enemy territories, when Churchill established a new and entirely separate organization to undertake sabotage and subversion in German-occupied Europe – SOE. And even SIS's most notable coup, the successful decryption of German signals sent via the Enigma cipher machine, was at first devalued because the military authorities instinctively doubted the reliability of what they presumed to be just another conventional (and therefore suspect) secret intelligence source.[5]

One of the few countries in mainland Europe where SIS enlarged their activities in the immediate aftermath of the outbreak of war was Yugoslavia. A new Passport Control Office had been established in Belgrade in the late 1930s.[6] In 1939 the Head of Station was Captain Clement Hope but in May 1940 his place was taken by Robert F. St George Lethbridge.[7] By 1941 Lethbridge's permanent staff numbered five officers – Parsons, Thom, Shires, James and Gerrish.[8] Britain also developed a network of regional consulates in Yugoslavia, from which SIS operated. Among the officials at the Split consulate were R. Sherwood, another 'passport control officer', and Desmond Clarke, who at first represented the Ministry of Information before being 'transferred to other duties'.[9] But the most important consulate, by virtue of its proximity to the southern frontier of the Third Reich, was located at Zagreb, the capital of Croatia, and was headed by T.C. Rapp. As one official submission put it:

> The outbreak of war with Germany has made the Yugoslav–German frontier…an important point for gleaning information about conditions in Germany and for keeping a watch on the trade and other relations between Yugoslavia and the enemy. Lord Halifax [the Foreign Secretary] therefore considers it eminently desirable to strengthen the staff of His Majesty's Consulate in Zagreb.[10]

The documents reveal strenuous efforts to enlarge the consulate's establishment in the later months of 1939, when it was re-designated a consulate-general.[11] And although appointees were nominally despatched to Croatia by the Foreign Office, they were in fact selected with the direct assistance of Commander Rex Howard, chief staff officer to 'C', the head of SIS.[12] The officer appointed SIS's senior representative at Zagreb was James Millar, a Scot who had studied modern languages at Cambridge before his recruitment. Millar, elder brother of the author George Millar, had previously served in the Passport Control Offices in Berlin and Copenhagen.[13] His assistants included William Stuart, a British citizen of mixed Anglo-European parentage, who had been born and educated in Yugoslavia, and a certain John Lloyd-Evans, the former SIS 'Z' officer at Prague.[14] But SIS's network extended far beyond the confines of official embassy and consular property. The surviving records show that British Council lecturers and former passport control officers were being considered for the same consular posts in Yugoslavia, and the British Council certainly provided one avenue by which SIS broadened its influence there.[15] Among the Council's Yugoslav staff were Kenneth Syers and John Ennals.[16]

During 1940 Belgrade and Zagreb became veritable hotbeds of espionage and intrigue. One notable SIS achievement in this period was the recruitment in Belgrade of an Abwehr* operative, Dusko Popov, who subsequently worked as a double agent for MI5.[17] And SIS's involvement in the coup d'état that unseated the Prince Regent in March 1941 and precipitated the German occupation is well recorded and requires no further coverage here.[18] Closer to the Reich, SIS's Zagreb operation was far more vulnerable to hostile countermeasures. The primary function of the consulate-general – espionage – would have been impossible to conceal and, given his previous employment in Berlin, James Millar's identity must have been well known to the Germans, who also harboured a profound suspicion of non-consular organizations like the British Council.[19] The position was further complicated by the presence of strong fascist and extreme nationalist movements in Croatia, which were deeply antagonistic towards Britain. German representatives in Zagreb unsuccessfully attempted to organize the assassination of one British agent; and early in February 1941 a member of a Croatian fascist group managed to detonate a bomb on the first floor of the consulate building. Fortunately all the staff escaped unhurt. Police investigations quickly led to the Europa Press, a news agency that flourished under the aegis of the German press attaché in Zagreb.[20] Yet in spite of the many hazards that confronted Millar's team, they succeeded in forging some important contacts – particularly in Slovenia, the territory actually bordering the Reich. By 1941 they had a source in Carinthia, on the Austria-Slovenia frontier, which supplied intelligence on the assembly of German forces for the invasion in April.[21]

The German invasion placed all of those with consular connections in Yugoslavia in considerable peril, but only Rapp, Evans and two others – ostensibly representatives of the British Council and the Shell Oil Company – were unlucky enough to fall into German hands.[22] A British Council party, which included Syers, left for Greece just before Germany's declaration of war, and then moved on from Athens to Cairo.[23] Lethbridge and the other passport control staff at Belgrade fled towards the Adriatic coast with the ambassador, Campbell, his staff and a number of non-diplomatic personnel (including British Council lecturers like Ennals).[24] Near Sarajevo they linked up with Millar and Stuart, who had escaped on foot from Zagreb in the nick of time.[25] After unsuccessful efforts to evacuate them from the Adriatic coast by submarine and flying boat, they gave themselves up to the Italians, Italy having agreed to repatriate any British diplomatic personnel captured on foreign soil on the strict understanding that Britain would fully reciprocate.[26] Notwithstanding such pressure as Germany presumably applied behind the scenes, the Italians observed the agreement and surprisingly extended its provisions to the non-diplomatic contingent, many of whom were in fact

---

* German intelligence.

linked to SIS or SOE.[27] Campbell's entire party was evacuated to Italy, where they were soon joined by the staff of the Split consulate.[28] From Italy they were transported in a special train across Vichy France to neutral Spain, from where they reached Britain via Portugal or Gibraltar.[29] According to the official history, no effective stay-behind networks survived in Yugoslavia following the German occupation.[30]

The collapse of their Yugoslav operation was the nadir of SIS's thoroughly inauspicious beginning to the Second World War. But by the time the German army entered Belgrade the Service was already in the process of rebuilding its intelligence-gathering capability elsewhere, as and when opportunities and resources permitted. The official historians record, for example, the creation of ship-watching networks on the Norwegian coast, a growing volume of intelligence reaching London from Denmark and the Netherlands, the penetration of southern France and north-west Africa, and improved measures for the exploitation of signals intelligence.[31] But one of the most important initiatives to rebuild SIS and restore their tarnished reputation was the foundation in June 1940 of a new station in Cairo, the city destined to be the focus of Britain's war effort for the next two years. The station was located in the 'Grey Pillars' GHQ compound, where it operated under the deliberately bland cover name the 'Inter-Services Liaison Department' (ISLD). It was headed by SIS's second assistant chief of staff, Captain Cuthbert ('Curly') Bowlby RN, an Oxford graduate who had served in the Coastal Motor Boat Flotilla during the First World War.[32] Bill Bremner, a pre-war SIS 'G' officer, became his deputy,[33] while other headquarters staff included John Bruce Lockhart, Archie Gibson and Major 'Titters' Titterington, King Farouk's personal chemist, who took charge of ISLD's technical section.[34] ISLD gradually extended their influence in the Middle East to such far-flung locations as Beirut, Baghdad and Aden. And an SIS station was also maintained on Malta operating independently from Cairo, presumably for security reasons. Control of the Cairo and Malta stations was eventually unified under Bowlby following the defeat of Axis forces in North Africa in May 1943, and ISLD headquarters then moved to Algiers.[35]

Several covert agencies were establishing a presence in the Middle East during 1940 and 1941. Apart from ISLD Security Intelligence Middle East (SIME) represented MI5, SOE perpetrated sabotage and subversion against Axis forces of occupation, MI9 organized escape and evasion activities, while 'A' Force specialized in strategic deception. On 13 August 1941 a so-called Committee for Secret Activities (SAC) was created 'to co-ordinate the work of the various secret organizations operating in the Middle East'.[36] The committee is said to have 'proved very valuable, particularly as it was set up at a time when the organizations represented were in the process of development'. It was regularly chaired by the Minister of State Resident in the Middle East, who thereby gained an insight into the activities of the secret organizations and into the best means by which their services could be employed. At the same time, as an ISLD memorandum subsequently recorded, 'he was able to facilitate our work by keeping us informed of the local and general situation on a high plane and in a manner not otherwise available to us'.[37]

While British – and in time American – strategy aimed to drive the Axis forces west from Egypt towards North Africa and Italy, ISLD played an important part in strategic deception activities designed to tie as many German troops as possible to the eastern Mediterranean.[38] A similar orientation – particularly towards Greece and Turkey – is apparent in the deployment of ISLD field agents. There were several reasons for this. SIS had maintained a presence in Greece and Turkey before the War;[39] their Athens station was closed when Greece was occupied in 1941, but covert operations began soon after the German invasion, and at least two ISLD missions were functioning in Athens by the end of the year.[40] Neutral Turkey became a focus for espionage during the War and also provided a conduit for the infiltration of field agents into German-occupied Europe.[41] The relatively open seas, island and mountain terrain of the eastern Mediterranean also facilitated infiltration and afforded operatives a valuable degree of protection.

As in Athens, ISLD remained active in Crete after the loss of the island in 1941.[42] One of their agents, Lieutenant Noel Rees, formerly of the Royal Navy Volunteer Reserve (RNVR), also founded a secret operational base at Khioste, on the Chesme peninsula in eastern Turkey, from where a regular caique* run was maintained to the northern Sporades:

> From Khioste, caiques were able to proceed to and from the coast of Turkey without let or hindrance. They continued to run, throughout the war, in flagrant defiance of all existing laws in Turkey, and those applicable to neutral states.[43]

In February 1942 another caique route was opened from Famagusta in Cyprus to Khioste to convey supplies to Noel Rees. By the end of the War these vessels had transported approximately 100 personnel and 50 tons of stores into Turkey.[44]

By contrast, ISLD made a slow start in the Middle East itself, and in more western territories. According to the official history, 'little had been achieved by the end of 1940 either by way of putting the SIS in the area on a war footing or in improving liaison with the Service intelligence authorities in the theatre'.[45] During 1941 an advance base was located in the desert, 'but its few reports dealt only with activity in the enemy's rear areas', and ISLD therefore 'contributed little to the collection of intelligence for the desert war'.[46]

---

* Bosporan skiffs, Levantine sailing ships.

It should not be thought that ISLD were uninterested in the desert campaign or in the western Mediterranean but transport aircraft were required to infiltrate agents into enemy-occupied north Africa, Italy and Yugoslavia, and a chronic shortage of such aircraft severely inhibited the development of clandestine activities in these regions. In 1941 there was no organization in the Middle East responsible for parachuting agents into enemy territory, and no aircraft were specially allotted to the task. If an air mission was needed ISLD had to make representations to the RAF, who might then allot an aircraft from the bomber force, if one could be spared. The aircraft might be one of a number of types, and could similarly be operated by one of several squadrons. None of the airfields involved was located less than 100 miles from Cairo. In these circumstances a single operation could only be mounted with considerable difficulty.[47]

ISLD initially sought permission to purchase their own aircraft and to create a special flight for their operations, but this was refused. 'Instead, instructions were received to negotiate with the RAF for the provision, maintenance and operation of this flight by them.'[48] At a meeting with the British Minister of State in Cairo on 27 September 1941, Bowlby indicated his desire to mount operations from Malta behind enemy lines in north Africa. He:

> said that the immediate problem so far as MI6 were concerned was the introduction of agents, at the C-in-C's request, into Tripoli. It was apparently proving difficult to find in Malta aircraft operationally suitable for this work, and he understood that the Governor of Malta had now taken the matter up direct with the Chiefs of Staff.[49]

ISLD afterwards prepared a memorandum proposing clandestine air drops into 'Balkans and Tunis from Malta...dropping or parachuting personnel, stores and pamphlets...from Egypt to Greece, Crete, Yugoslavia and Cyrenaica' and 'landing or collecting agents and stores off enemy coasts like Greece, Tunis, Balkans, Italy, [and the] Black Sea', employing flying boats or sea planes. They were hoping to base two aircraft in Malta and two in Egypt for these purposes.[50]

Misfortune dogged this project from the start. In the absence of suitable British aircraft the RAF rather improbably assigned four Heinkel 115 seaplanes (formerly the property of the Royal Dutch Air Force) to Malta for ISLD operations. The first was lost on only its second flight, and a Swordfish temporarily loaned by the local RAF Command likewise went 'missing' after completing one operation. The second Heinkel was destroyed at its moorings during an air raid in February 1942 without flying a single sortie, and neither the third nor the fourth ever reached Malta. The only alternative lay in conducting these missions from the Middle East using long-range aircraft but unfortunately hardly any were available at this stage of the War. In May 1942 a flight of four Liberators from 108 Squadron (based at the Nile Delta) was made available for special operations. Their sorties were only flown nightly in moonlit conditions, and their success was dependent on good visibility: many operations were aborted because of adverse weather, particularly during the winter months. They could not possibly satisfy the combined infiltration and supply requirements of the various clandestine organizations, particularly those of SOE.[51]

The flow of operational intelligence from the desert improved dramatically in the later months of 1942. 'Good coverage' of the western Mediterranean was allegedly being provided in the weeks before the Allied landings in French north-west Africa in November 1942, and in the following months ISLD collaborated with the SIS station in Algiers 'to supply some intelligence of operational value' to the First and Eighth Armies.[52] But it is hardly surprising that they remained heavily reliant on maritime transport to support their Turkish and Greek operations, or that their efforts to restore an SIS presence in Yugoslavia only proceeded slowly.

Following the Belgrade Station's closure in April 1941 SIS located their Yugoslav operations section with ISLD in Cairo, but the division of authority between London and Cairo was not very sharply defined. The 'chief passport officer' for Yugoslavia remained in London, and it is unclear from the documents precisely where his powers ended and Cuthbert Bowlby's began; jurisdictional disputes were by no means uncommon.[53] James Millar became head of the operations section in Cairo, while Bill Stuart and Desmond Clarke functioned as his deputies. Kenneth Syers, who had joined the RAF in Egypt, eventually found his way into Millar's team, while John Ennals manned SIS's Yugoslav desk in London.[54]

In the meantime two separate resistance movements emerged in Yugoslavia. One, the so-called 'Chetniks', was overwhelmingly Serbian and royalist, and was led by a Yugoslav army colonel (later general), Draza Mihailovic. The other, which was multi-ethnic and spanned north-western Serbia, Bosnia, Croatia and Slovenia, was predominantly communist and operated under the leadership of Josip Broz Tito, half-Croat, half-Slovene head of the Soviet-backed Yugoslav Communist Party. Although they fought under the self-styled title of the Yugoslav Army of National Liberation (JANL) his followers were invariably labelled 'Partisans'. There was initially some collaboration between the Chetniks and the Partisans, but relations subsequently deteriorated, and open conflict erupted between them in November 1941.

British policy was oriented towards Mihailovic for two reasons: firstly, Churchill's government believed him to represent the chief source of resistance within Axis-occupied territory; secondly, Britain actively supported the Yugoslav government-in-exile, which likewise backed Mihailovic, and initially had little knowledge of the Partisan movement. No doubt their communist affiliations were also distrusted in many quarters.[55] As early as January 1942 'C' was said to be 'anxious to introduce agents and W/T [wireless/telegraphy] sets into Yugoslavia for the purpose of obtaining information', and so ISLD set out to make contact with Mihailovic and other associates of the government-in-exile, working through government ministers, through their diplomatic corps and through royalist officers who had escaped to the Middle East in 1941.[56] Although records from this period are fragmentary, it is clear that their activities were by no means unsuccessful. At the end of July 1942, for example, an agent named Captain Naumovic was infiltrated into General Mihailovic's headquarters, from where he submitted daily reports to ISLD on enemy troop movements along particular lines of communication. In March 1943 Ennals told the Foreign Office: 'This information is considered by the Service Departments to be of considerable interest and importance, and Captain Naumovic is regarded as being a most valuable and reliable collaborator.'[57] In the same period SOE located British liaison officers with Mihailovic, and began dropping small quantities of arms, money and other supplies to the Chetniks. During the early stages of these operations ISLD handled SOE's radio communications, thereby obtaining automatic access to all signals emanating from SOE sources in the field.[58]

North-west Yugoslavia was inevitably more difficult to penetrate, but by December 1942 ISLD were claiming to 'possess channels into Slovenia good enough to enable them to arrange a [parachute] dropping pinpoint'.[59] In March 1943 an agent was successfully infiltrated through this connection, a Major Novak, who was Mihailovic's representative in Slovenia, and radio contact duly began on the 23rd.[60] A clandestine radio link was also organized between SIS's London headquarters and leading members of the Slovene National Committee (known as 'Zavesa') in Ljubljana, a body representing non-communist political parties in Slovenia. According to one SIS memorandum these sources 'provided information of some value'.[61]

From the limited documentation available it is difficult to establish SIS's precise thinking on Yugoslavia's resistance movements between 1941 and 1943. Some writers have accused officers such as Ennals of harbouring left-wing prejudices, which allegedly caused them to slant their intelligence appreciations against Mihailovic and in favour of the Partisans.[62] In fact, as already suggested, SIS did not display any reluctance to work with Mihailovic and his supporters; and while Ennals could be critical of the Chetniks he dutifully circulated raw intelligence to the Foreign Office that presented an extremely negative view of the Partisans. In May 1943, for example, he supplied copies of resolutions by Zavesa which called on the Partisans to 'stop killing Slovenes, burning down their houses and looting' and which at the same time described Tito's followers as 'an insignificant minority' who 'do not fight against the occupier'.[63] In Cairo ISLD distributed critical information about the Partisans to SOE. Hence, in March 1943, Desmond Clarke sent them one of Novak's signals claiming that the Partisans had 'killed about 3,000 non-communist Slovenes and not more than 100 of the occupying troops. They have burned down many Slovene villages and schools', he continued. 'They are fighting for the Bolshevization of Slovenia.'[64] In short, SIS cannot legitimately be accused of suppressing anti-Partisan intelligence.

It is nevertheless true that several members of their Yugoslavia section developed a strong pro-Partisan position within 12 months of the German occupation. In April 1942 one of these officers prepared a political report entitled 'The Partisans in Yugoslavia'. Although not overtly unsympathetic towards Mihailovic and the Chetniks, this document did maintain that the Partisans were responsible for most resistance activity in Yugoslavia and that they enjoyed 'the confidence of a large part, and that, probably, the most potentially active part of the population'. They were destined to play an important role in Yugoslav affairs both during and after the War. In an oblique reference to signals intelligence, which probably included actual or summarized Enigma decrypts, it was claimed that the report was based on all the evidence to which SIS had, at that time, had access, but simultaneously acknowledged that very little hard information on the Partisan movement had been received. There was, for example, 'no reliable indication of the strength of the Partisans'.[65]

While it is impossible to identify the author of this document with complete certainty, the fact that he had 'lived for many years in Yugoslavia' strongly suggests that it was William Stuart.[66] Through such arguments SIS were persuaded of the necessity to despatch agents to the Partisans and, true to form, began a search for émigrés with left-wing contacts inside Yugoslavia. Stuart was sent to North America with the aim of recruiting from among the many communists of Yugoslav origin who had emigrated to Canada in the 1930s, and Yugoslav Canadians already serving with the Commonwealth Armed Forces were likewise encouraged to join ISLD.[67] A number of suitable personnel were also found among some 25 European Jews recruited in Cairo through the Zionist organization, the Jewish Agency for Palestine.[68]

A further SIS appreciation of the internal situation in Yugoslavia prepared in August 1942 reflected the presence of Naumovic at Mihailovic's headquarters, while again drawing on signals intelligence. It was suggested that Mihailovic aimed 'to conserve Serb resources and not to expose his countrymen to annihilation in reprisal for ill-timed attacks on the Axis'. He was said to have shown himself to be a resourceful leader and a shrewd and realistic politician. 'In view of his undoubted qualities, his caution, and his considerable prestige, it seems very probable that his influence and strength... will continue to increase in Serbia, Montenegro, Sandjak, Bosnia, Herzegovina and perhaps in parts of Dalmatia.'[69]

More negatively, Mihailovic regarded the Partisans as a more immediate threat than the Axis forces of occupation, and was said to be 'in touch with Chetniks fighting the Partisans in North West [sic] Bosnia'. There was also evidence that he was 'in indirect touch with the Italians, at least to the extent of the Italians assisting his associates to break up the Partisans'. Most of all, his movement was overwhelmingly Serbian and nationalist. There was 'little likelihood of his establishing any effective organization or influence in either Slovenia or Croatia proper'.[70]

The ambivalence which characterized this assessment was no less apparent when SIS turned their attention back to the Partisans. To their credit Tito's followers were said to be 'sincerely and bitterly opposed to the Axis'. Their movement was 'the natural outlet for the ideological as opposed to the narrowly Serb nationalist opposition to the invader'. But at the same time they allegedly suffered from a lack of cohesion and from a tendency towards over-optimism and precipitance. They had 'failed to retain popular support in Serbia or Montenegro'. They were not expected to maintain a significant presence in such Chetnik strongholds, nor were their prospects considered very much more hopeful in Bosnia. Only in Croatia did it seem possible that Partisan activities might increase.[71]

But in the following months SIS's uncertainty about the Partisans was dispelled by a marked expansion of Axis, and particularly German, operations against them, largely revealed by high-grade signals intelligence. Apart from showing a steady build-up of Axis deployments in Partisan territory, this intelligence provided regular information on railway sabotage undertaken by the Partisans in a variety of locations, and disclosed that these activities were causing grave concern to German commanders. SOE's representative at Mihailovic's headquarters, Bill Hudson, and another agent located there, were also becoming increasingly critical of the Chetniks, supplying further evidence of their inactivity and of their collaboration with the Italians.[72] And SIS's contacts in Slovenia disclosed that neither Novak nor the other non-communist political groups were actively opposing the Axis forces of occupation.[73] However, just as it appeared that British intelligence appreciations were shifting decisively in the Partisans' favour, SOE replaced Hudson with a more senior liaison officer, Colonel Bailey, who promptly began submitting signals and reports reaffirming Mihailovic's operational potential, and casting doubt on Partisan prospects in Serbia and Bosnia.[74]

Between December 1942 and March 1943, partly on the evidence of Bailey's reports, several top-level British intelligence and military bodies reaffirmed their faith in Mihailovic. They included the Military Intelligence branch of the War Office, the Joint Intelligence Sub-Committee of the Chiefs of Staff, and the Chiefs of Staff Committee itself.[75] In London, SIS were intensely displeased to find that the authority of their intelligence sources was being directly challenged by information emanating from a British officer in the field. At a meeting with the Foreign Office and SOE in February:

C [SIS] representatives declined to accept information contained in D/H2's [Bailey's] telegrams regarding A/H31's [Mihailovic's] strength and organization and claimed that these were exaggerated. In general they pressed [the] Partisan case and emphasized their resistance in East Bosnia.[76]

They also argued that Bailey's position was inconsistent with the intelligence they obtained through 'Most Secret sources' – that is, Enigma and other decrypts.[77] The depth of SIS's concern is reflected in one particular extract from their representative's submission to this meeting. He declared that Bailey was not in a position to be well informed on conditions in Partisan-occupied territory, or on the 'strength of the pro-Partisan and anti-Mihailovic feeling...which our sources show to exist throughout the country. We do not think his reports can be taken as a basis on which to frame British policy towards Yugoslavia.'[78]

SIS responded to this situation in two ways. Firstly, they apparently began to pass an increasing amount of signals intelligence on the internal situation in Yugoslavia directly to the Prime Minister. Certainly, by the summer of 1943, Churchill was receiving a considerable number of Enigma decrypts from the Chief of SIS, and they played an important part in persuading him that the Partisans represented a very potent military force. On the basis of this intelligence he wrote to General Alexander in July of 'the marvellous resistance put up by the so-called Partisan followers of Tito in Bosnia'.[79] Secondly, SIS revised its long-cherished strategy of working only through foreign émigrés: clearly it was essential to despatch British agents into the field. The problem, of course, was that they barely possessed any suitable officers. Early in January they decided to recall Stuart from the USA and to send him to Mihailovic's headquarters, where he was to relieve Bailey of his intelligence work and prepare for the reception of further agents. 'We are convinced that great improvements can be effected in Mihailovic's system of Intelligence', SIS informed SOE with questionable sincerity, 'and this is of course a direct responsibility of "C".'[80] Predictably enough, SOE did not receive this proposition with enthusiasm. They contended that there was limited potential for improving the Chetnik intelligence organization, and that the collection of intelligence could in any case be adequately handled by Bailey and his subordinates. Stuart's invaluable experience and qualifications would be wasted with Mihailovic; instead, SIS should consider sending him on a mission to the Partisans in Croatia.[81]

Less concerned over the paucity of intelligence from Mihailovic's headquarters than over the pernicious influence of Bailey's reports in London, SIS were not at first persuaded. Moreover, they did not yet believe that the time was ripe to send a British officer to the Partisans.[82] Only broader strategic developments caused it to revise its position.

By the beginning of 1943 the desert war was moving west, the conclusion of the North African campaign was in sight and Allied planners were devising new strategies for opening a second front in mainland Europe. Following the Casablanca conference in January 1943 plans were drawn up for the invasion of Italy through Sicily ('Operation Husky'). The implications of Operation Husky for British policy towards Yugoslavia were indeed profound. As a direct result, Croatia and Slovenia assumed a far greater importance in British thinking than Serbia. Both territories bordered Italy, while Slovenia additionally shared a common frontier with Austria. The region was also vital both to Italy's communications with the Balkans and to Germany's communications between her armies in Greece, and her allies in Bulgaria, Romania and central Europe.[83]

The Partisans were known to be responsible for virtually all resistance activity in Croatia and Slovenia.[84] Churchill therefore sought to establish closer contact with Tito's movement, and to increase the volume of supplies being parachuted into Yugoslavia.[85] SIS and SOE were directed to assign priority to the northern Mediterranean theatre in support of this strategy.[86] As the chiefs of staff put it:

> Prospect of Operation Husky has made it more than ever imperative that our sources of information from Husky-land [Italy] and adjacent territories should be best possible. To meet this situation SIS must develop more sources by means of more agents and better communications.[87]

Again, much depended on the availability of air transport. During the winter of 1942/43 a number of requests reached London for more long-range aircraft suitable for mounting special operations from the Middle East. In February 1943, for example, the Foreign Secretary, Anthony Eden, was warned that without additional aircraft 'ISLD will probably be unable to make any contacts in Croatia and Slovenia'.[88] Following Casablanca both Churchill and Eden brought intense pressure to bear on the Air Staff to meet SOE and ISLD demands, Eden insisting that operations to gain contact with resistance forces in Croatia and Slovenia should commence as soon as possible.[89] By this time the four special duties Liberators had been completely separated from 108 Squadron to form a single flight (christened 'X' Flight), placed entirely at the disposal of ISLD, SOE and the Political Warfare Executive (PWE). An immediate consequence of Churchill's and Eden's demands was the formation of a new sub-committee of the Joint Operations Staff (JOS), the top military co-ordinating body in the Middle East, representing the three armed services and the secret organizations, to establish air transport priorities between them.[90]

The sub-committee was convened on 27 February 1943 at Headquarters RAF Middle East, but the efforts of SOE, ISLD and PWE to co-ordinate their respective air transport requirements at first proved less than harmonious.

This was not unpredictable, for 'whereas the activities of these organizations were increasing daily and consequently their demand for aircraft was also growing, there was no corresponding increase in the number of aircraft available for these duties'.[91] Squadron Leader Armitage-Smith, representing ISLD, asked for 'three sorties to Slovenia and Croatia' and stated 'that they were of urgent priority'. But he was challenged by Lord Glenconnor of SOE, who demanded priority for his organization and for operations in support of Mihailovic.[92] Glenconnor's arguments were rejected by JOS: 'Although he may be the largest user he was not necessarily the most important user, consequently priorities would be allotted by JOS.'[93]

Early in March an RAF officer from Mediterranean Air Command (MAC), Squadron Leader L.B. Hore, visited ISLD and discussed the air transport situation with Bowlby and Armitage-Smith:

> In a series of conversations which lasted, in and out of office, till midnight, I gained a good background of their activities... Their relations with the RAF are very friendly and mutually helpful, and on general lines they are satisfied with the present set-up, and have no important modifications to suggest.[94]

He also recorded, however, that ISLD were perturbed by the demands being made on special duties aircraft: 'I believe they are sending a signal home.'[95]

These tensions were gradually alleviated by the allocation of additional long-range aircraft for special operations. The four Liberators of 'X' Flight were augmented by six, then ten suitably modified Halifax bombers, and a new special duties squadron, numbered 148, was formed at Gambut; in April they moved to Derna. Weather permitting, they operated every night during each moon period, and every other night in non-moon periods, the Halifaxes concentrating on missions over Greece, Albania and southern Yugoslavia while the precious Liberators were reserved for long-range missions over northern Yugoslavia and Italy.[96] By June the number of Halifaxes had increased to 22.[97] As more aircraft became available, ISLD were able to plan on a more ambitious scale. At a meeting with the Senior Air Staff Officer (SASO) of MAC, on 5 June – attended by Bowlby, Armitage-Smith and ISLD's Middle East and Yugoslav Operations staff – the minutes again record their plans for sorties into Slovenia and Croatia, as well as northern Italy.[98]

With Allied strategic priorities now favouring the Partisans, ISLD finally agreed to send Stuart to Tito's headquarters in Montenegro as part of a joint mission with SOE codenamed 'Typical'. Accompanying Stuart was a Royal Marine sergeant, John Campbell, who was to act as bodyguard, and a radio operator, Peretz Rosenberg, one of the recruits from the Jewish Agency. His SOE counterpart was Captain William (later Sir William) Deakin, Churchill's former research assistant.[99] Stuart was instructed to

5. A Halifax bomber in north Africa being loaded with supplies for the Partisans. As few such aircraft were available for special operations in 1943, only a trickle of stores reached Yugoslavia.

assess and report on the military situation both on the Partisan and enemy sides, whereas Deakin was to consult with the Partisan leadership on joint operational tasks, and to supply SOE with his own impressions of the strength and structure of their movement. They each had separate radio sets linking them to their respective headquarters in Cairo.[100]

Stuart and Deakin were despatched about a month after an SOE team established initial contacts with the Partisans in Croatia (see below). It is possible that this first SOE mission conveyed in their signals to Cairo a somewhat misleading impression of the security of Partisan formations elsewhere in Yugoslavia; or it may simply be that Typical Mission was deployed in too much haste.[101] ISLD would certainly have been desperate to prevent SOE from monopolizing contacts with the Partisan leadership, and such considerations perhaps caused them to pay insufficient attention to Stuart's safety in the field. Whatever the truth is, the mission dropped into the middle of 'Operation Schwarz', a German offensive against the Partisans in Montenegro, and disaster struck when Stuart was killed in an air raid on 9 June.[102] He could not be replaced until the end of August, when Kenneth Syers arrived by parachute.[103] Three weeks later Syers and the other members of the British mission were joined by Brigadier Fitzroy Maclean, Churchill's personal envoy to Tito, who had been attached to SOE.[104]

ISLD experienced rather more success elsewhere. By July 1943 they had added a contact with the Partisans in Slovenia to their links with Zavesa and Novak. According to one contemporary report, '"C" have wireless communication with all three groups and it is through their link with the Partisans that targets for sabotage have been agreed with the Middle East'.[105] By contrast, SOE were only in touch with the Partisans.[106]

ISLD's early activities in Croatia are more obscure. In February 1943 it advised SOE that its contacts were 'developing favourably there' but offered no more specific information.[107] In the following months they worked through an established political party, the Croatian Peasants Party (Hrvatska Seljacka Stranka – HSS), which was thought to have connections with the Partisans. In collaboration with the government-in-exile in London, they employed a Croat official of the Yugoslav diplomatic corps in Jerusalem, who knew personally 'all prominent members of HSS' in Zagreb. The latter, in turn, were in contact with a 'reliable Croatian friend' in Budapest, from where there were clandestine links with SIS and SOE in Istanbul.[108] The Croatian diplomat was relocated to Istanbul early in 1943, and he duly succeeded in obtaining at least some information from HSS in Zagreb.[109] But the documents do not record that ISLD made contact with the Partisans via this circuitous route.

In the meantime, SOE despatched its first mission 'blind' (that is, with no pre-arranged reception party) to Partisan headquarters in Croatia, comprising three Yugoslav émigrés named Pavicic, Erdeljac and Simic.[110] They succeeded in making contact with the Partisans, and established that agents could be deployed in Croatia in conditions of relative safety. As soon as this was confirmed they were asked by SOE to propose to the Partisans the infiltration of British officers into their headquarters.[111] On the night of 18/19 May they were duly joined by Major Anthony Hunter, a Scots Fusilier who had commanded a patrol of the Long Range Desert Group, and Major Jones, a one-eyed Canadian, 'a picturesque figure, whose personal courage was only equalled by the violence of his enthusiasms'.[112] Hunter became British liaison officer at Partisan headquarters, Croatia, operating under the codename 'Fungus', while Jones proceeded by land to Slovenia to assume an equivalent position.[113]

For ISLD the arrival of Fungus Mission in Croatia was a distinctly mixed blessing. In some respects it made eminent sense for SOE to assume the role of vanguard in forging initial contacts with the Partisans. Their officers were usually military men, thoroughly schooled in the arts of irregular warfare, whereas SIS agents were information gatherers rather than soldiers, and were rarely prepared for combat by training or experience. Stuart's tragic death could only have reinforced ISLD's reluctance to despatch agents into the field before the security of their operating environment was established beyond reasonable doubt, and in 1943 SOE was the only British agency capable of providing this confirmation. Their officers in the field could also be called on to organize parachute drop zones and reception teams.[114] On the other hand, events earlier in the year had demonstrated all too clearly how SOE could usurp ISLD's intelligence-gathering functions in Yugoslavia. Once Fungus Mission had been established, ISLD therefore decided to send an intelligence officer to join Anthony Hunter in Croatia. 'For reasons of pride and politics they didn't want to be left out of the picture.'[115]

NOTES

1.   Hinsley *et al.*, *British Intelligence in the Second World War*, vol. 1, pp. 17–18, 48–51, 57; West, *MI6*, pp. 80–2, 110, 130–7; Cave Brown, '*C*', pp. 208–21.
2.   West, *MI6*, pp. 139, 148–9.
3.   Hinsley *et al.*, *British Intelligence in the Second World War*, vol. 1, pp. 276–7; West, *MI6*, pp. 164–75.
4.   Hinsley *et al.*, *British Intelligence in the Second World War*, vol. 1, p. 275; West, *MI6*, pp. 215–16.
5.   Hinsley *et al.*, *British Intelligence in the Second World War*, vol. 1, pp. 138, 278; West, *MI6*, pp. 185–7.
6.   West, *MI6*, p. 210.
7.   FO 366/1126, Sykes to Rance, 25 April 1940.
8.   FO 371/30261, Nichols to Broad, 17 May 1941. Some sources list another officer named Morgan, although elsewhere he is identified as an SOE operative.

9. FO 369/2550, Hutcheon to the Secretary, Ministry of Information, 7 December 1939; FO 371/30264, British Embassy Lisbon to Foreign Office, 16 June 1941. Some sources state that Sherwood was attached to the Zagreb consulate.

10. FO 369/2550, Scott to the Secretary of the Treasury, 16 September 1939.

11. FO 369/2550, Belgrade Chancery to Foreign Office, 27 October 1939.

12. This correspondence is contained in FO 369/2550. Howard's signature has been cut out of one of the letters in this file (letter to A.B. Hutcheon, 23 September 1939) in order to conceal his identity. See also West, *MI6*, pp. 164–5, 397, 404.

13. G. Millar, *Road to Resistance: an Autobiography* (London: The Bodley Head, 1979), pp. 70–1; FO 366/1125, encl. 2 to letter EG/F089, 16 January 1940; *The Times*, obituary of James Millar, 20 August 1986. In *Road to Resistance* George Millar went to considerable lengths to conceal the secret nature of his brother's employment, never mentioning SIS and even changing his brother's name from James to 'Hamish'.

14. FO 371/30260, Washington to Foreign Office, 30 April 1941; FO 371/30261, US Embassy London to Foreign Office, 9 May 1941; D. Martin, *The Web of Disinformation*, p. 108; West, *MI6*, p. 129. The Commonwealth War Graves Commission Debt of Honour Register gives Stuart's full name as William Yull-Stuart, son of Charles Yull-Stuart and Hedwig Yull-Stuart (née Baroness Henneberg).

15. FO 369/2550, loose minute, 14 September 1939; telegram from Campbell, 20 and 23 September 1939.

16. BW 66/6, Tollington to Rapp, 3 June 1940; FO 371/30261, US Embassy London to Foreign Office, 10 May 1941.

17. M. Howard, *British Intelligence in the Second World War*, vol. 5 (London: HMSO, 1990), pp. 16–17; West, *MI6*, pp. 340–2. According to West's account, Popov and his brother Ivo were but two of six volunteer double-agents recruited by the Belgrade Station.

18. Hinsley *et al.*, *British Intelligence in the Second World War*, vol. 1, pp. 369–70.

19. BW 66/6, Director of Studies, Zagreb, to Everett, 17 May 1940.

20. FO 371/30202, Rapp to Campbell, 12 February 1941; Rapp to Foreign Office, 19 February 1941.

21. Hinsley *et al.*, *British Intelligence in the Second World War*, vol. 1, p. 371; *The Times*, obituary of James Millar, 20 August 1986.

22. FO 371/30261, Nichols to Broad, 17 May 1941.

23. BW 66/6, Belgrade to Foreign Office, 3 April 1941; letter from Burn, 17 April 1941.

24. FO 371/30260, Foreign Office minute, 29 April 1941; FO 371/30261, US Embassy London to Foreign Office, 10 May 1941.

25. BW 66/6, undated report to the British Council by D.S. Lisbon entitled 'Evacuation from Belgrade, 1941'.

26. FO 371/30264, Commanding Officer, HMS *Regent*, to the Vice-Admiral, Malta, 28 April 1941; Campbell to Eden, 1 June 1941; FO 371/30263, US Embassy London to Foreign Office, 14 June 1941; FO 371/30261, de Aragao to Eden, 7 May 1941.

27. FO 371/30264, Italian Minister of Foreign Affairs to US Embassy Rome, 9 June 1941; Foreign Office minute, 19 June 1941.
28. FO 371/30260, Foreign Office minute, 29 April 1941; Washington to Foreign Office, 30 April 1941.
29. FO 371/30263, Dixon to Cadogan, 31 May 1941; FO 371/30262, Foreign Office minute, 6 June 1941.
30. Hinsley *et al.*, *British Intelligence in the Second World War*, vol. 3, pt 1, p. 144.
31. Hinsley *et al.*, *British Intelligence in the Second World War*, vol. 2, p. 19; see also West, *MI6*, p. 186.
32. *Who Was Who*, 1961–70.
33. 'G' officers were individual case officers who supervised incoming intelligence from the stations in their geographical region.
34. F.H. Hinsley and C.A.G. Simkins, *British Intelligence in the Second World War*, vol. 4 (London: HMSO, 1990), p. 152; West, *MI6*, pp. 215–16. According to his entry in *Who's Who*, Bruce Lockhart was a linguist who had taught at Rugby before acquiring a TA commission in 1938 and being called up in 1939. He subsequently found his way into ISLD, presumably because of their need for personnel with both military and linguistic qualifications. Gibson was a professional SIS officer, a pre-war 'passport control officer' who had been stationed in eastern Europe; see West, *MI6*, p. 81.
35. AIR 23/8631, minutes of a meeting of the Joint Operations Staff, 21 June 1943; note by AOC-in-C, undated, approximately 9 July 1943.
36. AIR 40/2605, record of a meeting at the Minister of State's Office, Cairo, 13 August 1941.
37. HS 3/59, ISLD memorandum (signature concealed under Section 3(4) of the Public Records Act 1958), 20 July 1943.
38. Howard, *British Intelligence in the Second World War*, vol. 5, pp. 85–6; West, *MI6*, pp. 312–23. The Committee for Secret Activities focused on Iraq, Iran, Turkey and the Caucasus during its early meetings; see AIR 40/2605, meetings of 16 August 1941 and 28 August 1941.
39. West, *MI6*, p. 210.
40. AHB file IIJ1/161/15, Summary of MI9 Activities in the Eastern Mediterranean, 1941–45, Section E, p. 13. Interestingly, both missions had joint functions: one, under a Captain Levides, also operated an escape and evasion section; the other, codenamed 'Homer', was a combined SOE-ISLD operation with sabotage and intelligence functions.
41. West, *MI6*, pp. 323–30.
42. AHB file IIJ1/161/15, Summary of MI9 Activities in the Eastern Mediterranean, 1941–45, Section E, p. 5.
43. *Ibid.*, p. 8.
44. *Ibid.*, p. 10.
45. Hinsley *et al.*, *British Intelligence in the Second World War*, vol. 1, p. 207.
46. *Ibid.*, vol. 2, p. 292.
47. AIR 40/2659, ISLD Air Operations, Mediterranean Theatre, 1942–1945, ch. 1.
48. AIR 40/2605, ISLD (signature concealed under Section 3(4) of the Public Records Act 1958) to Minister of State, 10 September 1941.
49. AIR 40/2605, meeting of the Secret Activities Committee, 27 September 1941.

50. AIR 40/2605, ISLD to Minister of State, 28 September 1941.

51. AIR 40/2659, RAF resources made available to SIS, 1939–45; AHB file II/17/7, Royal Air Force narrative, Special Duty Operations in Europe, pp. 9–11.

52. Hinsley *et al.*, *British Intelligence in the Second World War*, vol. 2, pp. 19, 483, 497, 500, 576. The documents record the successful infiltration of a joint ISLD-MI9 Field Section near Tripoli, and suggest that ISLD deployed other operatives into the western desert. See AHB file IIJ1/161/15, Summary of MI9 Activities in the Eastern Mediterranean, 1941-1945, Section F, p. 12.

53. Given the relatively small number of documents relating to SIS in the National Archives the quantity of evidence concerning this jurisdictional overlap is striking. Examples include: HS 5/907, London to Mideast, 17 December 1942, which appears to show the 'chief passport officer' Yugoslavia initiating an operation to Dalmatia from London; telegram from Cairo, 15 January 1943, which indicates ISLD's agreement with SOE in Cairo to an operation that had not been approved by SIS in London; HS 5/908, telegram from Cairo, 9 May 1943, which concerns another disagreement over the infiltration of agents between ISLD and SIS in London; FO 536/6/3144E/43, unsigned memo to Foreign Office, 16 May 1943, which shows that SIS in London was in direct radio contact with an agent in Ljubljana; and HS 5/909, minute (signature concealed under Section 3(4) of the Public Records Act 1958) to AD/1, 3 July 1943, which covers a telegram from SIS in London rejecting ISLD's proposals for co-locating intelligence officers with SOE liaison officers.

54. Interview with Reed, 4 November 1989; Lees, *The Rape of Serbia*, pp. 35, 37.

55. Hinsley *et al.*, *British Intelligence in the Second World War*, vol. 3, pt 1, pp. 137–9.

56. HS 5/913, A/D.3. to A/D, 27 January 1942. This minute recorded a meeting between SIS and SOE to discuss co-ordination of liaison with the Yugoslav government in London.

57. FO 536/7/G3627/43, Ennals to Rendel, 16 March 1943.

58. HS 5/913, A/D.3. to A/D, 27 January 1942.

59. HS 5/907, D/HV to D/H70, 23 December 1942.

60. WO 202/158, telegram to London, 26 March 1943.

61. FO 536/6/3144E/43, unsigned memo to the Foreign Office, 16 May 1943.

62. Lees, *The Rape of Serbia*, p. 37. Lees was also suspicious of James Millar who, like Ennals, was a graduate of St John's College, Cambridge; it is notable that Lees waited until both Millar and Ennals had died before making his allegations.

63. FO 536/6/3144E/43, Ennals to Rendel, 17 May 1943.

64. WO 202/158, Clarke to Davidson, 30 March 1943.

65. WO 208/2014, SIS report (numbered CX/35400) to the Foreign Office, 13 April 1942. The incorporation of 'most secret' material into this report is confirmed by HS 5/905, L/IC1 to D/H, 15 June 1942.

66. *Ibid.*; Deakin, *The Embattled Mountain*, p. 215. SIS assigned the number 35000 to their Yugoslav operations. The head of its Yugoslav station-in-exile would have been given the number 35100; 35400 would therefore have been a fairly senior deputy, such as Stuart.

67. Lees, *The Rape of Serbia*, p. 35; Martin, *The Web of Disinformation*, p. 108.

68. Lindsay, *Beacons in the Night*, p. 361.

69. HS 5/938, SIS CX report entitled 'The Position within Yugoslavia', 23 August 1942.
70. *Ibid.*
71. *Ibid.*
72. Hinsley *et al.*, *British Intelligence in the Second World War*, vol. 3, pt 1, pp. 140, 144–7.
73. WO 202/158, Millar to Davidson, 6 December 1942. As early as August 1942 SIS knew of an agreement among 'influential circles' (including Zaveza) 'that an opportunist policy of Slovene collaboration with the Italian authorities should be adopted'. This was considered to be 'the only way of preserving the nation from destruction and gaining breathing space'. Mihailovic apparently concurred with this position, as it was 'impossible to improve the Slovene Military Force at present'.
74. FO 371/37607, SOE to Foreign Office, 13 January 1943; SOE to Foreign Office, 20 January 1943; Deakin, *The Embattled Mountain*, pp. 178–9.
75. Hinsley *et al.*, *British Intelligence in the Second World War*, vol. 3, pt 1, pp. 142–3.
76. HS 5/942, telegram to Cairo, 20 February 1943. Although the abbreviation 'C' is commonly thought to refer to the head of SIS, this term was also frequently coined in preference to 'SIS' or 'MI6' to denote the Secret Intelligence Service as a whole.
77. HS 5/942, remarks on 'C''s comments on Bailey's report, 25 February 1943.
78. CAB 101/126, 'Yugoslavia', by Miss J. Dawson, pp. 17–18. Soon afterwards, Bailey also became disenchanted with Mihailovic; by April his reports were describing open collaboration between the Chetniks and the Italian forces of occupation; see Deakin, *The Embattled Mountain*, p. 191.
79. HW 1/1474, C to Prime Minister, 17 March 1943; Gilbert, *Churchill*, vol. 7, pp. 440, 448–9. In July 1943 Churchill asked Menzies for a digest 'of the "Boniface" about Yugoslavia, Albania and Greece during the last two months or thereabouts, showing the heavy fighting and great disorder going on in those regions'. *See also* D. Stafford, *Churchill and Secret Service* (Woodstock/New York: Overlook Press, 1999), p. 264. A search of HW 1, the class of documents in the National Archives containing signals intelligence passed to the Prime Minister, located only nine references to Yugoslavia in 1942, but 51 in 1943.
80. HS 5/907, SIS (signature concealed under Section 3(4) of the Public Records Act 1958) to D/HV, 14 February 1943.
81. HS 5/907, telegram from Cairo, 15 January 1943.
82. HS 5/907, SIS (signature concealed under Section 3(4) of the Public Records Act 1958) to DH/V, 9 February 1943; SIS (signature concealed under Section 3(4) of the Public Records Act 1958) to D/HV, 14 February 1943.
83. Hinsley *et al.*, *British Intelligence in the Second World War*, vol. 3, pt 1, pp. 141–7; Gilbert, *Churchill*, vol. 7, pp. 318–19.
84. Gilbert, *Churchill*, vol. 7, pp. 318–19. This was the message Churchill received during his well-known meeting with Captain (later Sir) William Deakin and Brigadier Mervyn Keble of SOE in Cairo on 28 January 1943. The conversations and the SOE paper prepared afterwards focused on Croatia and Slovenia (rather than the whole of Yugoslavia) precisely because of their proximity to Italy.

85. *Ibid.*, p. 338; AHB file II/17/7, Royal Air Force narrative, Special Duty Operations in Europe, pp. 20–1.
86. AIR 20/8349, Easton to Hockey, 7 April 1943.
87. AIR 20/8349, Medhurst to Tedder and Douglas, 19 April 1943.
88. AIR 23/8631, Keble to Lloyd, 23 February 1943.
89. AHB file II/17/7, Royal Air Force narrative, Special Duty Operations in Europe, p. 23.
90. AIR 20/8349, Headquarters, Royal Air Force Middle East, Air Staff Instruction 1, 11 March 1943.
91. AIR 23/8631, minutes of a meeting at HQ RAF ME, 27 February 1943 to discuss activities and programme for SOE, ISLD and PWE.
92. *Ibid.*
93. AIR 23/8631, note by SASO, 8 March 1943.
94. AIR 20/8349, Hore to CISO, MAC, 18 March 1943.
95. *Ibid.*
96. AHB history of 148 Squadron.
97. AHB file II/17/7, Royal Air Force narrative, Special Duty Operations in Europe, pp. 23–5.
98. AIR 23/8631, minutes of a meeting held at ISLD, 5 June 1943.
99. West, *MI6*, p. 383; Deakin, *The Embattled Mountain*, pp. 215–17.
100. Deakin, *The Embattled Mountain*, p. 215.
101. *Ibid.*, p. 214.
102. WO 202/339, signal from Typical, 12 June 1943. Deakin signalled, 'Stuart killed by bomb Wednesday. Inform ISLD; report follows; Tito and self wounded slightly.' Stuart has no known grave. According to the Commonwealth War Graves Commission's Debt of Honour Register he is commemorated on the Athens memorial. The Register wrongly states that he served with the Intelligence Corps.
103. WO 202/339, signal from Typical, 25 August 1943. A small file of Syers' signals is located in the archive of the Imperial War Museum.
104. Hinsley *et al.*, *British Intelligence in the Second World War*, vol. 3, pt 1, p. 149.
105. HS 5/932, meeting at the Foreign Office, 20 July 1943.
106. *Ibid.*
107. HS 5/907, SIS to DH/V, 9 February 1943.
108. HS 5/941, telegram to London, 25 January 1943; telegram to London, 30 January 1943.
109. FO 536/7/G3614/43, Ennals to Rendal, 25 May 1943.
110. HS 5/908, DSO(b)1 to D/HV, 2 April 1943; Deakin, *The Embattled Mountain*, pp. 201, 211–13; B.S. Vukevich, *Diverse Forces in Yugoslavia, 1941–1945* (Los Angeles, CA: Authors Unlimited, 1990), pp. 127–8, n. 40.
111. HS 5/944, SOE memorandum entitled 'The Partisan Movement in Yugoslavia', 24 May 1943.
112. Maclean, *Eastern Approaches*, p. 251.
113. Hunter's early signals from 'Fungus' are contained in WO 202/436.
114. SIS's reluctance to drop agents 'blind' into enemy-occupied territory has been noted by earlier historians; see, for example West, *MI6*, p. 252.
115. RP, Reed interviewed by J. Lane, 'Oral History of the BBC'.

4

'The Department that deals with Liaison between Different Services'

In July 1943 Owen Reed decided that his days with the BBC's Middle East organization were numbered. Given his dissatisfaction with life in Cairo and with his status as a 'base wallah', all evident in his correspondence since March, it might well be asked why he remained there so long. There are several reasons. Firstly, he recovered from jaundice only very slowly: as late as June he was back in hospital for tests, although he eventually received a clean bill of health.[1] Secondly, while the War in North Africa continued he managed to convince himself that the BBC's contribution – in the form of news and propaganda – was of some importance, as was his personal role in their office, given the chronic shortage of staff and the atmosphere of crisis prevalent during the early months of the year.[2] Thirdly, he had received an excessively pessimistic assessment of his future prospects in active service, which undoubtedly discouraged him from seeking alternative employment.[3]

By July much had changed. Although his health remained a cause of some concern, a strict regime of exercise and sunbathing and a marked reduction in his work-load at the BBC were making his outlook more positive, and were regenerating a sense of physical well-being lacking since El Alamein. Following the successful conclusion of the North African campaign he became increasingly conscious of, and troubled by, his growing distance from the front, and by the manifest irrelevance of the BBC's Cairo office to the war effort. Moreover, any 'crisis' within Liveing's lavishly resourced and over-staffed organization was now demonstrably self-inflicted.[4] 'I long for some sort of a job that has (a) nothing whatever to do with what I do in peacetime and (b) keeps me in fresh air and (c) has some sort of relationship with winning the war', he wrote on the 21st.[5] The new BBC location – close to GHQ and the embassy – brought him into contact with influential officers and officials, opening previously unknown windows of opportunity.[6] One such window led directly to ISLD.

Reed's search for new employment began with an interview with the head of Public Relations at GHQ (nominally his commanding officer since January), who attempted to persuade him to stay in broadcasting and to head a revitalized MEBU.[7] He refused and was promptly referred to the Appointments Department, which he visited at the end of July. Again he heard that he was too old to return to an active unit:

> There followed a series of interviews with different colonels in different offices on the scent of another job, in the department which deals with liaison between different services. All very hush. So much so that I found it quite impossible to get enough to go on.[8]

At length he was told to visit a particular address after nine o'clock that evening, to knock three times at the door and to ask for a certain colonel.

> It was the full sort of corny film works: a grill in the door slid back revealing bars, and an evil oriental face appeared and I identified myself, and heavy padlocks were undone and the door creaked open, and inside was a very agreeable man in a colonel's sort of army uniform.[9]

This was Cuthbert Bowlby, who would tell him little except that, if he joined ISLD, he would have no identity. 'It is extremely secret', Bowlby continued, 'and really you have to hand yourself over to us in a quite unqualified way.'[10]

Reed was then directed to another address, where on the following day he was to ask for Bowlby again. During this second meeting Bowlby (now clad in naval uniform)[11] promised him a majority and advised him that he would be sent to Palestine for a course in intelligence and staff work if he accepted the position; he would then return to Cairo for further training, mainly in languages. But the precise nature of his ultimate assignment was shrouded in mystery. 'I'm completely in the dark', he wrote:

> but I'm promised that it will have some connection with facts and that it will keep my brain busy, and that it won't mean living in oriental townships, which I regard as a greater danger than crumbling Axis war machinery.[12]

That was enough. Within a week he was back in Palestine, joining three other officers and several NCOs in an encampment near Nazareth, located in a valley between high mountains, 'a tiny cluster of tents under a grove of fig trees where crickets shout all night'. The first week was simply an army 'toughener' – two hours of physical training every morning, followed by a bathing expedition to Haifa in the afternoon. Thereafter he was schooled in languages, double-transposition codes and radio communication. In the few letters dating from this period he made absolutely no mention of combat training. He may deliberately have remained silent on that subject for reasons of security, or possibly to avoid alarming his family, who would naturally have preferred him to remain in broadcasting. Or it may simply be that combat training was thought inappropriate for intelligence officers. It is certainly far from clear at this stage that he expected to be despatched into a potentially hostile environment. 'If I make any headway with languages', he wrote, 'I may get a job as liaison officer with some Allied unit or I may be thrust back into GHQ and resume an office chair'.[13]

Gradually the true identity of his new employers became clearer. At first, amusingly, he had taken the ISLD cover name at face value but by the end of August he no longer harboured any illusions. 'It stands for Inter-Services Liaison Department', he recorded. 'It's a branch of intelligence and therefore wears its finger on its lip and is most fearfully hush hush.'[14] His language training began at about this time, as did the task of 'piecing together all the mosaic of information that the army gets about enemy-occupied territory', so it seems safe to assume that his ultimate destination and the clandestine nature of his duties had been finalized.[15] His total lack of Serbo-Croat at first seems problematic, to say the least, but Reed had other relevant qualifications to compensate. As a professional BBC broadcaster he was already very thoroughly trained and experienced in the collection and presentation of information, and in the Army he had demonstrated an ability to work alone in remote areas of the desert, and to navigate his way through poorly mapped and inhospitable terrain. He had also been attached to a brigade headquarters as a junior staff officer for several months. ISLD may have considered these skills to be equally, if not more valuable than any linguistic accomplishments. In any case, they would not have found very many suitable officers if they had restricted their recruitment to Balkan language specialists. Reed at least boasted a proven linguistic aptitude, having studied both Latin and classical Greek at school and university. So it was decided that he should simply be 'crammed' for a few months before his departure, and despatched with a Yugoslav émigré assistant, who was to act as his interpreter.[16]

One particularly important part of the training given to ISLD officers is recorded in detail in the official documents: this was the instruction they received in the planning of 'pick-up' operations. Pick-ups involved either clandestine air sorties to concealed and often makeshift landing strips in enemy-occupied territory, or more systematic air transport to and from semi-permanent and relatively well-organized airfields held by Partisans. The former sorties, typically employed to infiltrate and evacuate agents, were commonly flown using Westland Lysanders; the latter, for larger cargoes of personnel and supplies, were invariably flown by Dakotas. ISLD's training programme for pick-ups covered the selection of landing grounds and the manner in which their locations and characteristics should be reported to headquarters. It also dealt with the construction of flare paths, the direction of landing operations from the ground, the exchange of passengers and luggage and the organization of so-called 'mail pick-ups', by which low-flying aircraft collected mail or documents from enemy-occupied territory without landing.[17] Many of these skills would prove vitally important to Reed in the months ahead.

Reed described ISLD as very 'Oxford': 'Christchurch dons and British Council types...Very unmilitary and unregimental. Most of them clapped into uniform as experts in strange fields...[R]ampant individualists with a passion for truth.'[18] And he soon discovered a marked divergence of opinion on the subject of the Partisans. Older SIS staff, such as Bowlby, had for many years been engaged in espionage against the Soviet Union and were naturally suspicious of Tito and his followers because of their communism. By contrast, most of the younger officers, like Millar and Clarke, were far more sympathetic towards the Partisan cause.[19] The simplistic impression they conveyed to Reed is graphically illustrated in one of his letters. Referring to the Partisans he declared (with astonishing candour) that they had 'been fighting Germans, Italians *and* Mihailovic for two years and beaten the lot, only being communist-run the Brit[ish] pub[lic] has been kept in the dark'.[20]

From James Millar, Reed finally learnt that his destination was to be Croatia, and that his mission would have two principal objectives. The first was to work through the Partisans to obtain intelligence on Axis forces in Yugoslavia, while the second was to report more generally on the Partisan movement, and on the military and political situation in Croatia.[21] It was an interesting brief. At the beginning of July, ISLD had in fact proposed to SIS in London that they should immediately attach intelligence officers to SOE missions 'for the purpose of reporting on enemy military movements'. But the response was largely negative. An evidently senior SIS personality replied to Cairo, 'We consider this primarily as duty of military reconnaissance units and not secret intelligence.'[22] In any case, by 1943 senior SIS officials were in fact very well informed about enemy activities in Yugoslavia through their privileged access to Enigma and other intercepts, which disclosed the identity, location and number of Axis divisions there. It also provided detailed coverage of the three main operations launched against the resistance forces during the first half of the year.[23] Conventional reports from the field might have aided the evaluation of these decrypts; in intelligence, two or more sources are always better than one. But they could rarely match signals intelligence for speed, accuracy or reliability.[24] Hence it might reasonably be concluded that ISLD attached as much importance to the second of Reed's objectives as to the first.

There were good reasons for this. ISLD had, of course, been directed from the very highest levels to make contact with Partisan forces in

Croatia and Slovenia but by the summer of 1943 the need for military and political intelligence on Tito's movement was even more pressing than in the spring. Balkan resistance movements were playing a valuable role in containing Axis divisions which might otherwise have been deployed against the Allies in Italy.[25] Moreover, British and American planners were seriously considering the possibility of invading or weakening Germany through a campaign on her southern flank, in central-southern Europe and the Balkans. Churchill himself keenly advocated such a strategy, which he hoped might be undertaken in collaboration with resistance forces within enemy-occupied territory.[26] Although the scheme eventually foundered on the rock of American opposition, the debate was far from settled in the months preceding Reed's infiltration, and he was thoroughly briefed on the possibility of Allied landings on the Yugoslav coast during his training.[27]

Through Reed, then, ISLD hoped to broaden its sources of information about enemy deployments in Croatia, to develop a clearer picture of the political and military situation there and to learn more about the Partisans and their military potential. But beyond the specific details of his assignment remained the more general but no less important concern that ISLD's responsibility for intelligence gathering should not be taken over by the SOE liaison officers already located at Tito's headquarters, and in Croatia and Slovenia. He was quick to appreciate the rivalry that existed between the two organizations and the ulterior motive that lay behind his mission.[28]

By early September Reed was living in a luxury apartment reserved by ISLD for its trainees. 'We have the best cook in Cairo and I a room of my own with a desk and a view. Lovely after that awful pension.'[29] But he was frantically busy, 'buried deep in technicalities, how to interrogate prisoners, how to identify hostile units, how to break down other peoples' codes – detective work'.[30] He learnt Serbo-Croat for two hours every day, and Italian for one hour, and laboured to master the intricacies of Balkan history and Allied strategy at the same time.[31] He was also given a short course with the RAF, and parachute training at Ramat David in Palestine.[32] Another course, this time with the Navy, brought him to Alexandria, where he was accommodated in the Cecil Hotel next-door to a suite occupied by Nahas Pasha. From there he wrote that he was studying harbour installations and naval intelligence:

> This firm [ISLD] is the *open sesame* to everything, and I am the repository of monstrous stores of secret information which makes me rather dizzy to think of but is enormously interesting. I have a wonderful pass which takes me everywhere...This morning I was a guest at the weekly naval intelligence conference and sat in awe-struck silence while pretty Wrens moved flags about all over Europe.[33]

On 17 September, back in Cairo again, he learnt that he was to be parachuted into Yugoslavia within a 'few weeks',[34] but ISLD's plans for him remained curiously uncertain until the very last moment. In the meantime the world he had known since December 1942 evaporated. John Welton's name unaccountably disappears from his correspondence, and both Chignall and Talbot were recalled to London. Although relieved to have freed himself from the BBC, Reed was sorry to see them depart.[35] A bonus of £50 in appreciation of his services to the Corporation came as a complete surprise, and helped him to moderate his opinions of Liveing and Pennethorne Hughes.[36]

On 1 October Reed was told to expect a long spell in Cairo, but the very next day found him hastily preparing for a move to North Africa, together with ISLD's entire Yugoslav department. As late as 8 October, only four days before his infiltration, he could write: 'I'm never told what the future holds and may be sent at a couple of days notice or not at all.'[37] But in fact, a few days earlier, SOE had relayed the following request to Fitzroy Maclean at Tito's headquarters, which by then had relocated to Bosnia: 'ISLD wish to send one officer and one wireless operator to Fungus area to collect information and assist with intelligence side of Fungus work. Do you approve early despatch of this mission? Fungus also informed.'[38]

Although there was apparently no response, the details of Reed's mission were now finalized at last. Operating under the codename 'Judge' he was to join Anthony Hunter at Fungus Mission – Partisan headquarters in Croatia – for about two months. Notwithstanding ISLD's signal, he was to be dropped with both a radio operator, Sergeant Paddy Ryan, *and* an interpreter, a Canadian of Yugoslav origin named Paul Stichman, who had served with the Royal Canadian Air Force before joining ISLD.[39] They were flown from Cairo to the north African coast to join 148 Squadron on 11 October – 'out of the vile city at last'.[40]

By this time the air transport position had improved considerably. A new Wing, numbered 334, was being formed in Algeria to operate all special duties aircraft, and 148 Squadron (which had moved to Tocra in Cyrenaica, bringing the Halifaxes within range of more northerly destinations[41]) and 624 Squadron (at Blida), were now each flying three to four ISLD sorties per month. A special operations section had also been formed at Air Forces Headquarters (AFHQ) to co-ordinate the requirements of the various organizations concerned.[42] Nevertheless, capacity was still at something of a premium. Several missions were planned for the night of 12 October 1943, and all were postponed due to adverse weather predictions. But clear skies were forecast over western Yugoslavia. Rather than waste a sortie the RAF therefore scheduled Operation Judge/Fungus at very short notice.[43] Having once again been discouraged from expecting an early departure, Reed, Ryan and Stichman were swimming in the sea near the airfield when 'somebody came running down the beach saying "you're off, it's tonight"'. And they scrambled their equipment together, 'wireless, canisters, revolvers, medical, and so on', and boarded an awaiting aircraft. After less than ten minutes in the air they realized that they had forgotten their parachutes and returned to Tocra.[44] Finally, at 22.05, Liberator AL510, flown by Flight Lieutenant Maurice Passmore of 148 Squadron, took off to infiltrate Reed's party into Croatia.[45]

It is not strictly accurate to describe wartime Croatia as 'German-occupied'. Following the German invasion in 1941 Hitler decided to found a Croatian satellite state and to govern it through the so-called 'Ustase', an extreme nationalist Croat separatist organization led by Ante Pavelic. The Ustase had been formed in 1930 as an underground movement, which regularly resorted to terrorism and the promotion of civil disorder in pursuit of Croatian independence. They had enjoyed Mussolini's support in the pre-war years, but it was German patronage that finally brought them to power. In the four years of the Ustase's rule – from 1941 to 1945 – they implemented a policy of genocide against the Serb minority in Croatia and Bosnia: many thousands were murdered or expelled, or were forced to convert from Orthodox Christianity to Catholicism. The Ustase also killed most of the Jews and Gypsies in Croatia, and thousands of their own political opponents.[46]

By 1943 the occupying German forces were working in conjunction with Ustase troops to hold the principal towns and lines of communication in Croatia, while substantial tracts of less accessible territory were entirely controlled by the Partisans. These areas were often by their very nature unsuitable for parachute landings. In a vivid account recorded shortly after the War, Reed described 'ridge after ridge of spiky limestone mountains with tumbled masses of stone boulders on every slope, and deep wooded gorges black with beech and pinewoods, and swept by wind and rain'. Dropping in total darkness into such terrain was inevitably a hazardous enterprise. Storms were forecast over the Mediterranean, so the Liberator pursued an indirect course via the toe of Italy, flying over Vesuvius and then heading north, following the Apennines before veering east across the Adriatic. After reaching the Yugoslav coast they climbed above the mountains and the temperature plummeted. 'Only eight hours before', Reed recalled, 'we had been sweating in the desert in our shirtsleeves. Paddy [Ryan] was still wearing under his battle dress the bathing slips he'd been swimming in that very afternoon, 1,000 miles away.'[47]

At only 23 years of age the Liberator's pilot, Flight Lieutenant Passmore, was one of the most experienced officers in 148 Squadron. A flight commander, with more than 1,500 flying hours and one full tour of special operations sorties to his name, he had established 'a record of successes in difficult conditions which made him trusted by the oldest hands'.[48] He took meticulous care to deposit Reed's party in the correct location, near Otocac, searching for the drop zone beneath the clouds, 'down and round... [as] thick mist streamed past outside the plane'. The engines quietened, then roared again and the Liberator levelled out:

One of the crew lifted the cover from a hole in the floor, and there, right below us through a gap in the clouds, we could see the tiny twinkling pattern of the fires which the Partisans were burning to guide us. We held on for all we were worth while the plane flung us around, banking steeply between the mountain slopes, lower and lower.[49]

Parachute harnesses donned, the three members of Judge Mission moved to the edge of the hatch while a red light glowed at them through the dark interior of the Liberator. At an altitude of around 2,000 feet the engines quietened again, Passmore announced 'action stations', the red light turned to green and one after another they jumped. 'A terrific volley of wind ripped and tore at my clothing', Reed recorded:

> The world and the mountains and the stars and the clouds whirled around me. Somewhere was the roar of the Liberator zooming away into the darkness ... Then my shoulders were held in the firm grip of the parachute harness and I saw the tight swaying canopy of my parachute cutting a dark circle out of the sky above me ... The white rocks on the hillside below suddenly loomed up ... I saw blades of grass in the moonlight. Then I felt a bump that knocked the breath out of my body and found myself rolling over and over ... on a soft bed of bilberries and heather. I had forgotten every rule I'd ever been taught about parachuting, but I was in one piece.[50]

So were Stichman and Ryan. In addition to the ISLD contingent the Liberator dropped 12 containers and 17 packages of military supplies. A signal from the ground confirmed that both men and material were in Partisan hands. The Liberator then flew back to Brindisi, where it landed safely at 7.20 on the following morning.[51]

NOTES

1. RP, OR to PR, 21 June 1943.
2. RP, OR to PR, 14 July 1943.
3. RP, OR to PR, 30 December 1942.
4. RP, OR to PR, 8 and 14 July 1943.
5. RP, OR to PR, 21 July 1943.
6. RP, OR to PR, 29 June 1943.
7. RP, OR to PR, 14 and 18 July 1943.
8. RP, OR to PR, 31 July 1943; 3 August 1943.
9. RP, Reed interviewed by J. Lane, 'Oral History of the BBC'.
10. *Ibid.*

11. *Ibid.* According to Reed, in an effort to lend weight to the ISLD cover name, Bowlby would never be seen wearing the same service uniform on two consecutive days.

12. RP, OR to PR, 3 August 1943.

13. RP, OR to PR, 10 August 1943.

14. RP, OR to PR, 29 August 1943.

15. RP, OR to PR, 2 September 1943.

16. Interview with Reed, 4 November 1989.

17. AHB file IIJ1/130, History of Special Operations (AIR) in the Mediterranean Theatre, 87–106.

18. RP, OR to PR, 24 September 1943.

19. Interview with Reed, 4 November 1989.

20. RP, OR to PR, 24 September 1943.

21. Interview with Reed, 4 November 1989.

22. HS 5/909, minute (signature concealed under Section 3(4) of the Public Records Act 1958) to AD/1, 3 July 1943, covering telegram to Mid-East of the same date.

23. Hinsley *et al.*, *British Intelligence in the Second World War*, vol. 3, pt 1, pp. 144–6, 501–3.

24. *Ibid.*

25. AIR 20/8054, CAS to Tedder, undated, approximately mid-July 1943.

26. Gilbert, *Churchill*, vol. 7, pp. 530–3.

27. Interview with Reed, 4 November 1989.

28. *Ibid.*; RP, Reed interviewed by J. Lane, 'Oral History of the BBC'.

29. RP, OR to PR, 24 September 1943.

30. RP, OR to PR, 2 September 1943.

31. RP, OR to PR, 24 September 1943.

32. RP, OR to PR, 2 September 1943; RP, Reed interviewed by J. Lane, 'Oral History of the BBC'.

33. RP, OR to PR, 15 September 1943.

34. RP, OR to PR, 17 September 1943.

35. RP, OR to PR, 2 October 1943.

36. RP, OR to PR, 17 September 1943; BBC R13/166/3, E.G.D. Liveing to OSEO, 27 August 1943. A few weeks before, Liveing had cabled the BBC in London recommending the bonus for Reed. 'From January to March', Liveing confirmed: '...he was to all intents and purposes acting as AMED [Assistant Middle East Director]. From the time of AMED's arrival at the end of March he continued to perform a variety of heavy duties...He was in fact a Near East Organiser, general programme assistant and accountant all rolled into one...If this mark of appreciation is granted, would you please cable Cairo to pay it on the spot. Reed is about to leave Cairo at any moment, having accepted a somewhat dangerous military appointment.'

37. RP, OR to PR, 2 and 8 October 1943.

38. HS 5/882, signal to Pikestaff, 4 October 1943.

39. Interview with Reed, 4 November 1989; Commonwealth War Graves Commission Debt of Honour Register.

40. RP, OR to PR, 12 October 1943.

41. AHB history of 148 Squadron.

42. AIR 40/2659, ISLD Air Operations, Mediterranean Theatre, 1942–1945, ch. 1.
43. WO 202/438, signal to Fungus, 16 October 1943.
44. RP, Reed interviewed by J. Lane, 'Oral History of the BBC'; O. Reed, *Junior English 3, A True Story of the Recent War*, transmitted 29 January 1947, BBC Home Services (Schools).
45. AIR 27/995, 148 Squadron Operations Record Book (ORB), October 1943.
46. For a succinct account of the Ustase era in Croatia, see M. Tanner, *Croatia: A Nation Forged in War* (New Haven, CT/London: Yale University Press, 1997), ch. 11.
47. RP, Reed, *Junior English 3*.
48. AIR 27/995, 148 Squadron ORB, November 1943; information supplied by AHB, quoting Wing Commander J. Blackburn, OC 148 Squadron, to Base Personnel Office, RAF ME, 10 November 1943.
49. RP, Reed, *Junior English 3*.
50. *Ibid*.
51. AIR 27/995, 148 Squadron ORB, October 1943. The Liberator refuelled at Brindisi before returning to Tocra.

Map 2. North-western Yugoslavia.

5

Judge or Fungus?

SOE's 'Fungus Mission' had been established at Partisan headquarters in Croatia during the summer of 1943. In October it was located in the town of Otocac, in the Lika district. A statement of SOE personnel at Fungus lists Anthony Hunter and at least four 'commandos and others', including a radio operator, Corporal Jephson.[1] But the Allied presence at the mission was sometimes temporarily enlarged by SOE officers *en route* to other locations, and by escaped POWs and shot-down airmen awaiting evacuation. The headquarters (known as GSH, or Glavni Stab Hrvatska – General Staff Croatia) was commanded by General Ivan Gosnjak, a veteran of the Spanish Civil War, and was the largest Partisan base in Yugoslavia, controlling four army corps numbered 4, 6, 10 and 11; its authority extended north from Croatia into south-eastern districts of Istria, on the border with Italy. The other leading Partisan personalities there included Andrija Hebrang, who effectively headed an embryonic Partisan government of Croatia known as ZAVNOH (Zemaljsko Anti-fasisticko Vijece Narodnog Oslobodjernja Hrvatska), and two political commissars, Rade Zigic and Dr Vladimir Bakaric.[2] Three specialist battalions conducted attacks on enemy lines of communication under the direction of Ilya Grmovnik, 'an experienced railway saboteur with an international reputation'.[3]

Italy's capitulation at the beginning of September 1943 allowed the Partisans to consolidate their position in Croatia and Slovenia. While they were already active in many regions, their forces had chiefly been confined to mountainous districts and their ability to operate more extensively was restricted by a lack of arms and equipment. But following the surrender the Partisans disarmed six Italian divisions, and many Italian soldiers joined Tito's followers, bringing their weapons with them. A series of offensives then quickly produced territorial gains in Istria, around the Croatian capital of Zagreb, and along the Adriatic coast, where the Partisans captured a number of smaller towns as well as cities like Split. From the coast they extended their influence across the numerous offshore islands. The Germans responded with characteristic determination by launching counterattacks in Istria and Slovenia, bolstering their position in and around Zagreb, and recapturing Split and other major ports on the Adriatic.[4]

Otocac seems to have been remarkably unscathed at this stage of the war, boasting a weekly market, a brewery, an electricity-generating station and several flourmills. Staple food items like bread were strictly rationed, however, and the town was home to a steadily growing army of refugees, which included many Jews.[5] The Lika had otherwise been devastated by fighting since April 1941. Two escaped British POWs who passed through Fungus Mission in September found all the Partisan villages destroyed, and many ordinary civilians living in the forests. The British were given beds near the headquarters, but Partisan officers slept on the floor or in cattle sheds. They saw Italians serving with the Partisans, and children as young as 12 carrying rifles. Hunter appeared to be extremely popular: 'as he passed, soldiers sprang to attention and saluted him'. But the Western Allies were also openly criticized for their alleged failure to send adequate supplies of arms and equipment, or to match the military achievements of the Soviet Union. When an air sortie was organized Hunter would inform the Partisan staff, who would despatch a guard of about 50 men to the drop zone, normally accompanied by a member of the British mission.[6] One such party awaited Reed, Stichman and Ryan on the night of 12 October.

Had he thought, Reed might have been somewhat surprised at the selection of a drop zone covered in large boulders. In fact the area was chosen because Hunter was expecting supplies rather than personnel. Although he had been approached over the infiltration of Judge Mission, he had absolutely no idea that its arrival was imminent. Nor, for that matter, had the Partisans. This was important, for no Allied personnel were supposed to join them without Tito's express permission. In the case of Reed's party, Tito's approval had been sought via SOE before their departure from north Africa, but not received.[7] To ISLD it seemed preferable to infiltrate them without formal authority than to sacrifice a precious Liberator sortie.[8] But to the Partisans the unexpected arrival of Reed, Stichman and Ryan represented a serious breach of protocol. When they reached the Croatian headquarters with the landing party, Zigic promptly contacted Tito and was told that he had never been approached over their despatch. On 17 October ISLD received a belated response to their request to send a mission to Croatia which suggested that the issue had only been raised with Tito in the most general terms. Moreover, he had clearly been unenthusiastic – 'slightly suspicious' – and had expressed a marked preference 'to see the arrival of more stores rather than personnel'. The signal continued:

> If sub-missions require additional officers or ORs they should signal ...giving details and reasons why required. We will then discuss with

Tito and if agreed ask to arrange despatch after we have agreed name
and rank of officer.[9]

For Reed, of course, these instructions came too late. Although the
members of Judge Mission were quite comfortably accommodated, they
found themselves confined to Hunter's quarters and were denied the use of
their radio set (although they could transmit through the Fungus set). 'We
are virtual internees', Reed signalled, 'Partisans completely mystified re
need for us and [I] cannot hope convince them or myself until bona fide
established.'[10] The position was no less embarrassing for Hunter. 'Whole
incident highly unfortunate', he complained to SOE, 'but am doing best to
soothe down ruffled feelings'.[11]

There followed a three-week delay while Reed's position was discussed
with Tito.[12] In the meantime tragedy struck when Passmore's Liberator, on
another supply sortie to Fungus, crashed and burned out. The entire crew
was killed. The aircraft had taken off from Tocra on the evening of 3
November and was next reported, on fire, over the village of Kosinjski
Zamost, about 20 miles south of its target area, at 9 pm local time. It
circled the village before crashing into a hilltop with such violence that the
wreckage was spread over half a mile.[13] The Liberator's demise was never
properly explained. Few special operations aircraft were lost over
Yugoslavia (18 during the entire war). German night-fighters were rarely
encountered and anti-aircraft defences were thinly spread. But the location
of ground batteries was unpredictable because of the fluid nature of
hostilities with the Partisans; there were many instances when aircraft were
targeted over areas that had previously been considered safe, and this was
probably the fate of Passmore's Liberator. The distance between the
Liberator's crash site and its intended destination is not significant; the fact
that it was circling suggests that it was searching for the drop zone. But
why, if the aircraft had been set on fire, did the crew not bale out? Did they
decide to complete their mission regardless, or did they underestimate the
severity of the flak damage? The answers will never be known.[14]

Fungus Mission was warned of the crash on 5 November and Partisan
reports of 'what sounded like a plane in distress' reached Otocac the
following day.[15] The remains of the aircraft were duly located and Reed was
then allowed to accompany Hunter to the site.[16] He was appalled by the scene
and signalled James Millar at ISLD asking for his deepest sympathies to be
conveyed to 148 Squadron on the loss of Passmore and his crew. 'They did a
magnificent job with us', he told Millar, 'and we have felt it as [a] personal
loss'.[17] The crew were buried in a nearby cemetery at Kosinj, and the
Partisans made a cross, and later a headstone, bearing their names.[18]

On 10 November Reed signalled Millar again:

No decision about us has yet reached this HQ and we have now for over one month been detained pending Tito's pleasure. Suggest we transfer to Mihailovic.[19]

On the following morning Tito's long-awaited permission was at last received. Reed and his staff were allowed to operate more freely and to use their own radio – a minute set which fitted into an attaché case, with a little crystal transmitter and a charger motor for the batteries.[20] From 12 November they began to signal ISLD in accordance with a pre-arranged schedule.[21] 'The faint, wavering little Morse signals that we managed to get from Cairo were our lifeline', Reed subsequently recalled.[22] It then became necessary to establish a *modus operandi* for the two British missions. In agreement, Reed and Hunter proposed close collaboration under one officer (Hunter), who would be responsible for all British personnel in the area, and recommended that intelligence acquired from the Partisans should be handled by Judge, leaving Fungus to deal with military matters, administration and supply drops.[23]

SOE and ISLD promptly accepted this arrangement, but it was not to last very long.[24] The documents show clearly that Hunter was becoming disenchanted with his role at Fungus. Relations with the Partisans had worsened as unrealistic expectations of Allied assistance were inevitably disappointed. The number of supply drops declined as winter weather led to the cancellation of numerous special operations sorties (see Table 1):[25]

Table 1.
AIR SUPPLY SORTIES TO JUDGE/FUNGUS MISSION,
OCTOBER 1943–JANUARY 1944

Date	Sorties to Judge/Fungus
6 October	1
12 October	1
17 October	1
19 October	1
27 October	2
7/8 October	2
8/9 January	3
10/11 January	1

Hopes that an Allied landing might be staged in Yugoslavia following the Italian capitulation came to nothing; the absence of much tangible evidence of Allied action was unfavourably compared with Soviet advances on the eastern front; and there was also the embarrassment of Judge Mission's unexpected and unsanctioned arrival.[26] When, late in October, American bombers mistakenly targeted a number of Partisan towns, Hunter complained bitterly: 'This mission's work has become exclusively explanation and apology and it becomes increasingly hard to laugh off one incident after another.'[27] A few days later he added that SOE's failure to keep him informed was undermining his standing among the Partisans. 'If you cannot support me', he went on, 'I shall lose their confidence and my usefulness here'.[28]

On 7 November he signalled his desire to reach Fitzroy Maclean in Bosnia, almost certainly to seek permission to relinquish his post at Fungus, and ten days later he departed, taking some of the other mission personnel with him.[29] He was evacuated to Italy on 3 December.[30] At Maclean's request Reed now became the representative of both ISLD and SOE at Partisan headquarters in Croatia.[31] 'Debt to Hunter and team immense', Reed signalled. 'Hunter specially kind and helpful and his experience, advice and contacts [are] invaluable.'[32] But some weeks passed before it was confirmed that Hunter would not be returning to the mission.[33] Anthony Hunter afterwards served in Montenegro before rejoining the Scots Fusiliers. He fought in north-western Europe after the second front opened, but, sadly, was killed in Holland in February 1945.[34]

Reed's mission now comprised only Stichman, Ryan and the Fungus radio operator, Jephson, an establishment maintained until 13 January 1944, when Paul Stichman left.[35] Reed simply recorded that 'our interpreter had joined the Partisans, which he'd been determined to do from the outset'.[36] He was killed fighting in Slavonia in May.[37] His departure left the joint mission with only three personnel and no interpreter. 'I was learning Serbo-Croat as fast as I could', Reed recalled, 'in order to keep my head above water'.[38] Not for the first time in that war Reed found himself doing two jobs simultaneously: he gathered intelligence for ISLD, which he passed through the ISLD radio, operated by Ryan, and commanded the British Military Mission for SOE, communicating with them through Jephson. Routine work with the Partisans was conducted daily through their liaison officers, who apparently spoke some English, and English speakers were also on hand when Reed dealt with Gosnjak or his staff. As his linguistic ability improved, these contacts became very much easier. 'I now talk here about as fluently as I did French at my prep school', he wrote at the end of March, 'but I can get along, and my floundering earnestness I think sometimes rather impresses our hosts'.[39] His role as the senior British officer at Partisan headquarters Croatia was formally recognized early in February, when he was promoted to major.[40]

The task of running both missions would probably have been impracticable even with Stichman's assistance. Without him it was over-whelming. Reed's full range of responsibilities encompassed intelligence gathering and presentation, the continuous encoding and decoding of signals, arranging supply drops, attending drop zones and landing grounds, organizing other supply routes, particularly by sea, liaison with the Partisans, meeting, accommodating and despatching SOE and ISLD agents

by air, land or sea, evacuating escaped POWs and shot-down airmen, and
many essential administrative chores. This extraordinarily wide variety of
duties had often to be executed in very close proximity to enemy forces, and
was frequently disrupted by fighting, by enforced flight to safer territory
and by air attack from the Luftwaffe units based at Zagreb. 'I'm wanted all
day for 50 different things in three different languages', Reed wrote on 8
February. 'My office work . . . is always days behind.'[41]

For Ryan and Jephson he had nothing but praise: 'No work is too hard for
them and they bear astonishingly with my temper.'[42] But when Jephson fell ill
later in February Reed warned that the mission could no longer operate unless
reinforcements were despatched by SOE or ISLD, and his demands for assistance became increasingly strident in March, when arrangements were made
to evacuate Jephson to Italy for medical treatment.[43] ISLD responded first by
infiltrating another NCO, Sergeant Pavelic, on 13 March, the day before a
Dakota picked up Jephson and a group of American aircrew from an
improvized landing strip at Krbavsko Polje, near Udbina.[44] There is little documentary record of Pavelic's background or activities at the mission although,
from his name, it may be surmised that he was of Yugoslav origin – almost
certainly another Canadian recruit. But a few months later, on 16 July, it was
Pavelic who rescued four passengers from a burning Dakota which had crashed while landing at another airfield near the mission. Among them were the
Prime Minister's son, Randolph Churchill, and the novelist, Evelyn Waugh.[45]

There was a longer delay before more SOE personnel arrived to staff
Fungus Mission. In mid-March one of the senior SOE officers in theatre, Peter
Moore, made representations to SOE headquarters on Reed's behalf,[46] but
when this yielded no very obvious response Reed confronted SOE himself:

> Your stores plan . . . will break down unless you send at once one
> officer and one operator to take whole stores organization off our
> hands. All your messages take for granted that Fungus Mission still
> exists. Reference your files, if any, will show that it has been extinct
> since Hunter left five months ago.[47]

A few days later he decided that given the 'increasing pressure [of] ISLD
and other commitments' it was 'impossible to cope further with 133 [SOE]
affairs except on basis of emergency'.[48] In the meantime, SOE attempted to
arrange for an American officer of the Office of Strategic Services (OSS) to
join Reed with a radio operator.[49] It was eventually decided to transfer
Major George Selvig, who since December had represented OSS at Tito's
headquarters in Bosnia;[50] he reached Reed's mission on 6 April.[51] But
Jephson was only finally replaced on 7 May. Until then Paddy Ryan
handled both ISLD and SOE signals traffic.[52]

Between November 1943 and his evacuation from Yugoslavia at the end of

June 1944, much of Reed's time was devoted to assisting the bizarre variety of clandestine warriors, spies, dignitaries, escaped POWs and distressed airmen who passed through Judge/Fungus Mission. Some of these personalities and their extraordinary adventures are described in the following chapter. Otherwise, his work involved collecting intelligence for ISLD, organizing military and other supplies and aircraft landings for SOE, and continuous liaison with the Partisans.

The task was profoundly influenced by the course of hostilities with the Germans and the Ustase. When Reed arrived in Croatia the Partisans still held substantial tracts of the coast – one reason for Churchill's interest in staging an Allied landing there. And while the volume of airborne supplies to the Partisans had been a source of some disappointment, plans were afoot to send a far larger quantity of stores from Allied-occupied Italy to Croatia by sea. On 18 November Reed sent SOE details of a number of ports that were ready to receive stores at 24 hours' notice. 'Suggest ships go from Vis to Sali on [the island of] Dugi Otok where pilot [is] ready for them.'[53] As well as bringing supplies, shipping sorties might also have helped to infiltrate more Allied personnel and to evacuate anyone – British agents, Partisan wounded, downed aircrew – with an urgent need to reach safer territory.

Inevitably, though, the Germans were quick to appreciate the strategic importance of the coast, and its recapture became their foremost priority. On 27 November they took the port of Karlobag, and by the beginning of December they were attempting to dislodge the Partisans from Dugi Otok.[54] But this first offensive then ground to a halt and on the 6th Reed reported that the threat to the coast road had greatly diminished.[55] The Partisans quickly regained much of their lost territory, and on 6 January the Germans evacuated Karlobag. By that time Allied ships were landing stores at the port of Senj, further to the north, which were rapidly moved inland to Otocac.[56] Their cargo included anti-tank and shrapnel mines, Italian machine-guns, mortars, Bren guns and 800 Sten guns, as well as diesel fuel and petrol.[57]

In mid-January the Partisans reported that a large body of enemy troops and tanks was concentrating to the south-east at Gospic.[58] They soon crossed the river Lika and began advancing north towards Otocac. The British mission packed up their equipment and waited nervously for the order to move.[59] On 18 January, narrowly avoiding a column of German tanks, they withdrew eastward with Gosnjak's headquarters to where the mountainous territory of the Mala Kapela forms an almost impregnable natural fortress. The next day Reed reported that Otocac had been captured by a force of 47 tanks and 4,000 troops, and that enemy units were converging on Senj, cutting the Partisan supply line to the coast.[60] They also attempted to pursue the Partisans into the mountains. 'Heavy bombardment all day', Reed noted in his diary on the 23rd. 'Battle very near to N[orth] W[est].'[61] Two days later they moved further east to Plitvice, where they were housed in a former pension overlooking the lake.[62] The Germans failed to penetrate the Mala Kapela, but they achieved their principal aim by reoccupying the Croatian coast.[63]

From then on, air sorties offered the only means of transporting supplies and personnel from southern Italy to Judge/Fungus Mission. And as, at that time, no Allied aircraft were landing in Croatia, any personnel requiring evacuation had to be conveyed south-east to an airstrip near Tito's headquarters in Bosnia.[64] Intelligence reports and captured enemy documents were sometimes also sent back to ISLD via this route, but the delay involved tended to reduce the value of any information they contained. Lacking other means of ensuring that intelligence reached ISLD in time for it to be of any use, Reed and Ryan spent interminable hours encoding such papers in their entirety so that they could be transmitted by radio.[65]

Of Reed's innumerable duties, intelligence gathering is the least well documented. Most of his intelligence signals and reports were despatched to ISLD, and while many of the signals on German dispositions and Partisan military operations have found their way into the National Archives, the majority of longer reports and appreciations were retained by SIS, and were probably destroyed long ago.[66] Nevertheless, three points are clear. Firstly, the volume of intelligence was at its greatest during periods of combat with the Germans, when prisoners and documents often fell into Partisan hands. Most of the (scrupulously uninformative) diary references to Reed's ISLD work were written during the German offensives of January and early February, and April and early May 1944. Secondly, Reed was critically dependent on the Partisans for the collection of intelligence. He later recalled that his work 'involved the whole of the Partisan Army as a kind of pair of binoculars. They had the information, they were in a position to watch all the key roads and railways.'[67] This inevitably imposed severe constraints on his capacity to obtain useful material, for the Partisan intelligence organization was rudimentary in the extreme, as was their appreciation of potentially valuable information. Reed was clearly passed a large volume of intelligence on the enemy order of battle and on troop movements and dispositions, but it is doubtful that this 'gen' (as he called it) was more valuable than the Enigma decrypts already available to the Allies. Thirdly, it is clear that his reports ranged over a wide variety of subjects and were not merely confined to military matters. During his time in Croatia he helped to improve ISLD's appreciation of the Partisan movement, describing in detail their organization and political activities. He also supplied more general updates on living conditions and economic activity in Croatia.[68]

Intelligence received from the Partisans took two basic forms. The daily situation reports furnished by Gosnjak's staff had a tendency to be vague and somewhat optimistic, but they were usually accurate; in time they became more balanced, admitting military failures as well as victories. Reed also found that useful information could be deduced from them. Hence a situation report describing an attack on a train might unintentionally reveal that the railway line concerned had been returned to use by the Germans after the previous Partisan attack. Nevertheless, verbal information and documents passed to him by the Partisan liaison staff were always more valuable. By January 1944 he had established excellent relations with the Partisan Chief of Information and had convinced his hosts of the importance of recovering paybooks from enemy dead, which enabled their units to be identified.[69] On the basis of such intelligence, Reed's early assessment of German dispositions in Croatia was as follows:

The majority of German units in the area are there either:

1. Because they are greatly under strength and need training and reinforcements, i.e., reforming before moving to other areas.
2. To keep open certain invaluable lines of communication.
3. To deny our forces such ports as would make a landing simple and quick.
4. As a strategic reserve to be used as a delaying force if we were to make a landing in the Balkans.[70]

One of his early tasks was to obtain an authoritative assessment of the enemy order of battle from the Partisans. This was duly supplied and sent to ISLD, who in turn despatched it to London.

Reed's prestige was considerably increased when ISLD London challenged the GSH enemy order of battle, and were eventually proved to be right, although this caused a certain amount of jealousy and heartburning on the part of the Partisans at the time.[71]

This was a dangerous strategy, for the information available in London was almost certainly based on signals intelligence. Nevertheless, as one contemporary report put it, 'the value of this exchange of information as compared to merely getting information from the Partisans cannot be overestimated'. Reed often found his senior officers unwilling to accept Partisan reports uncritically, and regularly received requests from ISLD for corroborative evidence.[72]

When it worked the concept of 'using the Partisans as a pair of binoculars' worked very well indeed. Hence, on 17 November 1943, 'extracts of Hun cipher key found in enemy aircraft' were passed to Cairo via the Fungus radio.[73] A month later Cairo signalled back: 'This document [is] a valuable scoop and is being well used. Good show.'[74] Croatia's central geographical position made it a natural focus for information from many other parts of Yugoslavia, which was passed to Reed for despatch to Cairo.

Reports from Dalmatia, Bosnia and Slavonia were regularly transmitted by the Croatian mission, and were gratefully received. 'Your sitreps [are] very valuable', Reed was told on 27 December, 'and [are] often only source of information on certain areas. Carry on the good work.'[75] To improve the flow of intelligence further, Reed was supplied with extra radio sets for the Partisans to place in Zagreb, Fiume and other enemy centres.[76]

The German offensive of January 1944 produced numerous captured documents, which appear to have been encoded and transmitted to ISLD by radio.[77] But it was also the occasion of an all-too-graphic example of the limits of the Partisans' intelligence capability. Among the various dangers confronting the Croatian Partisans, a particularly serious threat was posed by Ustase infiltrators, who regularly attached themselves to Partisan formations. The two groups may have differed in their political and military allegiances, but racially and linguistically they could be indistinguishable. Together with aerial reconnaissance, signals intelligence and interrogation, these agents played a vital role in the Axis intelligence effort, and their identification required constant vigilance and scrupulous security measures, which inevitably were often lacking.[78] Nevertheless, on 15 February 1944, Reed was informed that an Ustase agent had been apprehended but that the Partisans had been unable to obtain any information from him. They approached Reed in the belief that, as an officer of the British Secret Service, he would be thoroughly skilled in the art of interrogation, and perhaps in methods of torture, and that he might therefore help to make their prisoner talk. In reality, of course, Reed had only received some very elementary instruction in cross-examining POWs before his infiltration the previous autumn.

It was definitely *not* the Partisans' intention that Reed should interrogate the Ustase officer himself and when he sought to do so they refused to co-operate, denying him the services of an interpreter. Reed eventually interviewed the luckless Ustase (who predictably displayed many signs of maltreatment at the hands of his captors) with the utmost difficulty, personally translating his Serbo-Croat sentence by sentence. He was at last persuaded to divulge a certain amount of information about the organization of the Ustase security services and their links with German intelligence, but his rambling and incoherent account added little to ISLD's existing knowledge. ISLD was nevertheless intensely interested in him, and went so far as to suggest that he might be evacuated for interrogation by its specialists. Although the logistics of this operation would have been extremely complex in the circumstances of February 1944, Reed dutifully conveyed their request to the Partisans and did his utmost to persuade them to co-operate. But his efforts were in vain, and he never saw the Ustase officer again.[79]

During the second half of February and through March 1944 there was a lull in hostilities which provided an opportunity to establish more reliable arrangements for supplying the Partisans by air. The American Dakota transport aircraft of 60 Group had, by this time, been added to 334 Wing's establishment of two RAF squadrons, and the entire wing had moved from north Africa to locations around Bari and Brindisi in Italy, dramatically reducing the transit time to Yugoslavia. ISLD moved there too, creating an operations centre at Bari which functioned under the name No. 1 I(U) Section; their headquarters was established at Naples.[80] After more than two months without any parachute drops, supplies to Croatia had been renewed on a limited scale in January, but 60 Group's Dakotas could land on even the most primitive strips provided that they were relatively flat and clear of obstacles, and both Reed and his superior officers at ISLD and SOE were keen to exploit this capability.[81]

As early as November 1943 Reed had advised SOE that a suitable landing strip was available at the historic battlefield site of Krbavsko Polje, and that a second field at nearby Bjelopolje could also be prepared.[82] He again recommended Krbavsko Polje to SOE in February 1944 in response to a request for information on airfields suitable for pick-up operations, but the RAF refused to authorize landings there until the strip had been inspected by one of their personnel.[83] Reed made no further progress until the beginning of March, when the need to evacuate Jephson, two other

6. Owen Reed photographed by Peter Wilkinson, Croatia, 19 March 1944.

SOE agents and a large group of downed American airmen created sufficient impetus for what turned out to be the only successful landing undertaken at Krbavsko Polje during his time in Croatia.[84] An RAF corporal, a specialist in pick-up operations, arrived by parachute to confirm the suitability of the airstrip, and to supervise the evacuation.[85]

To complicate matters the operation had to be co-ordinated with Pavelic's infiltration on the previous evening. On 13 March Reed, Jephson and a group of Partisans journeyed on horseback through deep snow to Crna Vlast, 'a fine ride and marvellous views and a terrific sunset as we arrived';[86] Pavelic was duly dropped at 1.40 on the morning of the 14th.[87] They then collected the Americans and made their way to Korenica, where they waited until nightfall before moving to Krbavsko Polje. It was a tense

7. A supply drop to the Yugoslav Partisans, typical of the many drops made to Partisan headquarters Croatia by the spring of 1944, when Reed was commanding the Judge and Fungus missions.

8. The supply parachutes litter the ground.

9. RAF Dakotas of 267 Squadron at Bari, Italy, in 1944. Flying from Italy in the summer of 1944 these aircraft dramatically increased the volume of supplies reaching the Partisans.

night. The Dakota eventually appeared and the correct identification signals were exchanged. But before the Partisans could light the flare path the aircraft unaccountably left the scene and there was a long delay before it returned. This time, to Reed's intense relief, it landed, and the evacuation then proceeded according to plan.[88] Having at last established Krbavsko Polje's potential, Reed promptly organized another landing there a few nights later, but the operation was repeatedly delayed and finally cancelled, and melting snow then rendered the airfield unusable.[89]

By mid-March the combination of increased aircraft numbers, shorter transit times and improving weather conditions was enhancing the potential for supply drops to the Partisans. Moreover, as Allied escort fighters based in Italy could establish and maintain air superiority over Yugoslavia for limited periods, daylight operations became practicable. At almost exactly the same time, after the months of hostilities following the Italian capitulation, famine began to threaten some northern districts of Croatia, adding food to the already extensive list of Partisan requirements.[90] On the 14th Reed was asked 'for saturation point [of] numbers [of] containers and packages, i.e., how many do you estimate you can receive [in] one night should mass sorties be laid on?'[91] On the 21st he was informed that a large number of daylight sorties was being considered and would probably be undertaken in the near future, and again SOE requested an estimated 'saturation point' for these missions.[92] But before time permitted any serious progress in this direction the Germans launched a further offensive against the Croatian Partisans.

This new attack came as a complete surprise. For some days Reed had been struggling with a backlog of signals and reports that had accumulated during his absence at the airfield, and with a second fruitless attempt to interrogate an enemy agent, this time an Abwehr officer, who had fallen into Partisan hands.[93] On 31 March he was anticipating another day in 'the office' when the lakeside headquarters' relative tranquillity was shattered by the sound of gunfire to the west. A Partisan liaison officer arrived shortly afterwards to announce that a move was imminent.[94] On 1 April Reed heard that the Germans had taken Vrhovine, about halfway between Otocac and Plitvice, and that Crna Vlast, one of the parachute drop zones, was in Ustase hands – information which he promptly relayed to ISLD.[95] The following days saw a succession of moves to more remote locations in the surrounding forest, and a narrow escape for Ryan and Pavelic, who were shot at near one of the waterfalls. Fortunately they both emerged unscathed.[96]

A break in the fighting luckily coincided with George Selvig's arrival at the mission on 7 April but did not last.[97] On the 8th Reed's diary records 'heavy firing all day...Packed once more and away 11 am.'[98] The adverse consequences of the offensive for the air supply programme became all too obvious when some 30 containers were mistakenly dropped to the Ustase at Crna Vlast. This was in itself an intensely worrying development for it suggested, firstly, that ISLD had failed to pass vital operational information to SOE and, secondly, that the Ustase had learnt of the ground-to-air recognition signals employed by the Partisans to confirm their identity to Allied aircraft, probably from German decrypts of Partisan radio traffic. Reed immediately changed the signals and suspended all sorties to Croatian headquarters pending the location of an alternative drop zone.[99] In the meantime intelligence acquired by Tito's staff revealed that the Germans knew the location of Gosnjak's headquarters and were intending to bomb it. The air raid occurred early in the morning on 11 April, when a single Fiesler Storch bombed the headquarters building with remarkable precision. Fortunately it was no longer occupied.[100]

The ensuing weeks were characterized by continued harassment from the Luftwaffe, further enemy attempts to seize Partisan territory and, notwithstanding these hindrances, sustained and predominantly successful efforts to enlarge the air supply programme. Troops and refugees congregated in the surrounding mountains and woods; the wounded accumulated steadily.[101] Bombing raids on the Partisan village of Leskovac on 13 and 17 April – the latter involving no fewer than 13 Stukas – kept the Croatian headquarters in a state of high alert.[102] But Gosnjak, 'an astute and impassive tactician who kept his hand in at the chessboard, always contrived to be one move ahead in the game of positional warfare'.[103] After a number of days sleeping in the open in tents improvised from parachute nylon, the ISLD/SOE contingent moved back to the former headquarters building, which they found 'much worse for wear', but renewed bombing drove them outdoors again.[104] There was one particularly close shave when a lone Henschel caught the Partisans off guard early on the morning of 30 April, and an enemy advance, which brought 'firing very near', forced another move north into the Kordun region the next day.[105]

Nevertheless, landing parties continued to stand by at the Korenica drop zone, and Reed maintained his campaign to reactivate the landing ground at Krbavsko Polje with George Selvig's wholehearted support. He also proposed dropping food directly into the famine area, to the north-west, where a new drop zone was organized near Ravna Gora.[106] There were successful supply drops to Korenica on the 22nd, 23rd and 28th, before the first large-scale operation to Ravna Gora, involving four aircraft, on 1 May.[107]

A remarkable interlude occurred early in May when the Commissar, Zigic, asked Reed if he would attend a three-day congress of Croatian cultural workers at Topusko. The middle of a German offensive appeared to Reed a most unsuitable moment for a cultural festival, but he nevertheless accepted the invitation and agreed to deliver a short speech. The following day he was driven north in a Fiat staff car to Topusko which, with its formal stucco-fronted Kursaal and dripping avenues of flowering chestnut trees, reminded him of British towns like Cheltenham or Leamington. The lobby of the Kursaal was lined with the work of Partisan artists, completed

10. Reed with Partisans and an unidentified British serviceman – possibly Ryan. Reed did his utmost to maintain cordial relations with his Partisan hosts, and in the process gained valuable intelligence during his two missions to Croatia.

and collected in the face of unimaginable difficulty, mainly sombre charcoal drawings and half-tints dwelling with nostalgic devotion on scenes of peacetime countryside, old barns and farms and ponds and fences, family faces and firesides, and all the domestic attachments that men cling to in countries ruined by war. There was one macabre display of war pictures and cartoons and posters, ferociously and defiantly commemorating the atrocities of invader and quisling. Many of them had photographs pinned beside them, as if no one could be expected to believe that what they saw was true. And all the time, as Reed walked round, the floor shook with the mortar and artillery fire from the river valley a few miles down the road.

That evening, in a concert hall aglow with the smouldering red and yellow of the Partisan banners and slogans, and hazy with cigarette smoke, pianists clad in battledress coaxed Chopin and Rachmaninoff out of a blackened and battle-stained Bechstein, which had been dragged by hand or truck or ox-wagon through six German offensives. Then came an old blind man who played the accordion, and a choir of tiny orphans clad in blue overcoats and caps. A play the next evening took the form of an impassioned declamatory dialogue between two spotlit figures on a pedestal, representing the Führer and the Spirit of Reaction – 'a hag-ridden and raddled old beldam straight from the Blasted Heath', in Reed's words. There followed a kind of choral ballet depicting in verse and movement the victorious history of the Red Army, and last came a comedy of manners – a period piece with a Hungarian setting in which the cast sported elaborate costumes stitched together from the variegated colours of British supply parachutes.

After his speech, which was greeted with rapturous applause, Reed found himself bombarded with questions. How had he liked the show? How did the standard compare with the Old Vic? Didn't he think so-and-so was terrific as the Spirit of Reaction? How was the British theatre reflecting the war? And then he remembered that, only the previous night, a supply sortie from Bari had delivered a mail bag containing, of all things, the interim report of his pre-war trades union, Equity, the British actors' association:

> Among the circle of interested faces behind the curtain it needed little imagination to believe that this scrap of paper, so heavily stamped with the marks of wartime paper economy, and so magically dropped in the night, was a message of greeting from all the actors and actresses of Great Britain. Anyhow, I knew that that was what every member of Equity would like it to be.[108]

And that is what the interim report became.

The enemy air and ground campaigns continued unabated during May, and the 'bomb jittery' members of the Judge/Fungus Mission went on spending as much time outdoors as possible. 'Pav and I encode all day under trees in wind', Reed noted in his diary on 6 May. 'Shot up by Dornier PM. Glad to see sun set.'[109] The next day the Germans captured the towns of Poljanak and Prijeboj to achieve their furthest advance yet into the Mala Kapela.[110] By the 11th they had pushed Gosnjak from Rakovica to Dunjak, taken Leskovac and overrun the drop zone at Korenica, and Reed's mission was reporting that Krbavsko Polje was 'threatened by a possible Hun thrust from the north... This [is] very disappointing to us.'[111] But no sooner had one drop zone closed than another opened, this time at Vrginmost, to the north-east.[112] Selvig was despatched there on the 15th to organize the reception of stores and on the 16th Pavelic assumed similar duties at Ravna Gora.[113] The information he supplied on his return allowed Reed to report to ISLD on living conditions around Ravna Gora and on Partisan stores requirements there. He also offered a brief and positive assessment of Partisan military activities in the region, describing how Pavelic had witnessed the sabotage of road and rail communications on his way back to Judge Mission.[114]

To direct operations Reed and Ryan remained at Partisan headquarters at Dunjak – an exceptionally hazardous location. On 18 May Reed recorded in his diary:

> Chicha [one of the Partisan liaison staff] suggests we move out. P[addy] and I recce after lunch. I stay on hill to work. 2 pm 12 Stukas appear. First raid on Kladusa. Then our turn. 2nd wave 3 pm. Hellish but I out of harm's way. At 5 looked round dizzily. Church, school, staff building, hospital and half cottages gone. Miraculous escape for me. Grim comparing of notes all day. Pack to quit pm. Quit 5 am next day. Get hasty mes[sage] away to firm [ISLD]. What a day! What a life!'[115]

The only consolation, apart from the mounting frequency of the supply drops, was the appearance of Allied bombers and their escort fighters, which made life increasingly difficult for the German and Ustase ground forces. Reed observed the waves of British and American aircraft flying over Croatia, but without any clear idea of their purpose or destination until 23 May, when the Germans launched a new offensive into the Kordun. As the Judge/Fungus Mission frantically prepared for yet another move Reed despatched a call for air support and on the following day formations of Allied aircraft, 'the biggest show yet', attacked a range of enemy targets to bring much-needed relief to the beleaguered Partisans.[116] From then on Gosnjak's staff passed him lists of potential targets, which were duly relayed to the MAAF headquarters via ISLD in Bari.[117]

Early on the morning of 25 May Reed emerged from his tent to observe a large body of enemy aircraft flying south from Zagreb.[118] News soon reached the Croatian headquarters that the Germans had launched a joint airborne and ground assault against Tito's headquarters at Drvar in Bosnia.[119] Reed signalled:

> 25 May combined glider and parachute troops attack on DRVAR believe involving 1 airborne div. Immense number aircraft flew south from direction ZAGREB dawn and dusk 25 May and dawn 26 May. All types including gliders. Simultaneously ground offensive on PETROVAC and DRVAR from BIHAC, LAPAC DONJE, DALMATIA, KNIN, LIVNO. No contact TITO since 5 GMT 25th May. Position very serious. Send all possible air support at all costs at once above area and attack ZAGREB bases. Most critical sector immediate DRVAR area.[120]

This was one signal that found its way into the upper-most echelons of government; a slightly summarized version quickly reached the Prime Minister, as well as the British Resident Minister in Algiers, Harold Macmillan.[121]

In fact, Drvar was entirely overrun, but Tito escaped to the Allied-held island of Vis, and in the following days the German ground forces were relentlessly harried from the air.[122] Between 26 and 30 May over 1,000 sorties were flown by RAF and USAAF (United States Army Air Force) units against

11. A South African Air Force Marauder bombing Banja Luka in June 1944. Reed supplied intelligence which helped guide many Allied bombers to their targets in this period.

targets in Yugoslavia. Reed's intelligence helped to guide bombing raids on to a number of key targets including Bihac, Knin, Livno and Drvar itself; a force of 55 B17s struck the Zagreb air bases on the 30th 'destroying 45 aircraft on the ground and damaging 96 others, [and] virtually eliminated the GAF as a combat force in Yugoslavia'.[123] At least 94 motor vehicles were also destroyed and more than 128 damaged.[124] One of Reed's signals to ISLD called for attacks on the enemy fortress at Cazin, and on a number of other locations. On 4 June he was asked to supply further information on the fortress' whereabouts and on the following day it was successfully targeted by 12 USAAF Marauders.[125] 'Cazin bombed early am' he noted in his diary with evident satisfaction.[126] An official account of these air operations prepared at the end of the War acknowledged that 'great credit must go to the officers in the field, who passed consistently good and correct information, under the most difficult circumstances'.[127]

After Tito's evacuation, SOE tried to cover his tracks by deceiving the Germans into thinking that he was in Croatia. To this end a new radio operator codenamed 'Bus' was to transmit false signals traffic from Partisan headquarters Croatia to the Allied base on Vis. The plan was approved by both Tito and Fitzroy McLean, but Reed objected, almost certainly in anticipation of Gosnjak's opposition.[128] It was well known that the Germans employed triangulation to pinpoint the precise location of radio transmitters in Partisan territory; if they were persuaded that Tito was indeed in Croatia further large-scale air and ground raids were almost certain to follow. Reed was particularly concerned over the many hundreds of wounded who had congregated in the area, who would have been extremely vulnerable in the event of a major German assault. Under pressure from SOE he finally approached Gosnjak and found him equally unenthusiastic. The general eventually conceded that if he were ordered to do so by Tito he would let Bus transmit, but only from a location well away from his headquarters and from the area where the various hospitals and storage depots were hidden.[129] The plan was eventually abandoned.[130]

Gosnjak's concerns over the possibility of a renewed German offensive are entirely understandable given the Croatian Partisans' experiences in the preceding months. But in fact the most desperate phase of the war in Yugoslavia was over by early June. Allied air superiority undoubtedly helped to turn the tide. But the opening of the second front in Europe on 6 June was followed by a particularly marked reduction in enemy activity and German troop withdrawals began almost immediately.[131] In Croatia the Partisan response was no less immediate, but it was a response which the Allies neither expected nor welcomed.

Among the formations controlled by the Croatian headquarters was 11 Corps, which was located in Istria, near the Italian frontier. Italian sovereignty over the border region of western Istria known as Venezia Giulia – dominated by the city of Trieste – had been a source of dispute between Italy and Yugoslavia throughout the inter-war years. Trieste had only been ceded to Italy after the First World War and contained a substantial Slav minority. After the Partisans took up arms against the Axis they had formulated detailed territorial claims in Venezia Giulia, which included the transfer of Trieste to Yugoslavia. Their ambitions had undoubtedly been communicated to SOE by January 1944, but do not appear to have been taken seriously.[132] The Allies' position was broadly that Venezia Giulia was Italian and Italy was now fighting alongside the British Empire and America; the territorial dispute was seen as a problem which would have to be solved after the cessation of hostilities, but there was little enthusiasm for handing over the region to a Soviet-backed communist regime. In the interim, the Partisans were manifestly not being supplied with weapons to enable them to pursue territorial ambitions bearing no relation whatever to the war with Germany.[133]

In June 1944, with Italian fascism defeated and Germany's forces in retreat, the Partisans saw their opportunity. In a matter of days the cry of 'Nasa je Trst' ('Trieste is ours'), had spread through the guerrilla units, encouraged by their propaganda organs and political commissars. Reed recalled later that he foresaw impending confrontation over Trieste between the Partisans and the advancing Allied armies in Italy: 'There was the danger of an unpleasant collision.'[134] His recollections may have been influenced by the Trieste crisis of 1945, which overshadowed his second mission to Yugoslavia. But it is certain that in June 1944 he reported the Partisans' determination to annex the city with the utmost clarity and in terms that ISLD felt were impossible to ignore. His warnings seem to have been greeted at first with surprise and then with mounting alarm. His diary records the rather strained attempts of his controller, Desmond Clarke, to obtain clarification and a 'second report for Des' on 14 June, after which it was decided that Reed should be withdrawn from the field to brief his superior officers in person.[135]

Only a few days after Krbavsko Polje fell into enemy hands, Reed and Selvig identified another potential landing strip at Gajevi, to the north-east, near Vrginmost and Topusko, and renewed their campaign for air transport sorties. The Partisans were desperate to evacuate their wounded, who were invariably shot if found by the Germans or the Ustase, and a number of downed American airmen had made their way to the mission and were awaiting a passage back to Italy; the commencement of pick-up operations would also greatly simplify the often complex incoming and outgoing of SOE and ISLD personnel. On 31 May the two officers sent a signal to all the interested Allied organizations, including the RAF and the USAAF, urging them to pool their resources in an immediate drive to evacuate the Partisan wounded and Allied airmen from Gajevi.[136]

The first Dakotas were expected at Gajevi on 10 June, but the first

major evacuation only took place on the 15th, as poor weather resulted in
the cancellation of all but one pick-up. In the meantime, the logistical
arrangements involved in evacuating the wounded *en masse* proved
extremely problematic. The Partisans normally accommodated their
wounded in hidden hospitals and assembly areas. Reed later recalled one
such hiding place, 'high up on the side of a great snow-covered mountain,
in thick forest. It was a cave which you reached through a hole in the
ground.' These locations were all some distance from the airfield, and the
aircraft were only allowed to wait on the ground for 30 minutes. The
wounded had therefore to be transported to Gajevi over several hours, well
in advance of the Dakotas' arrival, and many completed the journey before
Reed was informed that the scheduled sorties had been called off; they had
then to be returned to their hiding places.[137] On the 15th Reed ran out of
patience and signalled to Bari:

> Fifty critically wounded Partisans have waited in vain five nights on
> airfield. Each man has to be brought separately by ox wagon from
> assembly area five miles away and whole process involves 100 oxen,
> three doctors and six hours agonising pain. If you cannot send plane
> you must warn us by 14.45 hours GMT, so as to spare all concerned
> this beastly ordeal and save me a 50-mile journey without transport.[138]

12. The flare path marking the landing strip at Gajevi, near Topusko.
Reed and his assistants were responsible for opening and operating the
landing strip in June 1944.

That night four aircraft finally landed, one every half hour, bringing with them some useful stores; they returned to Italy with 65 wounded and 230 used supply parachutes.[139]

This success encouraged Reed to organize a more ambitious evacuation, which was to coincide with his own departure from Croatia. Unfortunately this second operation was characterized by precisely the same problems as the first, due to some unseasonable weather. Signals from the mission on 20 June confirmed that 130 wounded were awaiting evacuation at Gajevi, but no aircraft came that night.[140] And then it began to rain. 'Thundery, nil to report', Reed wrote in his diary on the 21st; the next day he wrote 'ditto'; on the next 'ditto, rain and thunder'; and on the next, 'bloody awful rain'.

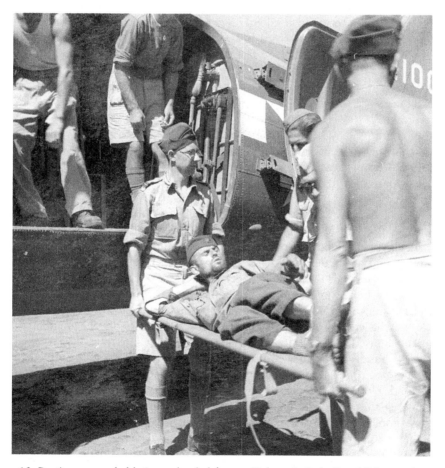

13. Partisan wounded being unloaded from a Dakota in Italy. In addition to the wounded, several hundred orphans were flown to safety under Reed's supervision at the end of June 1944.

On 24 June he was caught up in a rehearsal for another cultural congress at Topusko, and on the 25th he delivered a speech which was still remembered years later by those who heard it.[141] 'I think there is no army in the world who would attach so much importance to culture', he told the audience in his now much improved Serbo-Croat, 'but you are right: a victory is no victory if art and beauty remain suppressed'.[142]

He attended the congress again the next day, but his thoughts were elsewhere: '190 wounded awaiting evacuation', he signalled to Bari. 'Standing by at Gajevi.'[143] On the night of the 29th he was advised to expect six aircraft, and promptly left for the airfield with Ryan. The wounded were brought down from their assembly areas with the usual difficulty, only for word to arrive that the operation had again been cancelled – to the fury and frustration of both Reed and the Partisans. Once more he remonstrated: 'To avoid needless mental and physical suffering you must firstly give T[ime]O[f]A[rrival] if aircraft coming. Secondly inform us on late sked if sortie cancelled.'[144] The operation was re-planned for 30 June, but the exasperated Partisan doctors now flatly refused to bring the wounded to the airfield until the aircraft arrived. Reed pointed out that the Dakotas were forbidden to remain on the ground for more than half an hour, which did not leave nearly enough time for the wounded to reach Gajevi from their assembly areas, but the Partisans were unmoved. 'I could see that they were right', Reed recalled later. 'The suffering their men had to stand simply wasn't worth it.' That night, to his utter consternation, a late update from Bari confirmed that no fewer than *eight* Dakotas were to land at Gajevi.[145]

The fiasco was slightly mitigated by the fact that the Dakotas were staggered at half-hourly intervals: a number of wounded had reached the airfield by the time the later aircraft arrived. But the first two or three to land found no wounded there at all. Their entire cargo would have consisted of Reed, Ryan, their baggage and more used supply parachutes had it not been for the quick thinking of one of the Partisan doctors. A short distance from Gajevi the Partisans had established an orphanage. During the enemy offensives of the previous six months the number of infants housed there had increased steadily until, by late June, they totalled several hundred. Their well-being was a major source of anxiety: they required constant attention and made heavy demands on scarce resources of food, clothing and medicine. Their immobility rendered them no less vulnerable to the enemy than the wounded. The doctor now proposed that they should be evacuated to Italy in the empty Dakotas.[146]

After obtaining the agreement of the aircrew, Reed promptly arranged for the first consignment of babies and toddlers to be brought to Gajevi, where they were loaded on board 'like one damp little parcel after another' and laid on improvized beds made from the supply parachutes. As he climbed into the first aircraft a small boy was thrust up at him out of the darkness. There was no room on the aircraft floor, so the child sat on his lap while the engines started and the Dakota taxied to the end of the field to take off. Through the window Reed saw the flare path, and the crowd of excited fire-lit faces on the edge of the field, and far away the outline of dark forests and mountain peaks. Then, in his words, the Dakota 'began to bump and slither over the muddy ground, faster and faster...until one last bump, and we were away'. It is not difficult to imagine the astonishment that greeted him in Bari early the next morning when he announced that he had been accompanied from Yugoslavia by 50 Partisan babies, and that 350 more were on their way.[147]

Judge Mission was at an end. Reed handed over to another ISLD officer named Byrd, who operated under the codename 'Advocate'.[148] The mission's epitaph is contained in a letter addressed by George Selvig to Bari a few days later, which enclosed a cutting from a local newspaper about Reed's speech to the cultural congress at Topusko. 'The guy should have stayed around', Selvig wrote, 'because he's almost a legendary hero now.'[149]

NOTES

1. HS 5/911, statement of SOE personnel in Yugoslavia as of 1 November 1943.
2. WO 106/3211, Partisan Order of Battle, HQ Croatia; HS 5/963, corrections of intelligence contained in briefing of Operation Rip Van Winkle in May 1944, by Captain F.G. Burnett, 17 June 1944; interview with Reed, 4 November 1989. Hebrang was formally Vice-President of ZAVNOH, but the President was merely a figurehead; see PREM 3/511/12, report by Major R. Churchill, MP, HQ Croatia, 12 April 1944, addressed to Winston Churchill. Bakaric was a lawyer who had edited a left-wing journal before the war; see 'Yugoslavia Basic Handbook', p. 65, AHB.
3. WO 202/513, Military Report on Slovenia and Western Croatia, by Lieutenant-Colonel P.N.M. Moore, RE, compiled at HQ Croatia, 23 January 1944.
4. HS 5/933, note on situation in Yugoslavia, by MI 3b, 27 October 1943.
5. WO 204/9673, information supplied by Private Hutton and Private...[name not recorded] of New Zealand Army, 20 January 1944.
6. WO 202/157, interrogation of Corporal Arnold and Private Woodward, 24 October 1943.
7. WO 202/437, signal from Fungus, 13 October 1943; HS 5/882, signal to 'Pikestaff', 4 October 1943.
8. WO 202/438, signal to Fungus, 16 October 1943.
9. WO 202/140, Yugoslavia signal out, 17 October 1943.
10. WO 202/437, signal from Fungus, 22 October 1943.
11. WO 202/437, signal from Fungus, 16 October 1943.
12. WO 202/437, signal from Fungus, 30 October 1943: 'For ISLD. Appreciate your difficulties but this prolonged silence most disheartening.' WO 202/438, signal to Fungus, 2 November 1943: 'For Judge. Have signalled Pikestaff

urgently to get Tito to clear up your position.'

13. Information supplied by AHB, quoting report by Wing Commander... [name not recorded], commanding 5 MREU, RAF, BTA, November 1947.

14. Passmore's navigator that night was Flight Lieutenant E.B. Elliott, a veteran of more than 80 operational sorties. The other crew members were Flight Sergeant J.H.S. Clarke, Flying Officer H.I. Crawford, Sergeant E.H. Toole, Sergeant R.E. Hawken and Flight Sergeant W.J. Dowle; neither Elliott nor Crawford were on Reed's sortie, but Clarke, Hawken and Toole were on both. See AIR 27/995, November 1943.

15. WO 202/438, signal to Fungus, 5 November 1943; WO 202/437, signal from Fungus, 6 November 1943.

16. WO 202/437, signal from Fungus, 9 November 1943.

17. WO 202/437, signal from Fungus, 10 November 1943.

18. WO 202/437, signal from Fungus, 7 November 1943; information supplied by AHB, quoting report by Wing Commander... [name not recorded], commanding 5 MREU, RAF, BTA, November 1947. The remains of the seven crew members were later moved to the British Military Cemetery at Belgrade.

19. WO 202/437, signal from Fungus, 10 November 1943.

20. RP, Reed interviewed by J. Lane, 'Oral History of the BBC'.

21. WO 202/437, signal from Fungus, 11 November 1943.

22. RP, Reed interviewed by J. Lane, 'Oral History of the BBC'.

23. WO 202/437, signal from Fungus, 11 November 1943.

24. WO 202/438, signal to Fungus, 13 November 1943.

25. WO 202/513, report by Moore, compiled at HQ Croatia, 23 January 1944.

26. WO 202/437, signal from Fungus, 18 October 1943.

27. WO 202/437, signal from Fungus, 26 October 1943.

28. WO 202/437, signal from Fungus, 30 October 1943.

29. WO 202/437, signal from Fungus, 16 and 17 November 1943.

30. HS 5/911, note on statement of SOE personnel in Yugoslavia as at 1 November 1943.

31. Reed's record of service.

32. WO 202/437, signal from Fungus, 19 November 1943.

33. WO 202/438, signal to Fungus, 20 December 1943.

34. Commonwealth War Graves Commission Debt of Honour Register.

35. RP, Reed diary, 13 January 1944.

36. RP, Reed interviewed by J. Lane, 'Oral History of the BBC'.

37. Author's correspondence with M. Gold, Stichman's grandson.

38. RP, Reed interviewed by J. Lane, 'Oral History of the BBC'.

39. RP, OR to PR, 27 March 1944.

40. RP, Reed diary, 3 February 1944.

41. RP, OR to PR, 8 February 1944.

42. RP, OR to PR, 13 March 1944.

43. RP, OR to PR, 27 February 1944; WO 202/439, signal from Fungus, 3 March 1944.

44. RP, Reed diary, 13–15 March 1944; WO 202/439 signal from Fungus, 3 March 1944; WO 202/438, signal to Fungus, 10 March 1944.

45. WO 202/283, R. Churchill to F. Maclean, 9 November 1944; Gilbert, *Churchill*, vol. 7, pp. 854–5. In all, 11 passengers died in the crash, including

the deputy commander of the Balkan Air Force, Air Commodore Carter. There were nine survivors.

46. WO 202/439, signal from Fungus, 13 March 1944: 'Personal for Deakin from Peter Moore. Evacuation [of] Jephson [on] medical grounds leaves Reed and one ISLD operator to handle all Fungus work plus heavy ISLD traffic. Early provision [of] assistant for Reed as recommended by Fitz[roy Maclean] and immediate w/t operator replacement essential to maintain efficiency.'

47. WO 202/439, signal from Fungus, 25 March 1944.

48. WO 202/439, signal from Fungus, 28 March 1944. SOE's organization in the Middle East came to be known as 'Force 133' during the early years of the War.

49. WO 202/438, signal to Fungus, 21 March 1944.

50. WO 202/438, signal to Fungus, 28 March 1944; Wilkinson, *Foreign Fields*, p. 141.

51. RP, Reed diary, 6 April 1944.

52. See, for example, RP, Reed diary, 20 and 21 April 1944.

53. WO 202/437, signal from Fungus, 18 November 1943.

54. WO 202/437, signal from Fungus, 27 November 1943; 2 December 1943.

55. WO 202/437, signal from Fungus, 6 December 1943.

56. WO 202/439, signal from Fungus, 6 January 1944; RP, Reed diary, 8 January 1944.

57. WO 202/513, report by Moore, compiled at HQ Croatia, 23 January 1944.

58. WO 202/439, signal from Fungus, 15 January 1944; RP, Reed diary, 12 January 1944.

59. RP, Reed diary, 13–16 January 1944.

60. WO 202/439, signal from Fungus, 19 January 1944; RP, Reed diary, 18 January 1944.

61. RP, Reed diary, 23 January 1944.

62. RP, Reed diary, 25 January 1944; RP, OR to PR, 8 February 1944; L. Rogers, *Guerrilla Surgeon* (London: Collins, 1957), p. 59.

63. WO 202/439 signal from Fungus, 11 February 1944.

64. WO 202/439, signal from Fungus, 24 February 1944.

65. RP, Reed diary, 29 January 1944; 2 February 1944; RP, Reed interviewed by J. Lane, 'Oral History of the BBC'. The problems of sending documents out of Croatia were referred to obliquely in a letter Reed addressed to his wife on 8 February: 'Fate has been unkind to our postman – he works with considerable efficiency to me but very badly to you. For this as for all evils the bloody Hun must take the blame.'

66. Summaries of some of Reed's signals from this period can be found in CAB 121/529, which contains intelligence updates from Yugoslavia sent by the commander-in-chief Middle East to the War Office; Reed is identified as the liaison officer at Partisan headquarters Croatia. See especially reports of 17 December 1943, 19 January 1944, 31 January 1944 and 2 February 1944.

67. RP, Reed interviewed by J. Lane, 'Oral History of the BBC'.

68. Interview with Reed, 4 November 1989.

69. WO 202/513, report by Moore, compiled at HQ Croatia, 23 January 1944.

70. HS 5/915, Report on trip from Caporetto to Otocac, by Major E.H. Gibbon, DSO, undated but approximately 10 March 1944, 'Evidence mainly from Capt Reed's attempts to identify German units in his area.'

71. WO 202/513, report by Moore, compiled at HQ Croatia, 23 January 1944.

72. *Ibid.*

73. WO 202/437, signal from Fungus, 17 November 1943.

74. WO 202/145, signal to Fungus, 16 December 1943.

75. WO 202/438, signal to Fungus, 27 December 1943.

76. WO 202/513, report by Moore, compiled at HQ Croatia, 23 January 1944.

77. RP, Reed diary, 29 January 1944; 1–5 February 1944.

78. On similar problems among the Slovene Partisans, see Lindsay, *Beacons in the Night*, pp. 184–5.

79. Interview with Reed, 4 November 1989.

80. AHB history of 148 Squadron; Air 40/2659, ISLD Air Operations, Mediterranean Theatre, 1942–1945, ch. 1.

81. Wilkinson, *Foreign Fields*, p. 149.

82. WO 202/437, signal from Fungus, 21 November 1943. In 1493 the Turkish army inflicted a decisive defeat on the Croats at Krbavsko Polje, after which eastern Croatia was effectively incorporated into the Ottoman Empire.

83. WO 202/439, signal from Fungus, 18 and 24 February 1944.

84. WO 202/439, signal from Fungus, 3 March 1944.

85. Wilkinson, *Foreign Fields*, p. 180.

86. RP, OR to PR, 13 March 1944.

87. RP, Reed diary, 13 March 1944.

88. RP, Reed diary, 14 March 1944; WO 202/439, signal from Fungus, 16 March 1944.

89. RP, Reed diary, 18–21 March 1944; WO 202/439, signal from Fungus, 25 March 1944; Wilkinson, *Foreign Fields*, pp. 181–2. On 22 March Reed wrote in his diary that he 'inspected airfield in six inches of water'.

90. WO 202/439, signal from Fungus, 18 April 1944.

91. WO 202/438, signal to Fungus, 14 and 21 March 1944.

92. WO 202/438, signal to Fungus, 21 March 1944. As already shown, Reed used these requests to insist on the assignment of additional personnel to Fungus Mission.

93. RP, Reed diary, 24–30 March 1944.

94. RP, Reed diary, 31 March 1944.

95. RP, Reed diary, 1 April 1944; WO 202/439, signal from Fungus, 16 April 1944.

96. RP, Reed diary, 1–4 April 1944.

97. RP, Reed diary, 7 April 1944.

98. RP, Reed diary, 8 April 1944.

99. RP, Reed diary, 11 April 1944; WO 202/439, signal from Fungus, 16 April 1944; Hinsley *et al.*, *British Intelligence in the Second World War*, vol. 3, pt 1, p. 164. Enigma decrypts were found to contain German decrypts of Partisan radio traffic, showing that the Germans had acquired information from this source about the aircraft recognition signals. British field officers were consequently instructed to change these signals frequently.

100. PREM 3/511/12, report by Major R. Churchill, MP, HQ Croatia, 12 April 1944.

101. RP, Reed diary, 22 April 1944; RP, Reed, *Junior English 3*.

102. RP, Reed diary, 13 and 17 April 1944.

103. RP, 'The Story of a Box of Grease Paint', undated post-war lecture to Equity.
104. RP, Reed diary, 21–23 April 1944.
105. RP, Reed diary, 30 April 1944; 1 May 1944.
106. WO 202/439, signal from Fungus, 18 and 27 April 1944.
107. RP, Reed diary, 22, 23 and 28 March 1944; 1 May 1944.
108. RP, 'The Story of a Box of Grease Paint'.
109. RP, Reed diary, 6 May 1944.
110. RP, Reed diary, 7 May 1944.
111. RP, Reed diary, 8 and 10 May 1944; WO 202/439, signal from Fungus, 11 and 13 May 1944.
112. WO 202/439, signal from Fungus, 11 and 13 May 1944.
113. RP, Reed diary, 15 and 16 May 1944.
114. WO 202/271, undated report on visit to Gorski Kotar, 15 May–25 June, prepared by ISLD.
115. RP, Reed diary, 18 May 1944.
116. RP, Reed diary, 23 and 24 May 1944.
117. WO 202/438, signal to Fungus, 4 June 1944: 'If possible send information on other places mentioned in JUDGE signal 68, specially on location of tank repair at KOSTAJNICA.'
118. RP, Reed diary, 25 May 1944.
119. RP, Reed diary, 26 May 1944.
120. HS 5/883, Major, G.S.... [signature illegible] to HQ SOM, 26 May 1944, covering Reed's signal.
121. PREM 3/511/6, telegram 398, 26 May 1944; FO 371/44256, Bari to Resident Minister Algiers and Foreign Office, 26 May 1944.
122. For an account of the attack by ISLD's liaison officer at Drvar see WO 202/314, report no. YO3538, 19 June 1944.
123. MAAF weekly summary, May 1944, AHB; Hinsley *et al.*, *British Intelligence in the Second World War*, vol. 3, pt 1, p. 166.
124. AHB file IIJ1/130, The History of the Balkan Air Force, prepared by Headquarters, the Balkan Air Force, RAF, CMF, July 1945, pp. 77–8.
125. WO 202/438, signal to Fungus, 4 June 1944; Mediterranean Allied Air Forces monthly summary of bombing operations, June 1944, AHB.
126. RP, Reed diary, 5 May 1944.
127. AHB file IIJ1/130, The History of the Balkan Air Force, p. 79.
128. HS 5/883, Lieutenant-Colonel J.G. Beevor, for Major-General Comd, HQ SOM, to AOC-in-C Balkan Air Forces, 14 June 1944.
129. HS 5/883, Judge to Force 266 via ISLD, 18 June 1944. 'Force 266' replaced 'Force 133' as SOE's cover name late in 1943, as the SOE operation in Yugoslavia (and Albania) evolved into a more orthodox military operation.
130. HS 5/883, Lieutenant-Colonel V. Street to Major Parker, Force 266, 20 June 1944.
131. HS 5/883, B1 to Fungus, 13 June 1944.
132. Wilkinson, *Foreign Fields*, p. 158. Wilkinson wrote that SOE's first liaison officer in Slovenia, Major Jones, had reported Slovenia's territorial claims to Cairo in such extravagant terms that they were not taken seriously; his own report only referred to these claims 'in very general terms'.
133. WO 106/3211, telegram from Foreign Office to HM Ambassador to Yugoslav

Government, 11 August 1944; AFHQ Italy to AMSSO, covering text of a memorandum sent to Tito, 12 August 1944; AFHQ Italy to AMSSO, account of the Prime Minister's conversations with Tito, 14 August 1944.

134. RP, Reed interviewed by J. Lane, 'Oral History of the BBC'; interview with Reed, 4 November 1989.

135. RP, Reed diary, 12, 14 and 27 June 1944; interview with Reed, 4 November 1989; WO 202/182, letter from Selvig, 27 June 1944.

136. WO 202/438, signal to Fungus, 18 May 1944; WO 202/439, signal from Fungus, 31 May 1944; K. Ford Jr., OSS *and the Yugoslav Resistance, 1943–1945* (College Station, TX: Texas A&M University Press, 1992), p. 142. The airstrip's location should not be confused with the village in northeast Bosnia also named Gajevi.

137. RP, Reed diary, 10–15 June 1944; RP, Reed, *Junior English 3*.

138. WO 202/439, signal from Fungus, 15 June 1944. On the 14th Reed noted in his diary, 'fearful motorcycle trip to l[anding] g[round] in vain'.

139. RP, Reed diary, 15 June 1944; WO 202/439, signal from Fungus, 16 June 1944.

140. WO 202/439, signal from Fungus, 20 June 1944.

141. RP, Reed diary, 20–25 June 1944.

142. RP, 'Topusko, 1944', by Sime Simatovic.

143. RP, Reed diary, 26 June 1944; WO 202/439, signal from Fungus, 26 June 1944.

144. WO 202/439, signal from Fungus, 30 June 1944; RP, Reed diary, 29 June 1944.

145. RP, Reed, *Junior English 3*. This extraordinary saga was vividly described by Reed in a radio broadcast for schools in 1947, but his account does not correspond entirely with his diary entries or the surviving documents in the National Archives, and may have been altered slightly to make it suitable for schools broadcasting. I have drawn on both the diary and the National Archives documents in an attempt to correct the broadcast version.

146. *Ibid.*; RP, Reed diary, 30 June 1944. The diary records that some wounded were evacuated from Gajevi that night.

147. RP, Reed, *Junior English 3*. RP, Reed diary, 30 June 1944.

148. WO 202/438, signal to Fungus, 1 July 1944.

149. WO 202/182, Selvig to Force 399, 6 July 1944.

Map 3. Yugoslavia and northern Italy, showing routes through Judge Mission
taken by Stump Gibbon and Peter Wilkinson.

6

Through Judge Mission

Until the early summer of 1944 Owen Reed's mission was the only Allied representation in Croatia. For this reason, and because of Croatia's central geographical position in Yugoslavia, the mission became a key staging post for the infiltration, transit and evacuation of Allied personnel. The total number assisted by Reed, his staff and the Croatian Partisans would be impossible to assess with any accuracy, but from his diary and the SOE signal logs it can be estimated conservatively that several hundred were involved. They were mostly SOE and ISLD agents, escaped POWs and shot-down airmen. This chapter briefly describes how a party of 60 escaped POWs, a senior SOE officer, a New Zealand doctor, the son of the British Prime Minister and the top Allied agent in Hungary all had occasion to pass through Judge Mission between October 1943 and June 1944.

STUMP GIBBON

One of the most famous books to be published on wartime escape and evasion was *Horned Pigeon*, by George Millar, younger brother of Owen Reed's senior officer at ISLD, James Millar. In *Horned Pigeon* Millar described how he was taken by train from Italy to Germany following the Italian capitulation in September 1943. After a short sojourn at a transit camp at Moosburg in Bavaria, Millar succeeded in escaping through the toilet window of a second POW train, and then made his way through France to Spain, from where he managed to reach Gibraltar. The train which conveyed Millar from Italy to Germany was also carrying a six-foot-six-inches tall bespectacled tank officer, Major E.H. Gibbon, known to friends and colleagues as 'Stump'. Stump Gibbon's escape from captivity was no less remarkable than Millar's and in certain respects more so. For when he reached freedom in December 1943 he was at the head of a party of some 60 escaped POWs, whom he had led with enormous courage and determination from northern Italy through Slovenia to Croatia, from where Reed helped arrange their evacuation.

Gibbon was held prisoner for 14 months at Gavi near Genoa. On 16 September 1943 the Germans moved him and 58 other officer-prisoners to Mantova, where they were loaded on to cattle trucks destined for Germany. Gibbon found himself in a truck with 15 subordinate officers, who immediately pooled their ideas on possible means of escape, and the few tools that they had succeeded in carrying with them from Gavi. The train journey began on the evening of 18 September and by midnight Gibbon and his companions had cut a man-size hole in one end of their truck. Through it they crawled out on to the buffer, before leaping down the railway embankment in pairs. Gibbon and his companion, a South African major named Ballentine, jumped second to last, in the early hours of the morning, between Rovereto and Trento. All the preceding pairs made their way unobserved, but the German guards were alerted by Gibbon's escape and one of the last officers to leave the truck was shot and wounded as he ran from the train. Nevertheless, it was not until the following day that the Germans opened the truck to find nothing but baggage.[1]

Gibbon and Ballentine soon met a friendly group of Italian soldiers, from whom they obtained food and civilian clothes. Then they pondered their situation. The nearest neutral state was Switzerland, but there they would merely substitute captivity for internment – a thought unpalatable to them both. A possible alternative lay in reaching Allied forces in southern Italy, but Gibbon harboured no illusions about his ability to pass himself off as an Italian in German-occupied areas. Then one of the Italians told them about the Yugoslav Partisans, who were active to the east, in Istria. Not only were they nearer, geographically, than the Allied Armies; they could also be reached via remote mountain paths and passes where there was no significant threat from the Germans. On this basis the two officers agreed to travel east, keeping to the mountains, with the aim of contacting the Partisans. Equipped only with a map furnished by the Italians and a compass manufactured from Gibbon's wristwatch, they made their way across mountain ranges and a series of river valleys – the Adagio, Brenta, Plave, Tagliamento – begging, stealing and borrowing from the local population as they went.

They finally made contact with the Partisans – Slovenes who had crossed the frontier after the armistice – at Saga, which they reached on 10 October. Gibbon described them as 'a gang of cut-throats ... wearing Italian uniforms covered with red stars'. From Saga they were moved to Caporetto, for interrogation, and then to Stupezza, where they met more escaped British prisoners. In all, there were about 60, 20 other ranks (ORs) at Stupezza itself and a further 40 fighting with the Partisans near San Tietro under the command of a Captain Griffiths, who had jumped from the POW train before Gibbon. Griffiths' first remark on seeing Gibbon was 'You are senior and you are in charge. Thank God you've come.'

The situation Griffiths described was far from satisfactory. The Partisans were inadequately supplied for their own purposes and, despite frequent protestations to the contrary, could not possibly provide for large numbers of escaped POWs as well. Half the British troops were wearing ragged civilian clothing, and their boots were worn out; with winter approaching they lacked both blankets and greatcoats. They found themselves being used to fulfil the unpopular task of requisitioning food and other supplies from the local Italian population, who therefore blamed the British for their sacrifices rather than the Partisans. The linguistic barrier and differences in training between the British and Partisan contingents rendered effective co-operation virtually impossible, and resulted in friction and confusion during operations, increasing the likelihood of casualties. For all these reasons, Griffiths' men were distinctly unenthusiastic about the prospect of a prolonged stay in north-eastern Italy. They openly admitted that they had only taken up arms out of a sense of obligation – as thanks for food and shelter – but the majority were contemplating desertion, including Griffiths himself.

Gibbon discussed the position with the Partisan battalion commander, and they decided that the British should be released. But four days of argument with the headquarters at Caporetto were required before they agreed to pass the POWs back to the Allies through Yugoslavia, during which Gibbon resolutely blocked one Partisan proposal that he should form a separate British battalion to fight alongside them, and rejected the request of another British officer that his men should join the Italian Partisans in the Garibaldi Brigade. Those who wished were allowed to stay and fight, but only four elected to do so. Gibbon subsequently acknowledged that his actions had an unfavourable political impact on the Partisans, undermining Britain's status as their friend and ally, but he felt that there was no alternative.

The number of escaped POWs at Stupezza was increasing almost by the hour. On 16 October Gibbon marched east with an Italian guide at the head of five officers and 80 ORs divided into four platoons; a second party was to follow them a few days later. Gibbon's group crossed the river Isonzo the following night with a strong Partisan guard, and then proceeded south-east to Cerkno, sleeping in barns and lofts along the way, and eating what little food the Partisans could spare. At Cerkno they found a British liaison officer, Major Darewski, who had recently received instructions that all escaped POWs were to be sent on to Major Jones, SOE's representative in Slovenia. German forces were deployed in substantial numbers along the way, to safeguard key lines of communication between the Reich and the Italian front. The journey would make severe demands on Gibbon's men, many of whom still lacked adequate boots and clothing, but the Partisans optimistically agreed to supply both. They suggested as well that the British should be further divided into two groups, partly so that those with boots and clothes could proceed without delay, partly because the intended route ran through German-occupied territory, which could not be safely negotiated by such large numbers. Gibbon accepted their judgement.

After leaving Cerkno on 22 October Gibbon and his men crossed the Ljubljana–Gorizia road and railway by night. They could hear gunfire nearby, but saw no sign of the enemy. On the east side of the railway their guide left them hidden in woods overnight, before leading them on to Cerknica the next morning. There they were presented to a Partisan divisional commander, who promptly despatched them by truck to a village about four miles away. They were just getting bedded down when contingents from the Partisan 13th Brigade arrived with orders to look after them, and news of a general German offensive in the area. The British were now armed and marched overnight to a forest camp some ten miles to the north-east. On the 27th Gibbon's party was joined by 22 members of the second group from Cerkno. Having received no boots and very little clothing from the Partisans they had left Cerkno under the command of a Captain Forsdich. They crossed the Ljubljana–Gorizia railway successfully enough, but ran into a German patrol in a village near Cerknica on the following afternoon and scattered in small groups into the surrounding woods. Two of these groups then managed to rejoin Gibbon.

The next day Gibbon decided to move on. The Slovenian uplands are cold and damp in late October, and snowbound thereafter, and the British – lacking tents, sleeping bags or coats – were increasingly at risk from the elements. Moreover, the Partisans wished to withdraw further north-east whereas Gibbon had to travel south-east. The Partisan brigadier and commissar objected strenuously to his departure, but he overcame their protests by claiming quite falsely that his men would desert if they continued to march north.

After making good initial progress to the next brigade, Gibbon learnt that Major Jones and the Slovene Partisan headquarters had been pushed further south by the Germans. Unable to proceed because of the close proximity of enemy troops, the British waited until 2 November, when they only just escaped from a German patrol bearing down on their hideout. Eventually they retraced their steps to a spot close to the forest encampment near Cerknica, which they had formerly shared with the 13th Brigade. They gained little from the week's endeavours except for a better knowledge of German dispositions and a half-Irish Slovene guide named Florjan, a 22-year-old university student who spoke excellent English, and who volunteered to accompany Gibbon's party from then on. To their credit, the Partisans willingly released him.

Gibbon was intent on reaching Jones, but increasingly conscious that his party was too large and slow-moving to stand much chance of avoiding the many German patrols between Cerknica and Crmosnjice, a village to the west of Metlika, where the Slovene headquarters was located. A number of his men were ill, and some still lacked adequate footwear. So, with the greatest reluctance, he again determined that they should split up. Those ORs who lacked boots or were sick were left with the Partisans at Cerknica: 'Gave them money and all the information I could', Gibbon wrote in his report. He could not have done more.

The second attempt to reach Jones ultimately proved successful. A series of marches and still further cat-and-mouse antics with the Germans brought Gibbon and his men, on 9 November, to a Partisan brigade who were in contact with Jones. They finally reached him at Crmosnjice on the 12th, bearing all the signs of their long and arduous march: 'Party very tired', Gibbon recorded, 'and sores, cuts and abrasions won't heal because of low diet. Twenty-six pairs of boots irreparable.' Nevertheless, they harboured high hopes that Jones might somehow arrange for their evacuation. Only slowly did it emerge that there were no practicable means by which 60 escaped British POWs could be conveyed back to Allied-occupied territory from Slovenia. The Partisans were able to repair some of their boots and to provide them with extra clothing and blankets, but food and supplies were generally scarce, and Gibbon eventually concluded that his men were no better off at the headquarters than they had been on the march. And so, on 24 November, with the permission of the Partisan staff and with 10,000 lira from Jones, Gibbon and his party set off south-east towards Croatia. Their route took them via Crnomelj to Vinica, just north of the river Kupa, which marked the border between Croatia and Slovenia. Although hopeful of receiving more boots and information about the journey ahead, they eventually reached Vinica without Partisan assistance.

The task of escorting a large party of escaped POWs across German-occupied Slovenia inevitably imposed an immense burden on both the Partisans and the indigenous population, who faced brutal reprisals if they were found to be assisting the Allies. For this reason the Slovenes sometimes seemed less sympathetic and helpful than Gibbon expected. Their attitude was not always easy for the British to understand but overwhelmingly reflected the close proximity of the enemy and the appalling atrocities perpetrated by the Germans to overcome Partisan resistance. By contrast there were far more extensive 'safe areas' in Croatia, entirely free from enemy occupation, and the British presence was therefore not nearly so problematic. Predictably, then, Gibbon found the Croat Partisans to be friendlier and more co-operative than their Slovene counterparts. At Vinica he located a Croat brigade, which helped his men to cross the Kupa by boat; all the bridges were held by the Germans or the Ustase. They were then passed south through Partisan territory, and after 'tiring but not too difficult walking' crossed the Mreznica and Korana rivers to Veljun, before marching south to Slunj. From Slunj they were taken by truck to Otocac:

Between Crnomej and Otocac for a distance of nearly 100 miles they found five out of [every] six villages destroyed and the peasants living in abject misery amongst the ruins. In these areas peasants...[had] lost nearly everything including their stocks of horses, cattle and pigs.[2]

SOE (warned by Jones) advised Reed of Gibbon's impending arrival on 26 November, and set a provisional target date for evacuation of 16 December.[3] Reed duly alerted ISLD, who immediately expressed the greatest interest in the British POWs, recognising that they would have acquired detailed and valuable intelligence about German and Partisan dispositions in northern Italy and Yugoslavia during their journey.[4] On the 29th they finally reached Otocac. 'Captain Reed gave us a tremendous welcome and he did all he could to make us comfortable with Partisan help', Gibbon recorded in his report. But the Germans were attempting to recapture the Croatian coast at precisely this time and had they succeeded it would have been impossible to evacuate Gibbon's party. So when they arrived at Otocac Reed asked Cairo to 'do utmost to accelerate ship as this HQ state coastal and island situation [is] liable to deteriorate'.[5]

The SOE and ISLD missions previously located at Cairo were by this time establishing new operations centres at Bari in Italy, through which Yugoslav matters were being handled. Unfortunately, SOE's Bari office was not optimistic about the prospect of organizing an evacuation from the Croatian coast. On the 30th they signalled to Cairo that it would be 'difficult to get POWs out...because as yet no successful operation [has been] despatched to Fungus coastline which [is] now compromised by Hun occupation'. They suggested instead that the POWs should be moved south-east by the Partisans with the ultimate aim of evacuation to Vis, the most outlying – and hence the safest – of the Adriatic islands. From there the Navy could take them to Bari.[6] Their proposals were duly relayed to Reed.[7]

Reed was unimpressed. For reasons described in the previous chapter the Western Allies' war effort was not highly regarded by the Partisans in the later months of 1943, and he knew that Bari's proposals would be interpreted as further evidence of British timidity. He then received news that the German offensive was petering out, leaving much of the coast in Partisan hands. On this basis, in consultation with General Gosnjak, he proposed that the evacuation should take place in British shipping from the Croatian port of Senj; the Partisans would provide a pilot vessel from one of the islands and full cover while the ship was in shore.[8] After several days of silence ISLD replied that the Royal Navy was flatly refusing to co-operate, and was suggesting instead that the POWs be brought in a Partisan ship to Bari, which could then return with supplies. 'I have refused', Reed signalled to SOE:

I have not the cheek to ask Partisans to undertake risks on behalf of British personnel which the Senior Service dare not face. It would drive the last nail into the coffin of our tottering reputation and leave us no answer to growing accusations of Allied half-heartedness. Our advice to you on routes, ports and pilots seems to have failed to reach Bari...This is a major issue. Vital you take it to a level that can authorize something better than this pusillanimous dithering.[9]

His views were wholeheartedly endorsed at SOE headquarters, but Bari could make no headway with the Royal Navy, who maintained that the operation was unfeasible because of the presence of German U-boats and mines in the northern Adriatic.[10] SOE decided they could not ask Reed to approach the Croatian Partisans again so instead they went directly to Tito, who duly agreed that the Partisans should evacuate Gibbon and his men to Vis.[11] On the 16th Gosnjak gave a public dinner in honour of Gibbon's party and the next day they were taken by truck to Senj. The final leg of their epic journey was conducted in three overnight voyages, the first by fishing boat south-east to the island of Kornat, the second (in the same boat) to Vis, and the third, in British naval vessels, from Vis to Bari.

At Bari, ISLD considered Gibbon's insight into the Partisan movement to be so valuable that they promptly organized his return to London; at the beginning of January he flew by Sunderland flying boat to Gibraltar with James Millar. There, in one of the War's most extraordinary coincidences, they entered the Bristol Hotel and found themselves confronted by Millar's younger brother, George, who had just completed his own escape through France and Spain.[12]

But when Gibbon reached London he conveyed an impression of the Partisan movement that was decidedly negative and heavily influenced by his experiences in northern Italy and Slovenia. In his view their value as a fighting force had been overestimated and had, if anything, declined since the Italian capitulation. He doubted that they were containing as many German divisions as was sometimes claimed, and suspected that they were hoarding Allied arms with the avowed intention of imposing a communist regime on Yugoslavia when the war with Germany ended. In an apparent reference to Jones he criticized British liaison officers in the field, who were 'inclined to swallow everything the Partisan unit to which they are attached tells them, with the result that an exaggerated picture is sent to England'. But his view of the Croatian Partisans was very much more encouraging and 'he stressed the importance of [SOE] concentrating in the north of Croatia as that was the road by which [they] could infiltrate into central Europe and north Italy'. And for Reed he had nothing but praise. He was 'quite first class', Gibbon told SOE. 'Just the type of man who is wanted.'[13]

CLOWDER MISSION

On 14 December 1943, a few days before Gibbon's evacuation, two British officers from SOE arrived at Otocac. Lieutenant-Colonel (later Sir) Peter Wilkinson and Major Alfgar Hesketh-Pritchard had formed a mission, codenamed 'Clowder', which was seeking to infiltrate agents into the Third Reich via its southern border with Yugoslavia, a task somewhat facilitated by the Reich's annexation of northern Slovenia in 1941. Visiting SOE's Cairo headquarters in the summer of 1943, Wilkinson had learnt of the Yugoslav Partisan movement, and of its links with an Austrian resistance group, which was reputed to be active in Styria and Carinthia. 'At first sight', he wrote later, 'this looked like the back door into central Europe for which I had been searching for the last two years'. In fact, Wilkinson received an excessively optimistic assessment of the potential for such an operation from a Captain Klugman, of SOE's Yugoslav section. Klugman was later discovered to be a member of the Communist Party, and was almost certainly spying on SOE for the Soviet Union. Wilkinson's task would prove very much more difficult than he anticipated, not least because of the near-total absence of an effective resistance movement in Austria.[14]

Clowder was run from SOE's London headquarters, and operated in complete independence from the main SOE mission to Yugoslavia led by Fitzroy Maclean. Wilkinson and Hesketh-Pritchard were landed by Dakota near Tito's headquarters in Bosnia early in December, and there obtained his approval for their mission. On the 9th they duly set out for Croatia, which they hoped would provide a base for their penetration of the Austrian frontier. The five-day journey to Otocac was accomplished by motorcycle, truck and pack-horse, and their experiences along the way quickly taught them the importance of travelling light; by the time they reached Otocac they had lost or discarded much of their equipment.

At Otocac, Wilkinson discussed his objectives with Reed in some detail. He was disappointed to learn that the Croatian Partisans had no direct courier lines to Austria, but noted in the Lika district areas suitable for establishing airstrips, through which transport aircraft might help to supply Clowder Mission if it was located further to the north in Slovenia. The story of Stump Gibbon's exploits also encouraged him to believe that his mission could be established there. And Gibbon's invaluable Irish-Slovene guide, Florjan, now offered Wilkinson his services. Florjan acted as Wilkinson's personal interpreter and liaison officer for the next three and a half months, and supplied much invaluable information to him on the Partisan movement in Slovenia and northern Italy, which he afterwards brought back to SOE in London.

Wilkinson and Hesketh-Pritchard set off from Otocac on 20 December. Travelling by car, on foot and in a farmer's gig borrowed by the resourceful Florjan, they reached the Partisan headquarters in Slovenia three days later.

There they were advised that the courier lines running into the area of northern Slovenia annexed by Germany were of such a tenuous nature that they would be of little use to Clowder Mission. But the headquarters of the Partisan 9th Corps, which was operating in the Slovene-speaking regions of north-eastern Italy, maintained regular contact with the substantial Slovene minority resident in southern Austria, south of the river Drava (Drau). Wilkinson should therefore proceed to 9th Corps to examine the possibility of establishing his mission there. Accompanied by a small Partisan escort, the two British officers completed this final leg of their journey on foot in about three weeks, eventually locating the 9th Corps headquarters in a village near Cerkno.

The Partisan commander at 9th Corps could offer little more optimistic information on courier lines into Austria than his counterpart in Slovenia. But he did satisfy both Wilkinson and Hesketh-Pritchard that his headquarters could provide a suitable base for the Clowder operation. Early in February Wilkinson took a small reconnaissance patrol across the border, an experience which he later described in his memoirs:

> I confess to having felt a modest satisfaction that I was probably the first British and possibly the first Allied officer to have taken an active patrol into the Third Reich during the Second World War. Even though, I told myself, it was only in annexed territory, a black and yellow signpost on the main road pointing to Munchen proclaimed my proximity to the *Vaterland*.

On his return it was agreed that Hesketh-Pritchard should remain with 9th Corps to establish a forward operating base for Clowder. Wilkinson was in the meantime to return to London via Italy to report on the mission's progress and to supervise the expansion of its activities. After an abortive attempt to organize his evacuation by submarine from the northern Adriatic, he began the long journey south, following Gibbon's route via Partisan headquarters in Slovenia, but veering further to the north-east to avoid a German offensive along their most direct route to Plitvice, where Judge Mission was by this time located.

Reed was warned of Wilkinson's impending arrival on 1 March, and the need to evacuate him brought decisive pressure to bear on the authorities in Italy to agree to a pick-up operation at Krbavsko Polje. The single successful Dakota landing undertaken there on 14 March was intended to convey Wilkinson to Italy but unfortunately, due to his north-eastern detour, he missed the pick-up and only reached Plitvice on the 16th. So Reed attempted to organize a second landing on the following night, the failure of which has already been noted. At the first attempt, he and Wilkinson waited all night at the airstrip for an aircraft that never came. Thereafter they lost radio contact with Bari for nearly two days, during which Wilkinson remained at the airstrip in case the aircraft arrived. By the

14. Reed and escaped British POWs including Major E.H. 'Stump' Gibbon (centre, with pipe), Otocac, 16 December 1943, shortly before their journey to Senj for evacuation (*Imperial War Museum, K 7027*).

21st the March moon period was over, making the pick-up impracticable. Wilkinson was told to proceed south to Tito's headquarters so that he could be evacuated during April.[15]

When he arrived back in London, Wilkinson prepared a report on his experiences in Yugoslavia and northern Italy which aroused the intense interest not only of SOE and SIS, but also of the Chiefs of Staff; it even reached the Prime Minister. His report was important not least for the reason that it emanated from a source entirely independent of the established British Military Mission to the Partisans, and could therefore assess the Mission's work and the Partisans' military potential in uniquely objective terms. In the following months Clowder Mission was duly enlarged, and it continued to function as a separate mission to the Partisans for the remainder of the year; in this capacity its achievements were by no means insignificant. But for reasons that lie beyond the scope of this book Wilkinson never achieved his ultimate goal of sabotage and subversion within the frontiers of the Third Reich. Hesketh-Pritchard acquired an almost legendary status among the inhabitants of the Korosko Odreds,[16] and was on one occasion credited with the improbable tally of 40 Germans to his own gun. But he disappeared without trace in December after crossing the river Drava and venturing into southern Austria with a group of Partisans, and the mission was withdrawn shortly afterwards.

DOC ROGERS, GUERRILLA SURGEON

For Reed, both Gibbon and Wilkinson were 'real heroes and straight out of Buchan'.[17] But an equally courageous visitor to Judge Mission was a New Zealand doctor named Lindsay Rogers. 'Doc' Rogers was, on his own admission, an adventurer.[18] After serving for three years in military hospitals in the Middle East, he grew tired of life behind the lines, and a search for more active employment finally brought him to SOE in Cairo with a proposal that he should work with the Partisans in Yugoslavia. Rogers managed to acquire two orderlies and undertook the usual period of training before his departure. Equipment was the next problem, as he recorded in his memoirs:

> The Medical Stores Department of the Middle East was extra-ordinarily obstructive and difficult in handing out any equipment at all. The colonel in charge had little time for these secret outfits, and what he called 'side shows'...However, I did manage to drag something from them...

Rogers was taken by boat to Vis, where his team was augmented by three Yugoslavs. Together they then retraced Gibbon's passage via

Kornat to Dugi Otok, from where they were ferried by night to the Dalmatian coast. Disaster struck on their very first day ashore: they were forced to abandon all their precious medical equipment after the Germans overran the village in which they had been staying. Thereafter they joined the Partisan 19th Division in southern Croatia and remained with them for more than a month, during which they were unable to practise. Only at the beginning of February 1944 were they finally taken to the Croatian headquarters at Plitvice.

Arriving, Rogers found two large two-storied wooden houses by the lake, and learnt that one of them was inhabited by a British officer:

> As we went up the stairs we met the officer coming down. He welcomed us; we sat down; he gave us some refreshments, and best of all, some clean clothes. He told us his name was Owen Reed, captain in the intelligence...I asked him his civilian occupation and he told me he was an actor. My opinion of the stage rose daily and throughout all my stay in the country...It was always Owen Reed who spoke the most sense, who bore the burden of hostility without weakening, and who remained our wise counsellor and friend.

As always, Reed (promoted major that day) was the model host. But Rogers' arrival in reality proved a serious embarrassment, for it had initially been planned that his team would work near Tito's base in Bosnia, and the Croatian headquarters had received no forewarning of his arrival. That evening Reed took him to see Gosnjak, who agreed rather coldly to communicate on his behalf with the chief of the Partisan medical staff and with Tito. Pending their approval of his mission he was to remain under house arrest with Reed. In the interim Rogers used Reed's radio to signal his controller: 'Lost all technical and personal kit due [to] enemy action... Prepare complete reduplication of surgical requirements including linen and personal stores.'[19] The next day Reed encoded and sent a detailed list of Rogers' requirements, but a message was received warning that the surgical 'instrument position [was] extremely sticky' and that the medical supplies were certain to be delayed.[20]

On 7 February Rogers was summoned by Gosnjak's staff and told that Tito's approval had been received. The general wanted him to tour some of the Partisan hospitals, observe their work and if necessary make recommendations for their improvement. So Rogers and his team set out to the medical headquarters located in a tiny mountainside village near Babin Potok, and there they were shown photographs of forest hospitals, some in caves, some in log cabins. Two such hospitals were located at the villages of Turnavic and Turiansky, and Rogers' memoirs present a graphic description of the dreadful conditions they found on reaching the latter:

The first collection of wounded was hidden in a peasant house and the adjacent cowshed. Indeed, only a makeshift partition separated the cows from the wounded...Just to see them, the pale toxic-looking faces in the evening gloom, their thin hands veined with blue streaks, the fractured femurs lying with back splints, and ankles with pressure sores, made us anxious to get to work and try and help... The old doctor, who had done his utmost with nothing, explained that he had been a gynaecologist in Zagreb and knew nothing of war surgery. Every bandage was threadbare, for all were washed at least ten or twelve times until they rotted and fell into dust. There was no soap and almost no instruments with which to work.

Rogers decided to work at Turnavic and Turiansky from then on. On 20 February he returned to Plitvice, submitted his report to Gosnjak and arranged with Reed for his equipment to be dropped directly to Turnavic. By the 26th it was ready for despatch.[21]

Rogers remained in Croatia during March and April, operating on many hundreds of wounded and doubtless saving many a life; and he did his utmost to raise the standard of Partisan medical care. But in May he was summoned to Bosnia by Tito himself. There, the Partisan leader personally asked him to work in closer proximity to his headquarters. And so Rogers remained in Bosnia, where the Partisans built a new hospital and medical school for him in a forest near Otocevas. Sadly, it was only to function for a matter of weeks before the German assault on Drvar ended Partisan resistance in the area. After hiding the wounded, Rogers fled northwards with the Germans in hot pursuit, and came desperately close to capture on a number of occasions. When he doubled back to his hospital in search of medical equipment he found it had been burnt to the ground.

Doc Rogers and his staff stayed in Bosnia for some weeks in increasingly difficult conditions before finally accepting defeat and leaving by Dakota from a landing strip at Ticevo. Later in the year they were re-infiltrated into Slovenia, where Rogers renewed his acquaintance with Reed and worked tirelessly in a number of hidden hospitals until March 1945. Following his return to New Zealand this extraordinary man was awarded Yugoslavia's Order of Bravery and Order of Merit in recognition of his daring and devoted service to the Partisans.

RANDOLPH CHURCHILL

Winston Churchill's son, Randolph, joined Fitzroy Maclean's mission to Yugoslavia at the end of 1943 and was parachuted into Bosnia with Maclean at the beginning of the following year. Randolph Churchill was a hard-drinking and outspoken Conservative MP given neither to tact nor discretion. Franklin Lindsay, an OSS officer who worked with Churchill in Yugoslavia, later described him as 'one of the most aggressively rude men I ever met'.[22] After serving with the Special Air Service (SAS) in the desert, Churchill had participated in the Salerno landings with the Commandos and had accompanied his father to the Teheran and Cairo conferences. But Maclean subsequently found him at a loose end and recruited him, allegedly because he was known to be 'thoroughly dependable' on operations, 'possessing both endurance and determination'. Maclean also admired Churchill's intelligence and political awareness and expected him to get on well with the Yugoslavs, 'for his enthusiastic and at times explosive approach to life was not unlike their own'.[23] However, Winston Churchill's official biographer suggests that there were strong political motives behind Randolph's attachment to Maclean's mission: it was hoped that he might assist in brokering an agreement between Tito and the Yugoslav government-in-exile, which Britain formally supported.[24] There are also indications that Randolph was working, in part at least, in co-ordination with the Ministry of Information and the PWE in an effort to improve the reputation of the Western Allies among the vehemently pro-Soviet Partisans.[25]

Randolph Churchill worked from the British mission at Tito's headquarters in Bosnia from January to March 1944. But one of his colleagues there was Major George Selvig of OSS, who had been infiltrated the previous December,[26] and when, at the end of March, it was agreed that Selvig should move to Croatia to work as Reed's assistant, Churchill decided to accompany him. They set out on foot on 2 April with Churchill's batman, an interpreter, an escort of two Partisan soldiers and three packhorses.[27] At their very first overnight stop Churchill's credentials as an Allied propagandist were heavily taxed by the local brigade commander and his staff. 'Mostly they want to know about the Second Front and what we think of the Partisans', he wrote to his father.

> Also why we still have dealings with the émigré 'Government of Traitors'. I skirt delicately around the political issues and tell them all I can about the British and American war effort. They seem surprised and incredulous when I tell them we have been fighting for nearly five years and that for one year we were all alone ... They are on the point of interrupting to ask 'What about Russia?' and then a cloud comes over their faces and they dimly recall that Russia, too, waited to be attacked. This saddens them because they have the simple faith that everything Russian must be perfect.

The following night, with a guard of 40 Partisans, they crossed the Knin–Bihac road – a key German artery, cutting the telephone line as they went. 'This is well worth doing', Churchill wrote. 'The repair party is so often ambushed that it needs an escort of 200 Huns to protect it each time repairs are necessary.' At their next staging post they learnt that the valley through which they had been intending to pass was flooded, and that they would have to cross the mountains to reach Croatia. After an exhausting climb through deep snow they arrived at two tiny houses perched on a high summit, where they slept for a few hours before making their way down the other side. A further seven hours of walking across lower mountains then brought them to a Partisan base at Mazine, in Croatia's Lika province, on the evening of 4 April.

From then on conditions were very much better. The Partisans provided a kola [a long, low, horse-drawn cart] to replace the exhausted pack-horses. It could carry two of Churchill's four-man party as well as all their equipment, so they took turns to ride. After an hour and a half they reached an area headquarters. In Churchill's words:

> Great ceremony attends our arrival and a luncheon of splendid proportions has been prepared. From here we can speak on the telephone to Major Reed, our representative at Croatian headquarters 50 miles away. We are plainly getting back to civilization!

A second kola was placed at their disposal the next morning, hastening their progress considerably. The final stages of their journey were then accomplished in turn by motorcycle and sidecar, two more kolas, motor car, and finally horseback, as the road to Plitvice was still blocked by snow. A brisk ten-minute canter brought them to the British mission, an attractive wooden chalet hidden in the forest, where they were given a clean and comfortable room. 'We dine with Major Reed', Churchill recorded, 'and quickly demolish a bottle of whisky, which he has kindly saved for us'. Reed's recollection, 'He drank my last bottle of whisky', was very obviously different in emphasis.[28]

Some years before, Reed had been badly snubbed by Churchill in a common room at Christ Church, and he had not forgotten the experience.[29] He was never very politically oriented and, with ISLD and SOE missions to run, the dissemination of British and American propaganda probably came last in his order of priorities, if it featured at all. His interest lay in gathering useful intelligence and in supporting Partisan military operations against the Germans and the Ustase, and he believed that the Western Allies' cause in Yugoslavia was best served by actions rather than words. On one occasion in February 1944 he signalled:

> Reaction here to ... bombing of Zagreb aerodrome has sent our stock soaring. Wish we could convey adequately how the wan and weary faces here light up when we hear big bombers over snow clouds. Tell air force we are cheering them daily.[30]

By contrast, extravagant claims about the triumphs of the British and American war effort could easily prove counterproductive. In March one of the BBC's Yugoslav broadcasts succeeded in antagonizing the Partisans by bragging that the German population was being forced to live off the most basic rations, and that Hitler's armies were so heavily outnumbered that they were recruiting children and pensioners. Reed, with his BBC background, was horrified. 'No good telling Partisans of all people that potatoes are staple diet in Germany', he complained, 'as [Yugoslav] peasants never eat anything else. Age of Hun troops doesn't mean a thing here. Boasting of our strength in troops only makes them ask why we don't use it. Results are the only answer.'[31]

After the difficulties that accompanied his arrival in Yugoslavia, Reed had laboured assiduously to establish harmonious working relations with the Partisans, convinced that this was the only basis on which his mission could function effectively. There were periodic disagreements, but they reflected genuine differences of opinion over isolated operational matters and never engendered any protracted animosity. At all other times he remained the very essence of diplomacy, meticulously avoiding political controversy, observing Partisan protocol and respecting his hosts' admiration for the Soviet Union.

Churchill's agenda was very different. He was not at this time responsible for a mission of his own, and he was only planning to remain with the Croatian Partisans for a short time. He treated this period as a perfect opportunity for inculcating among them a Western perspective of the War, demonstrating in the process a complete disregard for their political sensitivities, and undermining Reed's painstaking efforts to cultivate their goodwill. Describing dinner with Gosnjak on 7 April, Churchill merely advised his father that it had been 'followed by four hours of question and answer along the usual lines'. But this was clearly something of an understatement. 'Famous and disgraceful Churchill electioneering dinner', Reed jotted in his diary that night. 'Me baffled, exhilarated, ashamed and disgusted. Just like Oxford.'[32] The next day Churchill departed with the commissar, Zigic, on a tour of the surrounding area. 'Thank God', Reed commented. 'The man who came to dinner!'[33]

But his troubles were by no means over. With a view to propagating his message to the widest and most influential audience possible, Churchill arranged to meet members of the Partisan civil government, their local newspaper editors and representatives of their youth organizations, and spent several days among them arguing his case. He remained throughout blithely unaware of the offence he was causing, even when the Vice-President of the Croatian government told him that he should 'spend 24 hours in a non-communist atmosphere'. That the Partisans tolerated his activities at all was a testament to their patience and stoicism. But they would probably have responded very differently had he not been the son of the British Prime Minister.

Yet for all his faults Churchill relayed an impressively vivid account of Partisan life in Croatia to his father, who was very appreciative.[34] On 10 April he was able to observe an attack on the Ustase stronghold at Cazin, and on the 13th he toured the divisional workshops, which he described as 'a miracle of improvization'.

> Housed in five wooden huts hidden deep in the forest, all its machinery has been captured from the enemy or bought on the black-market in Zagreb and smuggled out. They have dammed the nearby stream and installed an Italian turbine to supply power and light. They repair rifles and machine-guns, watches, fountain pens and typewriters. They make sights for mortars and breech-blocks for captured field guns. They are always ready to move off at two hours' notice.

Churchill returned to Bosnia on 14 April, leaving Selvig at the Croatian headquarters. Travelling on horseback he reached Drvar little more than a day after his departure – a marked improvement on the four and a half days required for the outward trip. Reed breathed a sigh of relief and set about repairing the damage.

VERESS

Among the many and varied travellers who passed through Judge Mission, none was more important than a Hungarian diplomat named Laszlo Veress, who fled from Budapest to Croatia after the Germans occupied Hungary in March 1944.[35] Veress was a key member of a group of Hungarian statesmen, diplomats and civil servants who decided in the early months of 1943 to dismantle their alliance with the Third Reich, following the crushing defeat of Hungary's forces at Voronesh and the Soviet victory at Stalingrad. At the same time they endeavoured to seek the goodwill of the Western Allies, as a reassurance against the growing might of the USSR. Their intention was to ensure that, in the event of Germany's defeat, Hungary should surrender to British and American forces rather than the Red Army.

From the beginning the group set itself a formidable task. They had no illusions about the dire consequences of openly opposing Hitler, and they lacked the support of many elements within the Hungarian political establishment and, crucially, the armed forces. Only the most limited measures were instigated to reduce co-operation with Germany. But in an effort to develop governmental links with the Western Allies, Veress journeyed to Istanbul and eventually made contact with SOE. The precise origins of his mission are uncertain. Veress told his British interrogators in 1944 that he had originally gone to Istanbul on his own initiative: 'He was not empowered to do so.' But he later recalled that he had been acting on the instructions of Hungary's Prime Minister, Kallay. Whatever the truth is, his mission was clearly very unofficial until the collapse of Mussolini's regime in Italy, which was accompanied by an upsurge in anti-German sentiment in Budapest.

At the beginning of August, Kallay was persuaded to appoint a staff officer with responsibility for the Istanbul contacts, which Veress was now formally instructed to resume. On his next visit, SOE arranged for him to meet with the British ambassador on a yacht in the sea of Marmora. There, Veress was naturally told that Hungary must surrender unconditionally before any substantive discussions began. The surrender was secretly transmitted to the British ambassador on 17 August and accepted on 9 September. The next day Veress returned from Istanbul to Budapest with two radio sets, which were hidden in his diplomatic baggage.

Throughout the winter he communicated on his government's behalf with SOE, who delivered his messages on to the Foreign Office in London and passed back the replies. There were protracted discussions of the means by which Hungary's surrender might be effected, and plans were initiated to establish a clandestine British mission there. But progress was slow: Britain was unable to enlist the support of the USA for a forward strategy towards Hungary and, with the Allied advance stalled in Italy, there were no practical means of sending troops into south-eastern Europe. In the meantime, the brutal reprisals perpetrated by the Germans in Italy after her capitulation deterred the Hungarian government from significant measures of overt resistance. Kallay's attempts to withdraw Hungary's Armies from the Soviet Union infuriated Hitler, and even limited measures of political liberalization were viewed in Germany first with suspicion and then with mounting alarm. In January 1944 the German Army High Command (Oberkommando des Wehrmacht – OKW) asked the Hungarian General Staff to find and terminate the radio link with SOE, and the Army Security Section duly located Veress' radio set. But the Foreign Ministry told the General Staff that it was used for contact between the government and Hungarian agents abroad. The codes were subsequently changed, but the conversations continued as before.

On 19 March German forces occupied Hungary. Veress fled on the 21st, shortly before the arrest of his radio operators. He cashed a large cheque, made one telephone call and then left for the nearest railway station, where he boarded a goods train for Transylvania, on the Romanian frontier. Shortly afterwards his apartment was searched and two German Abwehr officers accompanied by an officer from Hungarian military intelligence went to the Foreign Office in Budapest with orders to arrest him. But the Under-Secretary of State denied any knowledge of his whereabouts and on 10 April Veress successfully evaded the German border guards and entered Romania, with the ultimate intention of crossing through Bulgaria to Turkey. Unfortunately, Bulgaria's frontier with Turkey was more effectively controlled and he was compelled to revise his plans. Travelling on his diplomatic passport, which the Germans had miraculously forgotten to revoke, he crossed into Yugoslavia and made his way to Zagreb. From there he walked out into the hills and on 28 May made contact with members of the Partisan 4th Corps, who duly advised Croatian headquarters of his arrival.

On 3 June Force 266 (the new name for the British Military Mission to Yugoslavia formerly run by SOE) were advised by ISLD in Bari that Veress had reached the Croatian Partisans, information they subsequently confirmed back to Fungus Mission: 'Reed repeat Reed reports Veress at your HQ. Will try to evacuate by air soonest.'[36] In fact, the need to bring Veress out as quickly as possible (along with 26 American airmen, four escaped POWs and 2 Czech agents) provided the impetus behind the first Dakota pick-up from Gajevi. Within a month such operations were virtually a matter of routine, but few of the evacuations conducted during Reed's mission to Croatia merited this description, and the Veress pick-up was no exception. Originally planned for 6 June, the sortie was then postponed until the 8th, when Reed and Selvig again decided to reschedule it, possibly because an important parachute drop was expected at Vrginmost the same night. Unfortunately their cancellation signal was not relayed down to squadron level, and a Dakota duly took off for Gajevi. Nearing their destination, the crew spotted the drop zone fires at Vrginmost and mistook them for the flare path fires at Gajevi. The result could have been truly disastrous, for many drop zones were located in undulating or rocky countryside. But the terrain at Vrginmost was relatively flat and free of obstacles and the Dakota landed there without incurring any damage. It did, however, run out of firm ground and came to rest, half-submerged, in a nearby bog.[37]

Reed immediately alerted Force 266 and asked for all possible fighter cover to protect the drop zone while the Dakota was extricated from the mud.[38] At first the Partisans tried to pull it out using manpower alone, but to no avail. Finally they roped together all the oxen and horses available and tethered them to the aircraft: 'At last, slowly, inch by inch, the great plane moved out on to firm ground.'[39] The records do not reveal how the Dakota managed to take off from Vrginmost, but it seems certain that the Partisans would have had to clear – and perhaps level – a somewhat larger area than the original drop zone. Nevertheless, in the early hours of the following morning, on 10 June, it successfully got airborne and five days later Reed received another signal from Force 266: 'Hungarian section most grateful for safe evacuation Veress.'[40]

Two weeks later Reed's own evacuation from Gajevi brought Judge Mission to an end. Although he had received some brief training in pick-up operations, in October 1943 he had little expectation that his mission would function as such a significant staging post and point of entry and exit for Allied personnel travelling between Yugoslavia and Italy; but in retrospect he had no doubt that this was one of its most important functions. Apart from acting as the conduit through which Gibbon's POWs or agents like Veress could be brought to safety, Reed's isolated outpost in Croatia played a key role in enabling other Allied officers to discharge their duties. Peter Wilkinson planned his journey to Slovenia and north-eastern Italy from Judge Mission, and obtained there his Slovene guide, Florjan, without whom his travels would have been infinitely more difficult, if not impossible. Doc Rogers, having lost all his medical supplies shortly after his arrival in Yugoslavia, arranged through Reed for their replacement. And all of those whom Reed assisted helped to improve Allied intelligence appreciations of Yugoslavia. Indeed, the reports prepared by Wilkinson and Churchill reached the Prime Minister himself. But it would be impossible to conclude this chapter without commenting on one final point: everyone who passed through Judge Mission formed the very highest opinion of the officer who commanded it. Wilkinson was particularly heartened by the warm reception he received from Reed, 'a most competent and conscientious officer and a delightful host';[41] Churchill likewise praised his hospitality; for Gibbon he was 'first class'; for Rogers a 'wise counsellor and friend'. Coming from such men, these were indeed extravagant tributes which underlined the success of Reed's first SIS assignment. Only time would tell if that success could be repeated.

NOTES

1. G. Millar, *Horned Pigeon* (London: Pan, 1970), pp. 126–41; unless otherwise stated this account of Gibbon's journey is based on WO 202/157, report on Escape from Germans in Northern Italy and Journey through Yugoslavia, by Major E.H. Gibbon, DSO, 20 December 1943, and RP, 'Story of an escape from Italy after the Armistice with that country in 1943', by E.H. Gibbon, 1948.
2. WO 204/9673, information supplied by Private Hutton and Private . . . [name not recorded] of New Zealand Army, 20 January 1944.
3. WO 202/438, signal to Fungus, 26 November 1943.
4. Interview with Reed, 4 November 1989.
5. WO 202/437, signal from Fungus, 29 November 1943.
6. WO 202/140, Bari to Cairo, 30 November 1943. While Vis was already seen as a relatively safe island at this time, it had not yet been formaly garrisoned by the Allies.
7. WO 202/145, Cairo to Bari, 2 December 1943.
8. WO 202/437, signal from Fungus, 2 December 1943; WO 202/145, Cairo to Bari, 2 December 1943.
9. WO 202/437, signal from Fungus, 7 December 1943.

10. WO 202/140, Bari to Cairo, 9 December 1943.
11. WO 202/335, signal from Rowena, 14 December 1943.
12. Millar, *Horned Pigeon*, pp. 341–2.
13. HS 5/934, note by SO to V/CD on interview with Major Gibbon, DSO, 1 March 1944.
14. Unless otherwise stated, this account of Clowder Mission is taken from Wilkinson, *Foreign Fields*.
15. RP, Reed diary, 17–21 March 1944.
16. Odreds were the original Partisan organizational units. They were local commands with authority over small units in areas where the Partisans controlled no territory, but simply lived in the forests or at isolated farms and carried out occasional raids against small German garrisons or supply lines.
17. RP, OR to PR, 22 June 1944.
18. Unless otherwise stated, this account of Rogers' mission is taken from Rogers, *Guerrilla Surgeon*.
19. WO 202/439, signal from Fungus, 3 February 1944.
20. RP, Reed diary, 4 February 1944; WO 202/438, signal to Fungus, 8 February 1944.
21. RP, Reed diary, 20–22 February 1944; WO 202/438, signal to Fungus, 28 February 1944.
22. Lindsay, *Beacons in the Night*, p. 235.
23. Maclean, *Eastern Approaches*, p. 320.
24. Gilbert, *Churchill*, vol. 7, p. 644.
25. WO 202/438, signal to Fungus, 17 and 24 April 1944.
26. Wilkinson, *Foreign Fields*, pp. 140–1.
27. Unless otherwise stated this account of Churchill's journey is taken from PREM 3/511/12, report by Major R. Churchill, MP, HQ Croatia, 12 April 1944, addressed to W. Churchill.
28. Interview with Reed, 4 November 1989.
29. *Ibid.*
30. AIR 23/1668, message received from BLO at Partisan HQ west Croatia, 23 February 1944.
31. WO 202/439, signal from Fungus, 6 March 1944.
32. RP, Reed diary, 7 April 1944.
33. RP, Reed diary, 8 April 1944.
34. WO 202/438, signal to Fungus, 17 April 1944.
35. Unless otherwise stated this account of Veress' escape is taken from HS 4/110, memorandum, Prelude to Unconditional Surrender, based on conversations with Veress, June 1944, and the brief account contained in M.R.D. Foot, *SOE – The Special Operations Executive, 1940–46* (London: BBC, 1984). His name is spelled Veress and Veres in the documents; I have used the former spelling here for standardization.
36. WO 202/438, signal to Fungus, 3 June 1944. Reed himself was almost certainly the recipient of this signal, which was presumably intended for his assistant, George Selvig. A signal from Fungus complained the same day that ten messages sent to Force 266 via ISLD had been repeated back to Fungus.
37. WO 202/439, signal from Fungus, 9 June 1944.
38. *Ibid.*

39. RP, Reed, *Junior English 3*.
40. RP, Reed diary, 10 June 1944; WO 202/438, signal to Fungus, 15 June 1944.
41. Wilkinson, *Foreign Fields*, p. 180; HS 6/17, report on Clowder Mission by Peter Wilkinson, 13 May 1944.

7

The Istrian Débâcle

The Secret Intelligence Service – that is, 'ISLD' – evacuated Owen Reed from Croatia at the end of June 1944 so that he could report firsthand on the Partisans' declared intention of annexing the north-eastern Italian territory of Venezia Giulia, and with it the city of Trieste. He spent a week being debriefed at ISLD's Bari operations centre, No. 1 I(U) Section, and was then taken by boat to Vis to report to Fitzroy Maclean. He spent 'all morning with Fitz' on 9 July, providing a full appraisal of the Partisan movement in Croatia, the military situation there, and the status of the British mission. Back in Bari the next day there was just time for 'hectic packing and cleaning up'; early on the morning of the 11th he boarded the aircraft that was to bring him back to Britain, via north Africa and Gibraltar, after an absence of more than two years.[1]

In mid-July 1944 London was under V-1 flying bomb attack. Reed spent two rather nervous days at SIS's headquarters where his report on Venezia Giulia was received with great interest at the very highest levels. His diary records at least one audience with 'the General', or 'C', as the head of SIS is more commonly known, Major-General Sir Stewart Menzies, and several meetings with David Footman, who headed SIS's political section, Section I, and was an expert on Soviet affairs.[2] Footman's personal involvement confirms that while SIS were still monitoring the German presence in southern Europe, they were becoming increasingly concerned over the potential for Soviet expansion there. It was agreed that following his return to Bari Reed should join the Partisans in Istria, the coastal peninsula which includes southern Venezia Giulia. His debriefing completed, he boarded a train to Wales and took two weeks well-earned leave.[3]

After returning to London at the beginning of August he spent another fortnight training with SIS and learning more about his next job. Once again, he was given a dual brief, involving the acquisition of intelligence on both the Germans and the Partisans. The Allied Armies advancing into northern Italy were particularly keen to obtain information on German dispositions and logistical arrangements there, and on enemy shipping movements in the northern Adriatic. In the summer of 1944 Istria was central to Churchill's strategy for the concluding months of the War. His hope was to launch an amphibious operation against the Istrian peninsula, from where Allied Forces could link up with the Eighth Army, then expected to be moving through the Po Valley and towards Trieste. From there they would strike north, through the Ljubljana Gap, to Vienna. Churchill believed such a strategy to be the best means of blocking Soviet expansion into southern Europe. In September he argued that Britain should have 'powerful forces in Austria and from Trieste northwards at the end of the German war, and should not yield central or southern Europe entirely to Soviet ascendancy and domination'.[4]

For precisely the same reasons, intelligence on the Partisan presence in Istria was of paramount importance. From a British perspective, handing Venezia Giulia, and especially Trieste, to Tito was no different from handing it to Stalin – the very eventuality that Churchill was so anxious to avoid. On 12 August he met Tito at Naples and disclosed not only the possibility of an Allied landing in Istria, but also his intention of establishing an Anglo-American Allied Military Government in Venezia Giulia following Germany's withdrawal. British and American troops would then administer the disputed border area, with civilian assistance, until the Italian frontier with Yugoslavia was agreed under the relevant post-war peace treaties. Tito was clearly unhappy with this scenario, and pointed out on the following day that his movement already exercised a large measure of control in Venezia Giulia. Although their discussions were good-natured, there was no meeting of minds between the two leaders, and they each subsequently determined to pursue their own incompatible objectives.[5] Tito aimed to confront the Western Allies with the *fait accompli* of Partisan rule, while Churchill sought US approval for an amphibious landing. On 9 September he told the Chiefs of Staff, 'Istria holds a very high place in my thoughts'.[6] On the very same day, Owen Reed and his faithful radio operator, Paddy Ryan, were parachuted on to the peninsula under the auspices of an ISLD operation codenamed 'Claret'.[7]

Reed had returned to Bari on 19 August. By then ISLD's operations in northern Italy, Yugoslavia and the Balkans had been significantly enlarged. Their air operations programme for August and September listed some 24 planned drops to Yugoslavia alone, almost all of which were assigned to officers co-located with representatives of the official British Military Mission, now known as Force 399.[8] Reed himself was to work with a Force 399 officer, Captain Prescott, who was to arrange for the sea-borne delivery of supplies from Italy. They were not to be based at 11 Corps headquarters (the Partisan base located in southern Slovenia, which had overall responsibility for Istria) but at the headquarters of one of its component formations, the 43rd Division, which was deployed in the mountains above

15. Owen Reed in Italy in 1944.

Fiume (now Rijeka).[9] Reed had been expecting to reach Istria in August, but his departure was delayed, perhaps by the non-availability of air transport, or by unsuitable weather conditions, and he found himself killing time in Bari. He was severely demoralized after returning from leave, but positive about his new job, which he described as 'interesting... vigorous and to the point', and eager to get started. 'I want to get working again with my beloved Jugs', he wrote on 31 August.[10]

While most ISLD officers and their staff were now drawn from the British Armed Services, there remained some foreign émigrés of Yugoslav parentage, who did not owe any direct allegiance to Britain. Hence the ISLD mission at Partisan headquarters in Slovenia was still entirely in the hands of Slovenes or Slovene émigrés in the autumn of 1944.[11] This arrangement had functioned smoothly enough while relations between the Western Allies and the Partisans remained reasonably cordial. But as the confrontation over Venezia Giulia and Britain's continuing support for the royalist government-in-exile engendered mounting suspicion and animosity between them, officers and ORs in this position found their loyalties dangerously divided. Urged by the Partisans to defect, they frequently faced threats and intimidation if they refused to do so.[12]

Reed himself was instructed to liaise with two Slovene radio operators codenamed 'Tomato' and 'Oil' (their real names are not recorded), who were already in Istria monitoring German shipping movements around Trieste, having been seconded to ISLD under an arrangement with Partisan naval headquarters.[13] It is probable that this was brokered by ISLD's representative at the naval headquarters, Captain Cooke. Cooke had served with the Partisan Navy since October 1943, and joined them on the island of Vis when Tito located his own headquarters there in the summer of 1944. He is said to have collected intelligence through Partisan channels and to have furnished a number of reports on German shipping movements which were 'of the greatest value to the Royal Navy and the RAF [and which] resulted in several successful naval and air strikes'. But early in September Tito suddenly demanded Cooke's immediate withdrawal, alleging that he had been exceeding his duties and carrying out private investigations into the Partisan armed forces.[14] It is not clear whether Reed knew of these events before his infiltration, but they clearly did not augur well for the success of his assignment.

On 9 September he and Ryan were finally taken to a nearby airfield, from where their aircraft took off at 9.30 in the evening. They found themselves in the hands of a young and inexperienced American crew, who were 'very vague' about their destination and fearful of enemy anti-aircraft fire.[15] 'The crew had one ambition', Reed recalled later, 'which was to get in, make the drop, and get the hell out again as fast as they possibly could, and they weren't too concerned about where we landed'.[16] Reaching the drop zone at about midnight, they were reluctant to descend towards the fires in case they were decoys lit by the enemy, and the two ISLD agents were therefore parachuted from a far higher altitude than in the previous year. 'Long drop ... petrified with fear', Reed wrote in his diary. But they landed safely, met up with the reception party and made their way to the divisional headquarters.[17]

In October 1943 Reed had been a key member of a small and select group of Allied officers infiltrated into north-western Yugoslavia; indeed, for some months he was the only Allied military representative in Croatia. The situation he found in Istria almost a year later could not have been more different: a veritable plethora of Allied special operations teams were active there. In addition to ISLD and the British Military Mission to Yugoslavia there was the American OSS, the British Special Boat Service (SBS) (who perversely operated on land), and two detachments from the Long Range Desert Group (LRDG), who by 1944 had run out of desert. 'The function of the men thus infiltrated is not clear', Reed reported at the end of his mission. 'In some cases it is not established that they have any function at all.' Together they converged on the headquarters of the 43rd Division, 'the members of each organization complaining complete ignorance of the activities of the other organizations'.[18]

In time, the LRDG performed valuable shipping reconnaissance work in

Istria and helped to provide intelligence on enemy dispositions along the northern Adriatic coast,[19] but their early deployments to Yugoslavia were chaotic. Their first group, under the command of a Major Reynolds, was infiltrated by air to Partisan headquarters in Slovenia and ordered to move south; the second, headed by another major, Pitt, landed on the Istrian coast with instructions to move north. Inevitably they blundered into each other travelling in opposite directions. Their adventures were observed with ironic amusement by the other Allied personnel in Istria, but also with acute embarrassment. For the LRDG's activities made onerous demands on the Partisans, and sometimes seemed almost calculated to antagonize them. At one stage it was necessary for the senior officer from Force 399 to ask the local Partisan commander to withdraw troops from active units to serve as couriers for Reynolds and Pitt.[20] The LRDG had also been very badly briefed before their departure: 'All seemed to think of the Partisans as "fifth-column wogs" rather than allies. All parties were grossly over-equipped and seemed to expect unlimited "bearers" and guides to be produced on demand.'[21] A third LRDG group, Italian interpreters for the first two detachments, arrived in Istria unexpectedly, dressed in civilian clothes and lacking both written authorization and identity papers.[22]

The unorganized infiltration of so many special operations personnel caused severe friction between the Partisans and Allied officers in the field. In one report Reed described how the Partisans' 'suspicion of the activities of Allied personnel' was 'growing daily stronger, carrying the latent threat that it [would] assume ugly proportions and become dangerous'. They were completely unable to understand why several different Allied organizations were working in Istria and were becoming increasingly reluctant to co-operate with them.[23] Although Reed found the Partisans' attitude both frustrating and disturbing, he nevertheless felt some sympathy for them. In his view, the problem could only have been solved by better liaison at the highest levels of the command chain, and he recommended that infiltration should be so arranged that every local Partisan commander knew the function of every member of the Allied parties in his area of responsibility. It was also vital for each Allied mission to be properly authorized by the Partisan high command. Reed concluded:

> Everybody should have with him, on his person, the means of proving to the jealous, bewildered, suspicious and self-righteous commander what his right is to be here, and what Tito thinks he has to contribute to their victory.[24]

Reed had ample opportunity to observe the situation at the head-quarters of the 43rd Division while he awaited the arrival of his Slovene radio operators, Tomato and Oil. He quickly made contact with the senior officer from Force 399, Major Breene, whom he liked, and with Prescott, 'and for a week or two had a real John Buchan job with a pair of field-glasses peering over cliffs at the foe'.[25] But his assignment could not begin in earnest until the ISLD team reached its full complement. In the meantime, events far beyond his control intervened decisively to determine the fate of his mission. On 18 September Tito left his island base at Vis without warning. Unknown to Britain or the USA, he was travelling to Moscow to arrange Partisan collaboration with the Red Army in the liberation of Belgrade. He reappeared in October, shortly before the victorious Partisan and Soviet forces marched into the Yugoslav capital. During his absence there was a particularly marked deterioration in Partisan relations with the Western Allies. His subordinates may have become over-cautious in his absence, or perhaps reluctant to act on their own initiative; or they may have been implementing orders to reduce co-operation with the various British and US missions. The truth will probably never be known with any certainty.[26]

But on 22 September Reed was peremptorily informed that all Allied personnel in Istria, his mission included, were to move to the 11 Corps headquarters in Slovenia prior to their evacuation from Yugoslavia. He was given 'half hour's notice to quit' by the divisional commander, who claimed that the order had been issued at corps level. He and Breene hurriedly threw their most important possessions into a car provided by the Partisans, leaving their radio operators to follow with a kola carrying the bulk of their equipment and supplies. Naturally, Reed was deeply perturbed by this unexplained turn of events, and fearful for the future of his mission. The proposed link-up with the two Slovene radio operators was thrown into jeopardy, although before leaving he sought assurances that they would be sent on to 11 Corps headquarters when they reached the 43rd Division. Initially he assumed that the Partisans had simply run out of patience with the various Allied organizations deployed in Istria. 'My sympathies remain with Partisans after shambles of recent events', he wrote in his diary.[27] But an interview with the 11 Corps commander later that day proved this supposition incorrect. Instead he was told that the order applied to the whole of Yugoslavia and affected all Allied personnel other than missions to corps and regional headquarters. 'Vital you confirm this', Reed signalled to ISLD. 'If true our further stay [is] clearly futile . . . Own belief is further co-operation impracticable. About 50 personnel involved. All movement stopped except with written assent from Tito.'[28]

At Bari, ISLD and Force 399 decided to take the hardest possible line in response to the Partisan order. Reed was instructed to remain at his post for as long as possible and to protest strongly. In Tito's absence, Force 399 first tackled his senior liaison officer, Bakic, who replied defensively that there were too many Allied officers in the field, that some of them had nothing to do, and that the British had lost count of their number. Tito's chief of staff, General Arso Jovanovic, was more conciliatory. He insisted that the

11 Corps commander had seriously misinterpreted his orders, and that no unreasonable restrictions would be placed on the movement of Allied liaison officers.[29] But his assurances led only to a revised order permitting the LRDG to remain in Istria, together with an officer who was organizing air operations at a nearby landing ground. Reed, Breene and Prescott were excluded from these new arrangements. In consultation with ISLD, Force 399 therefore decided to suspend forthwith the delivery of supplies to 11 Corps, and the evacuation of their wounded.[30]

On 25 September Reed and Breene each received identical directives from Bari, which they duly read out to the corps commander in an 'atmosphere freezing with formality':[31]

> We have received the following orders from the officers commanding our organizations:
> 1. The order to withdraw all mission personnel from Istria and Slovenia was made without consulting the British Military Mission to Yugoslavia.
> 2. The British Staff takes the view that it was a most discourteous and untimely act in view of the fact that all personnel with the Partisan army were approved by Marshal Tito.
> 3. The British commander-in-chief is therefore protesting very strongly to Marshal Tito.
> 4. The Head of the Allied Mission to Istria, Major Breene, and the Head of the British Intelligence Service attached to Istrian HQ, Major Reed, are ordered to protest to the commander, 11 Corps, against their removal from their posts, and to ask for the protests to be sent to the Vrhovni Stab [General Jovanovic].
> 5. Until the commander-in-chief receives a satisfactory explanation, all flights of stores to and evacuation of wounded from the area concerned will cease.[32]

Both Reed and Breene delivered this directive with the very gravest misgivings. Indeed, Reed subsequently addressed an uncompromising critique to his senior officers, which they did not appreciate, recording his conviction that their action was 'calculated to worsen [the] situation'. Halting the evacuation of wounded while the Partisan order was still under discussion was, in his view, an 'inhumane and dictatorial gesture'. Moreover, it was futile to retaliate against the corps commander, who might simply have been obeying orders from Tito's staff. It 'merely puts added strain on already embarrassed local relations', Reed continued. 'Unfortunately we have no way of showing to Staff that this retaliation originated in Bari. They think we suggested it.' To make matters worse, the senior US officer at 11 Corps received different instructions: he was to comply with the Partisan order and no precipitate action was to be taken in the field for the time being.[33] Reed stated that he had done his best to 'dissociate' himself with the British directive, a phrase which earned him a stinging rebuke from Bari a few days later. In response he denied that he was 'saboteur [of] official solidarity' but acknowledged that the phrase 'dissociate' was ill chosen, and confirmed that he had 'expressed no opinion to Partisans nor opened [his] mouth independently of Breene'. At their joint interviews they merely stressed that the ban on the evacuation of wounded was a directive from Bari. 'Otherwise', he maintained, 'it would have been construed locally as a piece of personal face-slapping by us'.[34]

On 27 September Breene was ordered to return to Bari to report;[35] his departure left Reed holding the unenviable position of senior British officer at 11 Corps. In the meantime the Partisans employed classic delaying tactics to frustrate all efforts to resolve the dispute. At Tito's base on Vis a more amiable Bakic assured Force 399 that a further directive would be sent to the corps commander permitting Reed and Prescott to continue with their work in Istria, but no perceptible change followed in the Partisans' stance at corps headquarters. 'Eleventh Corps profess no knowledge of any such cancellation', Reed signalled to ISLD on 5 October. 'Latest ruling from Tito HQ was on September 25th ... and order for our withdrawal and detention still stands.'[36] Reed was by this time convinced that the Partisans' claim to Trieste lay behind their actions. Allied officers – particularly ISLD officers – moving freely around Istria with their radio operators would, at the very least, submit detailed reports on Partisan activities there, and might undertake a reconnaissance role in advance of an amphibious landing.[37] He was deeply frustrated and disheartened, and had lost any residual enthusiasm for his assignment. Brief notes in his diary refer to his sense of futility, and to his 'cheerless and pointless life'.[38] He was also clearly frightened: relations with the Partisans were at their lowest possible ebb and the atmosphere at 11 Corps was 'almost openly unfriendly'. Understandably, in this environment, he became deeply concerned for the safety of Allied mission personnel, himself included.[39]

Reed's very worst fears were soon realized. On 2 October he was informed that Prescott had arrived at the 43rd Division. Prescott had been involved in a reconnaissance operation with the LRDG some days earlier when a signal reached him via the Partisans recalling him to the divisional headquarters. Believing that the order emanated from Allied sources, the local Partisans had not compelled him to comply with it, and he had therefore continued with his mission until 25 September, when the divisional commander insisted on his return. At the 43rd Division he was duly told that no Allied personnel were to remain with formations below corps level, and that he was to move to 11 Corps forthwith.[40] Reed promptly arranged for his transfer with corps headquarters. Leaving nothing to chance, he gained permission for Prescott to be escorted by the senior officer from Force 399,

Captain Burnett; the next morning Burnett left for the 43rd Division and the two officers returned together a few hours later.[41]

But Prescott brought with him alarming news. He had seen the two Slovene ISLD radio operators, Tomato and Oil, being 'badly bullied and detained at HQ 43 Division', where they had gone in search of Reed. The Partisans there had also 'taken their [radio] sets and codes'. Signalling ISLD, Reed continued: 'Am taking up strongly here and trying to extricate them...Unless can induce total change of heart here, ISLD prospects in Istria are nil.'[42] Reed took up cudgels with the 11 Corps staff on 4 October and received an assurance that Tomato and Oil would be transferred immediately from the 43rd Division. On the 7th he was told that they were on their way, and that they would arrive later that day. On the 8th, when there was still no word, he demanded to see them. He now began recording his interviews with the Partisan staff in his diary in some detail:

> 8 October. Saw Lac [a senior member of the Corps staff] about Tomato and Oil. Stated he must ask commander about my seeing them. Returned obviously relieved to say commander out. Then said they were Partisan bodies and subject to Partisan discipline and would ask commander about my seeing them.[43]

The next day Prescott received orders to return to Bari; he was shortly to be followed by the LRDG.[44] The British operation in Istria was disintegrating. Reed's sole concern now was to ensure that the two Slovene radio operators emerged safely from the débâcle. His diary takes up the story:

> 9 October. Saw [corps] commander about Tomato and Oil. Clearly lying. Said they were not here. I said Lac knew I wanted to see them. He said they were only here [a] few hours and then went on. I said nonsense. [They] arrived two days ago. He said he was away and knew nothing about it. I asked why, as I had particularly asked to see them, they had sent them away. He said because they had orders from [Partisan] Naval Headquarters handing them and sets over to 11 Corps and it was none of my business. I said I was gravely dissatisfied with whole picture and would ask for instructions. Also asked why they had taken sets and codes. He replied also gift from Navy HQ. I said I required return of both [personnel] at once and would ask for their explanation of why Navy HQ had broken agreement.[45]

Throughout the meeting the corps commander wore around his neck a pair of standard ISLD-issue binoculars. Reed had no doubt that they had been confiscated from Tomato and Oil, and he withdrew to his quarters fearing the worst. Predictably enough, further enquiries through ISLD were unable to establish whether the Partisan Navy had in fact offered the radio operators and their equipment to 11 Corps. When Prescott returned to Bari he reported that the two Slovenes were thought to be under arrest, but Reed always harboured far more sinister suspicions about their ultimate fate.[46]

The end was now in sight. Some days earlier, on 29 September, Reed's former counterpart in Force 399, Major Breene, had submitted to his own organization a report on the Istrian situation. He recorded his gratitude for the help he had received from the ISLD team there, and professed himself 'most happy' to have worked with Reed. 'However', he continued with some understatement, 'there is NOT sufficient scope for him'. He was keen to discuss with his own commanding officer Reed's position at 11 Corps headquarters, 'with a view to … making recommendations to ISLD'.[47] ISLD were in the meantime receiving an almost identical message from Reed himself. Then, during the first week of October, their representative at Partisan headquarters in Slovenia, Captain Leonard, suddenly announced that he and his three staff wished to join the Partisans. So ISLD decided that Reed and Ryan should replace them.[48] Reed was jubilant. 'Great news about Slovene job', he wrote in his diary. He informed the corps commander of his new assignment on 11 October and left discrete instructions for the two Slovenes in case, by any chance, they should reappear after his departure.[49] On the 13th he and Ryan packed, said their goodbyes and took their leave.[50]

NOTES

1. RP, Reed diary, 1–14 July 1944.
2. RP, Reed diary, 15 July 1944; West, *MI6*, pp. 145–6.
3. RP, Reed diary, 16–18 July 1944.
4. Gilbert, *Churchill*, vol. 7, p. 948; Cave Brown, 'C', p. 617.
5. J.R. Whittam, 'Drawing the Line: Britain and the Emergence of the Trieste Question, January 1941–May 1945', *English Historical Review* (April 1991), pp. 360–2.
6. Gilbert, *Churchill*, vol. 7, p. 948.
7. RP, Reed diary, 9 September 1944; WO 204/12838, ISLD Air Operations Programme for August/September, prepared by Squadron Leader Ops 1 at 1 I(U) Section, 19 August 1944.
8. WO 204/12838, ISLD Air Operations Programme for August/September, prepared by Squadron Leader Ops 1 at 1 I(U) Section, 19 August 1944; Hinsley *et al.*, *British Intelligence in the Second World War*, vol. 3, pt 1, p. 178. SIS is said to have had about five agents and radio operators in enemy-held territory in Italy by the end of 1943, a number which had increased to about 35 by the end of the War. According to the official history, the intelligence they supplied on the German order of battle and troop movements 'was well received by the 15th Army Group and … valuable reports on the effects of Allied air attacks on enemy communications were supplied in answer to special requests for such intelligence'.

9. Interview with Reed, 4 November 1989; WO 202/212, No 1 I(U) Section, Bari, to Lieutenant-Colonel Street, Rear HQ 'M' Military Mission, 5 October 1944.

10. RP, OR to PR, 24 and 31 August 1944.

11. WO 202/212, No 1 I(U) Section, Bari, to Rear HQ 'M' Military Mission, 9 October 1944. Several of Reed's signals to ISLD on Istria were copied to Force 399 and have been preserved in this file in the National Archives.

12. According to one source, Tito ultimately issued a blanket prohibition against Allied personnel with family ties in Yugoslavia, although the author has not located any reference to such a prohibition in the official documents. See Lindsay, *Beacons in the Night*, p. 183.

13. RP, Reed diary, 9 October 1944. The Partisans operated a small naval force in the northern Adriatic consisting mainly of gunboats, some of which were captured from the Italians and the Germans, some of which were little more than converted civil craft.

14. *See* WO 202/189, Lieutenant-Colonel Maxwell to Rear HQ 'M' Military Mission, 24 September 1944. A British lecturer named Adrian Cooke was teaching at Zagreb University at the time of the German occupation in 1941 and may well have been another of James Millar's recruits; see FO 371/30261, Nichols to Broad, 17 May 1941.

15. RP, Reed diary, 9 September 1944.

16. Interview with Reed, 4 November 1989.

17. RP, Reed diary, 9 September 1944.

18. WO 202/212, No 1 I(U) Section, Bari, to Rear HQ 'M' Military Mission, 13 October 1944.

19. AHB file IIJ1/130, The History of the Balkan Air Force, Headquarters, Balkan Air Force, July 1945, p. 71.

20. RP, Reed diary, 16 September 1944; WO 202/521, report by Major Breene, 29 September 1944.

21. WO 202/521, report by Major Breene, 29 September 1944.

22. WO 202/212, No 1 I(U) Section, Bari, to Rear HQ 'M' Military Mission, 13 October 1944.

23. *Ibid.*

24. *Ibid.*

25. RP, Reed diary, 12–16 September, 1944; RP, OR to PR, undated, postmarked 25 February 1945.

26. Lindsay, *Beacons in the Night*, p. 195; Maclean, *Eastern Approaches*, p. 382; Whittam, 'Drawing the Line', p. 362.

27. RP, Reed diary, 22 September 1944; interview with Reed, 4 November 1989; WO 202/521, report by Major Breene, 29 September 1944; WO 202/212, signal from Claret, 23 September 1944.

28. WO 202/212, signal from Claret, 23 September 1944.

29. WO 202/212, Maxwell to Street, 23 September 1944; WO 202/212, Rear Macmis to Macmis, 23 September 1944 (two signals).

30. RP, Reed diary, 25 September 1944; WO 202/212, signal from Claret, 5 October 1944.

31. WO 202/212, signal from Claret, 26 September 1944.

32. RP, Reed diary, 25 September 1944.

33. WO 202/212, signal from Claret, 26 September 1944.

34. WO 202/212, signal to Claret, 1 October 1944; signal from Claret, 5 October 1944.

35. RP, Reed diary, 27 September 1944.

36. WO 202/212, Macmis to Rear Macmis, 27 September 1944; signal from Claret, 5 October 1944.

37. RP, OR to PR, undated, postmarked 25 February 1945.

38. RP, Reed diary, 27 and 28 September 1944.

39. WO 202/212, signal from Rip Van Winkle, 1 October 1944; No 1 I(U) Section, Bari, to Rear HQ 'M' Military Mission, 13 October 1944. Rip Van Winkle was Force 399's mission at 11 Corps headquarters, at this time commanded by Captain Burnett.

40. WO 202/521, report on reconnaissance of Istria, by Captain D. Prescott, 4 October 1944.

41. RP, Reed diary, 2 and 3 October 1944.

42. WO 202/212, signal from Claret, 5 October 1944.

43. RP, Reed diary, 8 October 1944.

44. RP, Reed diary, 9 and 10 October 1944.

45. RP, Reed diary, 9 October 1944. In helping to monitor German shipping movements and to co-ordinate the delivery of sea-borne supplies, the two Slovenes were working with the Partisan Navy, as well as with ISLD and Force 399.

46. WO 202/521, report on reconnaissance of Istria, by Captain D. Prescott, 4 October 1944; interview with Reed, 4 November 1989.

47. WO 202/521, report by Major Breene, 29 September 1944.

48. WO 202/212, No 1 I(U) Section, Bari, to Rear HQ 'M' Military Mission, 9 October 1944.

49. RP, Reed diary, 10–11 October 1944.

50. RP, Reed diary, 13 October 1944.

8

Slovenia

Owen Reed's assignment to Slovenia was conducted against a background of steadily worsening relations with the Partisans which arose from three fundamental problems. The first was Britain's continuing support for the Yugoslav monarchy and for the government-in-exile, while the second was the steadfast refusal of the Western Allies to accept Yugoslav sovereignty over Trieste. The third was a new development – the landing of British forces in Greece in October 1944 following Germany's withdrawal from the Balkans, and their subsequent intervention against the communist movement there.[1] British involvement in Greece was inevitably viewed with alarm and suspicion by Tito and his followers, and encouraged the belief that some similar action might be contemplated in support of British political objectives in Yugoslavia. The stakes were shortly afterwards raised further when Belgrade was liberated and Tito established his new regime there. As the threat from Germany declined and attention turned to Yugoslavia's post-war order, these various differences between the Western Allies and the Partisans assumed a greater prominence in their relationship, completely overshadowing the common objectives that had united them in earlier years. The Second World War was nearly over; the Cold War was about to begin.

In October 1944 Partisan headquarters in Slovenia was under the command of General Stane Rozman, an almost legendary figure in Tito's movement. Rozman 'was a youthful veteran of the Spanish Civil War with a formidable fighting record and clearly knew his business'.[2] His forces had enjoyed some success in both taking and holding territory from the Germans and the so-called 'White Guard' nationalists who collaborated with them, and in disrupting their lines of communication from Austria into northern Italy.[3] But, by the autumn of 1944, Rozman was facing renewed pressure, as the Germans sought to remove any Partisan threat to the road and rail routes conveying their retreating armies back to the Third Reich. Shortly before a major Partisan counterattack in November he was tragically killed by the premature explosion of a mortar shell.[4] His replacement, Dusan Kveder:

> was thoroughly committed to the Partisan revolution and appeared to consider the larger conflict between the Western Allies and Germany as of lesser importance. Of the Partisans, he was one of the most rigid in what appeared . . . to be a pro-Russian and anti-West attitude.[5]

Kveder's outlook was shared by the chief commissar at Slovene headquarters, Boris Kidric. Kidric was one of the founders of Slovenia's Partisan movement. A pre-war leader of the Slovene Communist Party, in 1944 Kidric was also a senior member of the Slovene Liberation Government and of Tito's inner circle. He has been described as 'the most powerful man in the Slovene resistance leadership'.[6] The antipathy manifested by Kveder and Kidric towards Britain and the USA was reflected in their treatment of Force 399 and ISLD field officers at the headquarters, and imposed a further severe strain on the already troubled relationship between the Partisans and the Western Allies. After his departure from Slovenia in February 1945 Reed described how he had been 'the victim of the most awful combination of icy courtesy and downright loathing'.[7]

Working in isolation, as he had worked in Croatia, Reed might have considered these circumstances intolerable. Mercifully he found himself among friends. At almost exactly the same time as his posting to Slovenia, Lieutenant-Colonel Peter Moore was appointed head of the British Military Mission there, operating under the codename 'Flotsam'. Moore was a Royal Engineer, who had played a key role in mine clearance during the battle of El Alamein.[8] An original member of the team that first accompanied Fitzroy Maclean to Bosnia in 1943, he had since worked with a variety of Partisan formations, advising their explosives and demolition units and participating in numerous attacks on enemy lines of communication.[9] In the early months of 1944 he had regularly transited through Partisan headquarters in Croatia, where he first met Reed, and they soon became firm friends.[10] Reed was delighted to learn that they were to be reunited.

Moore was not the only familiar face in Slovenia. During the summer Doc Rogers had arrived there with his assistants and had since been treating Partisan wounded at a hospital concealed deep within a forest near the village of Ajdovec. On visiting the Slovene headquarters in October to organize his supplies he learnt of Reed's impending arrival. 'I decided I would come down again in a fortnight's time', he wrote, 'and we would have a party'.[11] And then there was Florjan, the half-Irish Slovene who had previously guided Stump Gibbon and Peter Wilkinson between Slovenia and Croatia. Florjan was by this time attached to the Partisan liaison staff at the headquarters and also functioned as an interpreter. Although an ardent member of the Communist Party, he was evidently unhappy about the obstructive and unfriendly manner increasingly adopted by his superiors towards British and US officers in Slovenia. But for obvious reasons 'he never went so far as to say so'.[12]

SOE had first established a mission to the Slovene headquarters during 1943. Their principal achievement in the intervening period was the organization of an effective airborne supply system for the Partisans, which employed two drop zones and three separate landing grounds.[13] A few sub-missions had also been located to the north and west of the headquarters by the summer of 1944. As usual, ISLD's operations in Slovenia are not so well recorded, but it is clear that they consistently proved both difficult and hazardous. A notable success was the establishment in late 1943 of a mission at Partisan headquarters which operated under the codename 'Moth'. Moth Mission was staffed entirely by Yugoslav émigrés, presumably recruited in North America, the senior officer being Captain J. Leonard. According to one early SOE report on Moth Mission:

> The field [for intelligence gathering] is so great that the ISLD party have been able to do great work particularly in respect of locations of factories, airfields, and descriptions of bridges, and their information sources extend well into northern Italy. The very valuable rail traffic reports from a Ljubljana source closed when Ljubljana was cordoned off. Leonard has done excellent work, but I was astonished to find that he had dropped without any previous intelligence training, and also knows nothing of the organization of the Germany army.[14]

By October 1944 Leonard was being assisted by Sergeants Sivec, Jelen and Mikuz. It has already been described how, in that month, they all sought and received permission to join the Partisans.[15]

ISLD's attention otherwise focused on the Primorska region, on the Italian border, and on Koroska and Stajerska, the northern Slovene territories annexed by Hitler's Reich – the official documents refer to the infiltration of at least two ISLD teams bound for Primorska and Stajerska during 1943. The first of these was quickly captured and both its members were killed. The fate of the other is not recorded but it seems doubtful that it met with much success for there is no record of any permanent ISLD presence in the Stajerska before the early summer of 1944, when a Major S.V. McNeff arrived there. He was soon followed by a radio operator, Lieutenant Dan Gatoni (whose real name was Dan Linar), one of the recruits from the Jewish Agency in Cairo, and was shortly afterwards replaced by Squadron Leader Mervyn Whitfield. Later in the year they were joined by Major Mathews and Lieutenant Edward Parks.[16]

As 1944 wore on, ISLD's field agents in Slovenia all found their objectives frustrated by the deterioration of relations with the Partisans. Through a combination of obstruction, intransigence, half-heartedness, incompetence and outright animosity they rendered the task of intelligence gathering virtually impossible.[17] To make matters worse, ISLD's only recorded effort to infiltrate agents into southern Austria from Slovenia ended in total failure and seriously compromised the position of other Allied personnel and of Partisan formations in the region. Two agents were involved, operating under the cover names of 'Smith' and 'Black'; Black was an Austrian national who had been recruited from a prisoner-of-war camp. They were dropped to the Allied mission in Stajerska with instructions to proceed north to Vienna, and were initially passed on to Peter Wilkinson's mission, Clowder, in Koroska. Their conduct at Clowder did not encourage any confidence in their intelligence, reliability or sense of security. 'The Partisans rightly refused to work with them, and they started back to Fourth Zone [in Stajerska] as the first leg of the trip back to Italy.' While resting outside a mountain farm they were surprised by a German police patrol. Smith escaped and reached the Fourth Zone only to report that Black had deliberately allowed himself to be captured. He was later seen by a reliable witness talking in friendly terms with the Germans and accompanying them to the Clowder base. A powerful enemy force soon afterwards launched an attack on the base, and Clowder's staff only narrowly evaded capture after a running fight lasting five days.[18]

By the end of the year ISLD's various initiatives in northern Slovenia had been brought to a complete halt by determined and ruthless German countermeasures. Whitfield alone evaded capture. Gatoni and a group of Partisans were surrounded and taken prisoner by German troops in the mountains of Stajerska. The Partisans were shot but Gatoni was separated from them, apparently for intensive interrogation, and subsequently managed to escape. Mathews and Parks were not so fortunate. Wounded and captured during a surprise German attack on the Fourth Zone headquarters in December, they were reportedly taken to a Ljubljana hospital. But later investigations found no trace of them there, and it was assumed that they were shot by their captors.[19] Operating further from the Austrian frontier, Reed and Ryan were never in such immediate danger. But they were not significantly more successful in collecting intelligence than ISLD's other agents in Slovenia.

Reed's journey from Istria to Partisan headquarters in Slovenia was accomplished by the usual mixture of carts, trucks and foot slogging. His diary records a 'slow trail on left bank of Kupa till nightfall' on 13 October and a 'back-breaking struggle up hill to Stari Trg' on the 14th with a heavy rucksack. Reaching the headquarters at Crnomelj early that evening, they were met by Leonard and Florjan and briefly introduced to the Partisan staff. 'Reception first class', Reed noted, 'but too tired to sleep'.[20] He had some explaining to do to his hosts, for ISLD had ordered him to leave Istria without obtaining the proper authority from Tito's headquarters for his relocation to Slovenia. They probably felt that it was pointless for him to remain in such a hostile environment, and were no doubt eager for him to assume Leonard's duties. Predictably, though, the Partisans insisted that he should not take over from Leonard without Tito's express permission; nor, in the interim, should he communicate directly with ISLD. All communication was to be made through the Force 399 radio.[21] This ruling was entirely in keeping with Reed's past experience in Yugoslavia, and he accepted it without demur. As he once told Doc Rogers, 'It's always a month before you can start to do anything in this country.'[22]

Reed apparently expected Peter Moore to be holding the required authority when he reached the mission on the 16th, but Moore arrived empty-handed.[23] And so Reed waited; the delay did at least provide him with ample opportunity to discuss his new responsibilities with Leonard.[24] After two weeks Moore confronted Commissar Kidric, telling him that 'Reed might well consider himself insulted by their attitude'. Kidric 'appeared to be full of apologies but pleaded explicit instructions from General Headquarters JANL and promised to signal General Headquarters again'.[25] On 2 November Reed's mission finally received official sanction, and he advised James Millar at ISLD that he would resume the 'Claret' signal plan on the 4th.[26]

Conditions for representatives of the Western Allies at Slovene headquarters were both inhospitable and restrictive:

> While the Russians lived in state in the best house in Crnomelj, the British lived in the worst in Packa . . . The Stab [the Partisan staff] also lived pretty well in their new wooden huts, but the old British mission, which was responsible for almost all their supplies, was allocated the dirtiest house in Packa.[27]

The 15 officers and ORs, representing Force 399, ISLD, 'A' Force and the Balkan Air Force (the formation established in June 1944 to control all Allied air units committed to Balkan operations), all cohabited in this single primitive dwelling. They were kept indoors for long periods by both work and weather – weeks of rain in November and December, and heavy snowfalls thereafter. Their only links with the outside world took the form of radio messages, intermittent mail deliveries and BBC broadcasts. Throughout his four daunting months in Slovenia, Reed regularly found solace in the familiar voices of his erstwhile colleagues, Frank Gillard and Godfrey Talbot, both of whom were now accompanying the advancing Allied Armies through France and the Low Countries.[28]

The Partisans imposed a blanket ban on any unaccompanied movement by British personnel outside the headquarters. Reed, Moore and their staff found that all their activities were closely monitored, and that any conversation might be reported to Kidric by the liaison staff, whose

commanding officer they soon christened the 'chief spy'.[29] Reed wrote later
that there was always 'a spy, official or disguised, tied to our tails. It was
that, I think, that made the Slovene job so monstrously exasperating.'[30] The
consequences were sometimes absurd. Reed, a keen motorcyclist before the
war, inherited a Triumph with a worn-out clutch from his predecessors and
promptly repaired it, making rudimentary friction plates from a piece of
khaki webbing. But the Partisans refused to allow him to ride it without an
approved pillion. He countered that this would represent a pointless waste
of their manpower and would overtax both the motorcycle and its rider on
the steep and muddy tracks through Slovenia's hills and mountains, but his
objections were dismissed out of hand. Only reluctantly did the liaison staff
agree that his escort should be the smallest and lightest pillion available, a
12-year-old boy. The boy accompanied Reed wherever he went, and duly
reported back to the liaison staff at the end of every journey.[31]

The Partisans also took, in Peter Moore's words, 'the most elaborate
steps to ensure that no British personnel should have access to the ordinary
peasant or soldier in the absence of a politically reliable Partisan
observer'.[32] On arriving at the Slovene headquarters, Reed learnt that
Leonard was to marry a girl from a nearby village early in November. He
was invited to the wedding, and to the riotous reception that followed it,
and he emerged in the early hours of the following morning with an entirely
positive view of the local populace. 'This is a very Shakespearean
community', he wrote, 'and as decent as *Twelfth Night*, with much the
same liberty of humour, and safely and firmly hooked to Mother Church'.[33]
As events transpired this was to be virtually his only contact with the
ordinary Slovene people for the duration of his assignment. At least one
senior member of the Western Allies' military staff in Slovenia believed that
there was widespread antipathy among the general population towards
Tito's movement. The Partisans were therefore 'very anxious that the extent
of opposition and the anti-Partisan feeling [should] not be known to us,
hence the attempt to isolate us'.[34]

Large-scale military operations against the Germans ground to a halt in
November. On the 14th, enemy forces struck simultaneously at Semic,
Crnomelj and Metlika, forcing a precautionary move on the Partisan
headquarters. But the offensive petered out within two days.[35] A Partisan
counterattack followed against Kocevje, where one of the main German
garrisons was located. With Allied air support the Partisans made two
unsuccessful attempts to enter the town and were then surprised by a force
of some 500 SS troops and compelled to withdraw. 'Much regret Kocevje too
big a nut for us to crack', Peter Moore signalled on the 21st.[36] Thereafter the
Partisans moved to a largely defensive posture and relinquished more
territory to the Germans and the White Guard. The enemy garrisons at
Kocevje and Novo Mesto were reinforced and used as bases for offensive
thrusts into the remaining Partisan areas; key lines of communication were

reopened; the White Guard became far more aggressive under German direction, and their *pokretni,* or commando battalions, similarly made some notable gains at Partisan expense. Although their German patrons were now certain to be defeated, their morale perversely appeared to be higher than that of Tito's followers. Against this background, Moore began to question the Western strategy of supplying the Partisans with military equipment, weapons and ammunition. He became convinced that they were hoarding military supplies and conserving their strength in order to impose their own rule on Yugoslavia when the Germans were finally defeated.[37]

Given the Slovene Partisans' unimpressive combat record during the last months of 1944, it is hardly surprising that their intelligence operation also left much to be desired. In Croatia, Reed had been relatively free to collect intelligence from a variety of sources; in Slovenia he was almost entirely dependent on the Partisan intelligence staff. According to one source, Tito had decreed during September that the supply of intelligence to Allied liaison officers was to be restricted to an official 'handout' dealing entirely with the enemy; by contrast, the Partisans became extremely secretive about their own activities.[38] The handouts Reed received sometimes covered enemy dispositions and the results of Allied bombing raids; important information also periodically arrived from Partisan contacts in occupied territory, notably from the Bishop of Ljubljana. But they were overwhelmingly concerned with German rail traffic passing through Slovenia. Soon after taking over from Leonard, Reed found himself completely submerged under these railway reports, all of which had to be encoded before their transmission to Bari via an extremely unreliable radio set.[39]

He was never very sure of their origin, and therefore lacked the crucial ability to verify their contents. 'I hadn't any idea how much of it was true and how much mere invention', he wrote later.[40] Moore was not quite so pessimistic. 'A great deal of valuable information about enemy movements and results [of] Allied air actions...is received here and is being transmitted by Reed', he signalled on 26 November.[41] He also assessed the railway reports to be 'of great value'. He nevertheless acknowledged that Reed was 'having a tough time' and that the reports would have been very much better had they not been 'messed about by an incompetent Partisan intelligence staff'. The head of the Russian mission in Slovenia took a similar view: in late December he 'expressed his disgust that [German] divisions had recently passed through the 4 Zone area without a single identification having been obtained'.[42]

It was difficult for Reed to improve the quantity and quality of intelligence in the absence of Partisan co-operation, but not impossible. As in Croatia, a steady flow of Allied personnel – downed airmen and occasional escaped POWs – reached the Slovene headquarters *en route* for Italy. On their way they often acquired information about German dispositions, and Reed found that by interrogating them he could obtain a useful check on the accuracy of the Partisan reports.[43] Otherwise, he had no option but to maintain persistent pressure on the intelligence staff, a thoroughly unpleasant task which achieved some success but did nothing to promote more cordial relations between them. On 3 January Moore reported: 'After vigorous protests by Reed to the intelligence staff they have swept out their drawers and at last produced some identification of units.'[44] As usual, though, their continuing refusal to reveal their sources made verification impossible.[45]

Early in January 1945 Reed's incessant struggle with the intelligence staff was overshadowed by an episode which perfectly illustrated the sheer futility of ISLD's work in Slovenia during the closing stages of the War, and which helped to persuade his superior officers that he could more usefully serve them elsewhere. With certain defeat now confronting Germany's armies, a growing number of her military personnel were beginning to contemplate desertion or surrender. They rarely surrendered to the Partisans, who tended to shoot German prisoners in the same way that the Germans shot Partisans who were unlucky enough to fall into their hands. But they sometimes tried to contact British military missions in northern Italy and Yugoslavia in the belief that the Western Allies could be relied on to arrange for their evacuation to the relative safety of a POW camp. This was precisely the intention of a naval petty officer named Hopf, who managed to contact a British officer near Venice at the end of October 1944. Hopf claimed to possess important information on German naval plans in the northern Adriatic, which he was prepared to divulge in return for passage to Allied-occupied territory.[46]

After an unsuccessful attempt to bring him out by air, Hopf was passed to a British mission in western Slovenia who in turn arranged for him to be moved to Slovene headquarters. It was hoped that he might be evacuated from the nearby airstrip, but no undertaking to this effect was obtained from the Partisans before his departure, nor were Reed or Moore warned of his impending arrival. Hopf travelled with an ISLD sergeant named Marlowe and on arriving at the headquarters was immediately placed under arrest by the Partisans, while Marlowe found his way to the British mission and alerted Reed. The terrified Hopf then addressed two letters to the local representative of 'A' Force urging his claim for evacuation on the grounds that he possessed vital intelligence on the German Navy.[47]

Reed duly sought guidance from ISLD's operations centre in Bari, where it was decided that the evacuation should be left to 'A' Force. ISLD's intervention might only complicate matters, revealing to the Partisans Hopf's potential value, and thereby encouraging the usual vindictive obstruction and delay; quite probably Hopf would be shot. 'A' Force consequently asked for permission from the Partisan staff to arrange Hopf's flight to Italy but received no immediate response. In the meantime, ISLD despatched a counter-espionage expert named Burdon to Slovenia in an attempt to establish whether Hopf was genuine or whether he was, in fact, an enemy agent. The Partisans at first prevented Burdon from seeing their prisoner; then, on 5 January, their chief security officer asked him to conduct an interrogation. Burdon eventually satisfied himself that Hopf was trustworthy.[48]

It soon became clear that the source of any request for Hopf's evacuation was immaterial; the Partisans would only co-operate with the utmost reluctance. The obvious alternative was to interrogate him at the Slovene headquarters, but this strategy was also problematic. Firstly, it was dependent on Partisan acquiescence, which was not initially forthcoming.[49] Secondly, it assumed Hopf's willingness to divulge the all-important intelligence before his personal safety was guaranteed. But Hopf was evidently no fool. He probably knew full well that his knowledge was keeping him alive and that it was his only bargaining counter. He was thus predictably unwilling to reveal his secrets while he remained in Partisan custody.[50]

The saga was then further complicated by the arrival of a second German prisoner. On the 10th the Partisans revealed that they were holding an *obergefreiter* named Hein, who claimed to have information on German measures for intercepting British naval signals traffic.[51] They even supplied Reed with a lengthy interrogation report, which he transmitted to ISLD together with Burdon's report on Hopf. 'Flood of gen from interrogated bodies', he wrote in his diary on the 11th.[52] The Partisans surprisingly agreed 'in principle' to evacuate Hein, but they continued to prevaricate over Hopf.[53] ISLD therefore told Reed to conduct an interrogation himself; the details remain obscure, but it is possible that they suggested offering Hopf an inducement of some kind – perhaps a foreign passport – if he agreed to divulge more of his information. Reed was clearly unhappy with ISLD's strategy, suspecting that Hopf would not be so easily seduced, and his doubts proved entirely justified. With the Partisans' grudging approval he conducted a 'dismal interrogation of Hopf' on 15 January, which yielded little intelligence of value.[54] Confronted by Partisan intransigence on the one hand and by ISLD's unscrupulous tactics on the other, Reed began to feel increasingly isolated, and he decided that he could do no more than continue pressing for the two prisoners to be evacuated.[55]

Although the Partisans had theoretically agreed to Hein's evacuation, Reed and Moore apparently believed that it might be possible to fly out Hopf instead, if Bari considered him to be more important. They did not expect the Partisans to sanction the evacuation of both Germans.[56] After consultation between ISLD, Force 399 and the Royal Navy, it was confirmed that Hein's evacuation should have top priority and Peter Moore duly conveyed this message to Commissar Kidric on the morning of 16 January.[57] To Moore's obvious astonishment, Kidric now calmly informed him that Hein had joined the Partisans. After further discussions with Reed, who had held a second interview with Hopf that day, Moore signalled to Bari:

> Reed and Burdon interrogated Hopf today and recommend his immediate evacuation. As Pzns will be unable to resist temptation to use Hein as a bargaining counter and have gone back on their word I recommend that we should raise our bid immediately and ask [Partisan] GHQ for evacuation of both as proof of the often expressed but rarely apparent desire of the Pzns to co-operate with us.[58]

Bari immediately approached Tito's headquarters to obtain permission to evacuate both Hein and Hopf, and received what appeared to be an affirmative response, 'unless liaison officer Slovene HQ has any special objection'.[59] Yet a fortnight later, on 3 February, GHQ's approval for the evacuation had not been received in Slovenia.[60] Soon afterwards the affair assumed the proportions of a fiasco when the Slovene liaison staff declared that Hein had escaped – a revelation scarcely consistent with their earlier claim that he had joined the Partisans. The British mission was invited to attend the court martial of his guards! On 18 February, when Reed left Slovenia, Hopf remained incarcerated in a Partisan cell and the liaison staff were still insisting that GHQ had not formally sanctioned his evacuation.[61]

Although this was unquestionably the most humiliating failure of Owen Reed's sojourn in Slovenia, it was but one of many instances when Partisan obstruction completely frustrated the work of the British missions there. While refusing to co-operate in the evacuation of the German prisoners, the Partisans also imposed intolerable constraints on other mission activities, and did so with barely concealed animosity towards mission personnel. They continued to accept military supplies from the Western Allies but maintained an entirely defensive military posture; their intelligence operation remained inefficient and unreliable. A major dispute erupted when they suddenly began taking medical stores intended for Doc Rogers' hospital. The issue was only resolved in Rogers' favour after he signalled Tito directly and threatened to leave Yugoslavia.[62]

By the end of December 1944, when the abortive struggle to evacuate Hopf was just beginning, Reed and Moore were already running out of patience. Reed 'typed pessimistic analysis of misgivings' for ISLD on the 26th and on 4 January Moore tackled Kidric head-on. 'Raised whole question of petty obstruction [of the] last three months by Slovene authorities here in 9th Corps and 4th Zone with commissar yesterday', he signalled:

Told him I and all other British officers in Slovenia were disgusted by
their attitude. Told him also that officers leaving Slovenia for Italy
during the last three months had all carried away extremely
unfavourable impression. Produced several examples whereby such
obstruction had in fact hampered our attempts to assist them.[63]

Kidric replied evasively that his subordinates had misinterpreted their
orders, and promised to investigate, but Moore was unconvinced by his
response and no tangible improvement resulted from the interview.[64]

On 7 January Doc Rogers made one of his regular visits to the mission
and a long conversation with Reed turned inexorably to the problem of
relations with the Partisans. Finally, Rogers declared that he could foresee
no change in the current situation, that the task of intelligence gathering
would consequently become even more difficult, that Reed's continued
presence in Slovenia was therefore futile, and that he should leave.[65] The
New Zealander went so far as to hint that he might supply ISLD with
medical grounds for Reed's (and Ryan's) withdrawal, and he did in fact
signal James Millar on 11 January recommending Reed's 'relief at the
earliest possible opportunity for examination by a medical specialist and a
period of rest'.[66]

Rogers' intervention appears to have been the catalyst for Reed's
departure from Slovenia. His diagnosis, while exaggerated, was by no
means entirely spurious, for Reed was not in particularly sound health in
January 1945. At the same time he had clearly lost faith in his task. He was
demoralized by the constant struggle with the Partisans and by the
conditions of daily life at the headquarters, and pessimistic about ISLD's
future prospects there. A signal informing him that he had been awarded a
Military OBE provided only the most temporary comfort.[67] ISLD likewise
almost certainly realized that an intelligence officer of Reed's calibre and
experience was wasted in Slovenia, particularly when there was still
important work to be done elsewhere. They were perplexed by the manner
in which the Partisans had turned against the Western Allies and anxious to
discover how prevalent anti-Western sentiment really was among the
Yugoslav population as a whole. While such information would be difficult
to acquire in north-western regions, there was still ample scope for
intelligence gathering in Croatia, where relations with the Partisans
remained relatively cordial. Reed, with his past experience of working at
Croatian headquarters, was admirably qualified for such an assignment.[68]

Throughout January a combination of enemy air activity and blizzard
conditions prevented pick-up operations from Slovenia. On the 20th, for
example, the landing ground was bombed and strafed by a force of 11
aircraft.[69] What Reed described as 'the great snow' began at about this time
and continued until the 31st.[70] But a thaw started early in February, and
Partisan teams then cleared the remaining snow from the landing strip.

Peter Moore left the mission over land on the 3rd and Reed's replacement, Whitfield, arrived by parachute three days later.[71] Rather than following Moore, Reed decided to wait for air transport, which was duly scheduled for 10 February. That morning six Dakotas landed, and Reed made his way to the landing ground confidently anticipating his evacuation to Bari. Unfortunately, the melting snow had left the runway in such poor condition that only two of the six aircraft succeeded in taking off, the other four being grounded while efforts were made to improve the surface of the strip.[72] The next day Reed returned to the landing ground to find that three of the four Dakotas had already left; he was offered a place on the fourth, but after surveying the condition of the runway again he declined.[73]

Reed looked on from a distance as the Dakota began to taxi for take off. A combination of mud and ruts left by the other aircraft impeded its progress and the pilot realized too late that he had insufficient speed to gain altitude. At the last moment he made a forlorn attempt to pull the nose up, and the Dakota then climbed for a few seconds before stalling and plunging into a deep bank of snow at the end of the airstrip. The Partisan landing teams rushed to the crash site and miraculously succeeded in extricating all the passengers – mainly their own wounded – and the crew, while a thin plume of smoke rose gently from the wreckage. Then suddenly, as the last of the wounded was pulled clear of the stricken aircraft, it was engulfed by flames. 'There but for the grace of God', Reed wrote in his diary. 'Back to mission intensely exhausted.'[74] He was finally evacuated a week later. The Dakota routed over Croatia in clear weather, allowing him to spot such familiar locations as Plitvice, Otocac and Krbavsko Polje, but attracting the attention of German anti-aircraft units in the process. 'Too near the ack ack', Reed scribbled, 'but no harm done'. He landed near Bari at 9.50 that morning and reached ISLD's office an hour later.[75]

NOTES

1. Gilbert, *Churchill*, vol. 7, pp. 881–2, 981–2, 1083–6.
2. Wilkinson, *Foreign Fields*, p. 155.
3. Lindsay, *Beacons in the Night*, p. 194, quoting a contemporary report by Lieutenant-Colonel Peter Moore.
4. RP, Reed diary, 7 November 1944; Rogers, *Guerilla Surgeon*, p. 208; Lindsay, *Beacons in the Night*, p. 360.
5. Lindsay, *Beacons in the Night*, p. 39.
6. *Ibid.*, pp. 35–6.
7. RP, OR to PR, undated, postmarked 25 February 1945.
8. B. Pitt, *The Crucible of War: Year of Alamein, 1942* (London: Jonathan Cape, 1982), p. 267. Apart from leading mine-clearance during a number of operations in 1942, Moore also ran the Eighth Army School of Mine-Clearance near Burg el Arab.

9.   Maclean, *Eastern Approaches*, pp. 249, 251–2.

10. WO 202/513, report by Moore, compiled at HQ Croatia, 23 January 1944;
     WO 202/439, signal from Fungus, 30 December 1943; WO 202/439, signal
     from Fungus, 6 January 1944: 'Colonel Moore held up here by heavy snow';
     interview with Reed, 4 November 1989.

11. Rogers, *Guerilla Surgeon*, pp. 145, 176.

12. *Ibid.*, p. 207.

13. WO 202/276, report by Moore, 14 February 1945.

14. WO 202/513, report by Moore, compiled at HQ Croatia, 23 January 1944.

15. WO 202/212, No 1 I(U) Section, Bari, to Rear HQ 'M' Military Mission, 9
     October 1944.

16. WO 202/276, report on Operation Livingstone II by Major Darewski,
     RAOC, undated. Lindsay, *Beacons in the Night*, pp. 49, 99, 204. Gatoni's
     name is spelled Catoni and his rank is given as sergeant in Wilkinson, *Foreign
     Fields*, p. 197. He was initially placed under the command of Peter
     Wilkinson's mission, Clowder, but was later transferred to the command of
     the senior ISLD officer at Partisan headquarters, 4 Zone. Both Lindsay and
     the contemporary sources record the name Edward Parks, but his full name is
     shown in the Commonwealth War Graves Commission Debt of Honour
     Register as Albert Edward Park, wrongly described as an officer in the
     Intelligence Corps. Mathews is said by Lindsay to have worked for the
     strategic deception organization, 'A' Force, but is described as an ISLD officer
     in at least one official document; see WO 202/473, signal to Flotsam, 27
     January 1945. McNeff had previously worked at the SIS station on Gibraltar;
     see West, *MI6*, p. 230.

17. Lindsay, *Beacons in the Night*, pp. 178–84, 204, 327.

18. WO 202/520, report on a mission to Carinthia (Korosko), May to September
     1944, by Major C.H. Villiers, November 1944; Lindsay, *Beacons in the
     Night*, pp. 158–9; Wilkinson, *Foreign Fields*, p. 198.

19. Lindsay, *Beacons in the Night*, pp. 326, 361; WO 202/473, signal to Flotsam,
     27 January 1945. The Commonwealth War Graves Commission's Debt of
     Honour Register records that Parks died on 26 December 1944. He has no
     known grave, and is commemorated on the Cassino Memorial.

20. RP, Reed diary, 13–14 October 1944.

21. RP, Reed diary, 14, 15 and 19 October 1944; WO 202/477, signal from
     Flotsam, 15 and 19 October 1944.

22. Rogers, *Guerilla Surgeon*, p. 154.

23. RP, Reed diary, 16 November 1944.

24. See, for example, RP, Reed diary, 22, 24, 25 and 30 October 1944.

25. RP, Reed diary, 29 October 1944; WO 202/477, signal from Flotsam (Moore
     to James Millar at ISLD), 1 November 1944.

26. RP, Reed diary, 2 November 1944; WO 202/477, signal from Flotsam (Reed
     to James Millar at ISLD), 2 November 1944.

27. Rogers, *Guerilla Surgeon*, p. 208.

28. RP, OR to PR, 28 November 1944.

29. Rogers, *Guerilla Surgeon*, p. 205.

30. RP, OR to PR, undated, postmarked 25 February 1945.

31. RP, OR to PR, 19 December 1944; interview with Reed, 4 November 1989.

32. WO 202/276, report by Moore, 14 February 1945; Lindsay, *Beacons in the Night*, pp. 179–80.
33. RP, Reed diary, 5 November 1944; RP, OR to PR, 8 November 1944.
34. Lindsay, *Beacons in the Night*, pp. 213–14.
35. RP, Reed diary, 14 and 15 November 1944.
36. WO 202/477, signal from Flotsam, 21 November 1944.
37. WO 202/276, report by Moore, 14 February 1945; Lindsay, *Beacons in the Night*, pp. 213–14.
38. *Ibid.*, p. 183.
39. RP, Reed diary, 3–5 November 1944. The reports are mentioned in his diary throughout November and December. In December Reed wrote that 'for sheer office slog I have never had any job equal to this'. See RP, OR to PR, 19 December 1944; RP, Reed diary, 21 November 1944; WO 202/241, report by Moore, 14 December 1944; WO 202/276, report by Moore, 14 February 1945.
40. RP, OR to PR, undated, postmarked 25 February 1945.
41. WO 202/477, signal from Flotsam, 26 November 1944.
42. WO 202/241, report by Moore, 23 December 1944.
43. RP, Reed diary, 24–26 November 1944; WO 202/477, signal from Flotsam, 15 December 1944.
44. WO 202/241, report by Moore, 3 January 1945.
45. *Ibid.*
46. WO 202/477, signal from Flotsam, 11 January 1945.
47. *Ibid.*
48. *Ibid.*; WO 202/241, report by Moore, 3 January 1945.
49. WO 202/477, signal from Flotsam, 11 January 1945.
50. RP, Reed diary, 15 January 1945.
51. WO 202/477, signal from Flotsam, 10 and 14 January 1945.
52. RP, Reed diary, 11 and 14 January 1945.
53. WO 202/477, signal from Flotsam, 14 January 1945.
54. RP, Reed diary, 15 January 1945. Reed referred to 'the passport question' in his diary, although its precise significance is impossible to ascertain.
55. RP, Reed diary, 16 January 1945.
56. WO 202/477, signal from Flotsam, 14 January 1945.
57. WO 202/477, signal to Flotsam, 15 January 1945.
58. WO 202/477, signal from Flotsam, 16 January 1945.
59. WO 202/477, signal to Flotsam, 21 January 1945.
60. WO 202/477, signal from Flotsam, 3 February 1945.
61. WO 202/477, signal from Flotsam, 18 February 1945.
62. WO 202/477, signal from Flotsam, 8 December 1944; 21 January 1945.
63. WO 202/477, signal from Flotsam, 5 January 1945.
64. *Ibid.*
65. RP, Reed diary, 8 January 1945; interview with Reed, 4 November 1989.
66. RP, OR to PR, undated, postmarked 25 February 1945; WO 202/477, signal from Flotsam, 11 January 1945.
67. RP, OR to PR, 2 January 1945. The Military OBE was normally awarded to personnel serving at commands or headquarters who were not engaged in direct combat with the enemy. While this was arguably appropriate to Reed's role in Slovenia, it very obviously understated his earlier activities in Croatia,

as he himself almost certainly recognized. In conversation with the author in August 1998 Sir William Deakin expressed his surprise that Reed was not more highly decorated.

68. RP, OR to PR, undated, postmarked 25 February 1945.
69. RP, Reed diary, 20 January 1945.
70. RP, Reed diary, 19–31 January 1945.
71. RP, Reed diary, 3 and 6 February 1945.
72. RP, Reed diary, 10 February 1945.
73. RP, Reed diary, 11 February 1945.
74. *Ibid.*; interview with Reed, 4 November 1989.
75. RP, Reed diary, 18 February 1945.

9

The Last Battle

Reed remained in Italy for less than a month. A full medical examination revealed no serious ailments beyond extreme fatigue, so he was granted a week of complete rest, during which he did little but sleep.[1] He was billeted in a luxurious apartment which had formerly belonged to a wealthy fascist dignitary, and which had since been appropriated by his mistress, who had in turn offered it to ISLD.[2] Although glad of the opportunity to recuperate, Reed was impatient to return to Yugoslavia, despite the mounting tension between the Western Allies and the Partisans which had so seriously complicated his task in Istria and Slovenia.[3]

One of ISLD's priorities was, as we have seen, to learn more about the communist regime then establishing itself in Yugoslavia as German forces withdrew; they were particularly concerned about the deterioration of relations with Tito's followers, and the reasons that lay behind it. Since 1943 Reed had held a dual brief to supply intelligence on both the Germans and the Partisans, so it was perhaps inevitable that the focus of his activities should have shifted increasingly towards the latter as the War neared its end. A similar reorientation was taking place at the very highest levels of the SIS hierarchy. For intelligence on Germany SIS preferred to rely on signals intelligence, and made few efforts to infiltrate agents into the Third Reich from liberated territories. Instead, they turned their attention to Europe's post-war order, and a new Soviet section, Section IX, was established in anticipation of a prolonged struggle with the USSR over the government of central and eastern Europe.[4]

Nevertheless, ISLD's plans for Reed were also closely linked to the final phase of military operations against Germany. The Yugoslav capital, Belgrade, had been liberated the previous October and was by early 1945 the centre of Tito's new government. German forces had withdrawn from much of Serbia, and from parts of the coast. But they continued to occupy central and northern Croatia, including the Croatian capital, Zagreb. At the end of February the Supreme Allied Commander Mediterranean

(SACMED) met Tito in Belgrade and it was agreed that a large-scale offensive should be undertaken in Dalmatia by units of the Yugoslav 4th Army under General Drapsin, which comprised the former Partisan 8 Corps and 11 Corps. From an Allied perspective, the primary objective of the operation was to clear the Germans and the Ustase from the Gospic and Bihac areas and then to liberate the northern Dalmatian coast and the islands. SACMED promised that the Balkan Air Force would provide the maximum possible air support for the offensive and that Allied naval craft in the Adriatic would also co-operate to ensure the maintenance of ample supplies to the participating Yugoslav formations.[5] What ISLD apparently wanted was an officer at Partisan headquarters who could report on the progress of the offensive and on the Partisans' activities in liberated areas. Reed, with his abundance of experience in Croatia, was the perfect man for the job.

But Reed could hardly have been infiltrated back into Croatia with the openly declared intention of gathering intelligence on the Yugoslav communist movement; the Partisans would never have permitted him to operate with such a remit. His intelligence work had therefore to be coupled with some more acceptable function, such as that of liaison officer. Fortunately, or so it at first appeared, a perfect opening existed at his former base, GSH–General Staff Croatia. GSH had by this time abandoned the Croatian mountains and had relocated itself in liberated territory on the coast at the port of Zadar, which was being used to ship Allied supplies to the Partisans.[6] By March 1945 a small British staff, representing all three Armed Services, had been located at Zadar, and plans were afoot to establish a fully fledged military base there, partly to supervise the supply effort but principally to operate an airstrip at Zemunik, from which Balkan Air Force squadrons were to support the Partisan ground offensive.[7] A liaison officer was required to represent British military interests at Zadar to GSH.

Reed expected the task to be very different from his earlier assignment in Croatia. 'This time', he wrote on 3 March:

> I shall be living in a town, will move army style on wheels, and will arrive by boat. It will be the exact reverse of my Jug life hitherto, with a large staff, and a formidable prospect of smoothing the seamy relations between the Jugs and the Navy, Army, and RAF wallahs on my side.[8]

What he did not expect was that, at this final stage of hostilities in Yugoslavia, he would for the first time encounter determined bureaucratic obstruction from other British officers in the field.

The rivalry between SIS and SOE was described in some detail earlier in this book. Yet their various disputes seem largely to have been conducted at headquarters level; in the field, officers from the two organizations worked in relative harmony. Reed had certainly enjoyed the closest and most co-operative association with SOE officers such as Anthony Hunter when he first arrived in Croatia, and the metamorphosis of SOE into the more orthodox Military Mission during 1944 in no way undermined this relationship. The problems that arose in 1945 were complex, but they resulted primarily from the fact that GSH had been co-located with one of the Partisan army corps. After the departure of the previous British liaison officer (BLO) at GSH, the BLO at the corps headquarters, Major Crichton, had automatically assumed his role. This effectively made him the senior British representative in Croatia, to whom the BLOs at other corps headquarters were responsible. He was not at first ordered by his superiors to relinquish his position at GSH to Reed, and clearly took the strongest exception to any proposal that he should do so, not least because it would require him to subordinate himself to an officer of equal rank from an entirely separate organization.[9]

The Partisan offensive was scheduled to begin on 20 March. Operating under the new codename, 'Outlaw', Reed had embarked on his last journey to Yugoslavia four days earlier, when he and Ryan were flown from an airstrip near Bari to the Allied base on Vis, from where they were taken by boat to Zadar. There they were met by two of Crichton's staff, who had organized transportation to the British mission. They finally reached the mission at about 7 pm, but they were not welcomed with open arms. 'Called on Crichton, [who] gave me evasive and embarrassed reception', Reed wrote in his diary.[10] They arranged a meeting for the following day only for Crichton to find excuses not to attend. Reed was more successful in making contact with GSH, who were delighted to see him. 'I was kissed all over by commissars and generals', he recorded. 'Long heart-to-heart with [General] Gosnjak and [Commissar] Zigic. 'Whole thing so spontaneous that [I] emerge on top of the world, doing some fierce comparisons with Slovenia.' Bakaric and the Chief of Staff, Pavlovic, were no less hospitable.[11]

But Reed's euphoria proved short-lived, as the true difficulty of his position became clear. Although he had held the necessary authority from the Partisans to enter Croatia, this was apparently granted on the basis that he would assume the post of BLO at GSH. With another officer, Crichton, fulfilling this function, Reed's precise status and his authority to operate were cast into doubt. To make matters worse, he found himself dependent on Crichton to resolve the situation and it quickly became clear that he could not be trusted to do so. At first, ISLD suggested that Reed might fill some alternative post, but to this plan Crichton's reluctance to co-operate also emerged as an insuperable obstacle. As early as 22 March Reed sent an 'ultimatum to James [Millar]' insisting that he should either take over from Crichton at GSH or else leave Croatia.[12] Millar responded by suggesting that the two British liaison posts that had been combined under Crichton should be separated again so that one of them could be assigned to Reed, and he apparently indicated that Crichton would receive orders from his superiors to this effect. But when Reed confronted Crichton on the 24th he blithely claimed that he never received orders but instead wrote his own, that no orders had arrived from Military Mission headquarters to separate the two liaison posts, and that their separation was not, in any case, a practical proposition.[13]

The wrangling about Reed's accreditation continued for the next two weeks. The possibility that he might resume his old job at Fungus Mission (now located at Partisan 4th Corps headquarters) was discussed at this time, but the BLO there was no more amenable than Crichton to the prospect of working as Reed's subordinate, and neither Crichton nor Military Mission headquarters were prepared to force the issue.[14] Reed also suggested to Zigic that he might work as the British mission's political attaché, but the commissar was predictably unenthusiastic.[15] While the arguments continued Reed lived on his accumulated goodwill with GSH, occupying 'an expensive holiday villa with private bathing beach, wine cellar, Jeep and Riviera view and climate'[16] and promptly set about gathering such intelligence as he could about the areas under Partisan control. He found himself free to travel to nearby towns, notably the port of Split, to meet civilians and to discuss with them political developments since the German withdrawal.[17]

Although he witnessed some severe war damage, he found many towns and villages on the coast virtually unscathed.[18] Inevitably, perhaps, close contact with the populace was limited to citizens of some substance, who had by fair means or foul maintained a relatively normal existence during the occupation, and who were distinctly perturbed by the prospect of a communist take-over. They protested vociferously about the Partisans' authoritarianism and administrative incompetence, about the threats and intimidation they directed at anyone with British or American connections, and about inflation and rigged municipal elections. But such complaints were to be predicted from pro-Western members of the liberal intelligentsia, and Reed was careful not to accept them uncritically. 'Must get evidence', he wrote, 'to back up impressions and clarify my mind'.[19] Early in April he managed to reach Otocac, GSH's location in October 1943, when he was first dropped into Croatia, and found his old parachute canisters precisely where he had left them, on the steps at the back of the local brewery.[20] Conditions in the Lika district were far worse than on the coast, for the Germans and the Ustase had systematically destroyed Partisan towns and villages there. Overcrowding was rife, and food supplies had almost been exhausted during the winter.[21]

He soon abandoned any hope of monitoring the progress of the Partisans' March offensive. Indeed, it transpired that both the Military

Mission and ISLD had misunderstood GSH's role in this final phase of hostilities, for it played no part in directing the offensive but prepared instead for a final thrust northwards to drive any remaining hostile forces from Zagreb and the surrounding territory. By contrast, the March offensive, propelled triumphantly forward by Allied equipment, supplies and air support, avoided most of the remaining enemy formations in Croatia and Slovenia and executed a two-pronged thrust into Istria, outflanking the German 97th Army Corps at Fiume to the east, and crossing to the peninsula via the Adriatic islands to the west. It quickly became clear that its objective lay not so much in liberating German-occupied areas as in reinforcing Tito's territorial claims to Venezia Giulia and, especially, Trieste, by establishing a strong Partisan military and administrative presence there before the Allied armies arrived from northern Italy.[22] This so-called 'race for Trieste' and the ensuing confrontation over the city hammered the final nail into the coffin of British and American relations with the new Yugoslav regime, casting a menacing shadow over the last weeks of Reed's assignment.[23]

Reed's struggle for accreditation was finally resolved in mid-April. A number of factors worked in his favour. Firstly, it is clear that ISLD attached considerable importance to his presence in Croatia. Without one of their own operatives in the field they would have been unable to maintain a detailed intelligence picture of the impending liberation and of the imposition of communist government which would inevitably follow it. Byrd, the officer who had replaced him the previous July, was well overdue for relief, and as a captain lacked the rank necessary to represent British interests to the most senior Partisan authorities. Moreover, his experience lay purely in intelligence, whereas Reed had worked as a liaison officer with GSH in 1943 and 1944. No one was better qualified to fulfil a combined liaison and intelligence-gathering role and ISLD therefore decided to press the issue of his accreditation at the highest levels of the Military Mission's command chain to overcome Crichton's obdurate refusal to negotiate a *modus operandi*. They were assisted by a high-level ruling that ISLD officers should take over certain liaison posts from the Military Mission as the cessation of hostilities drew near.[24] The officers who had obstructed Reed's appointment were consequently overruled, withdrawn or re-assigned, and by the middle of the month he was once again functioning as the joint representative of ISLD and the British Military Mission at GSH. Fungus Mission was also placed under his command.[25] As before, he reported to ISLD on intelligence, and to the Military Mission on military liaison and supplies. Soon afterwards he learnt that he was to act as British consul in Croatia when the war with Germany ended, a post he would hold pending the establishment of more formal British consular machinery there.[26]

Reed left Zadar on 17 April and followed GSH north to Gospic.[27] The former German and Ustase stronghold, where hundreds of Serbs had been massacred, used, he wrote, 'to sit glowering at us from just over the horizon, a place of threats and doom'. Now it was just 'a featureless dusty little place with a few thin children and bewildered old women'.[28] On the 23rd they proceeded to Otocac.[29] While the Fourth Army's offensive thrust rapidly north-west, the formations under GSH's command now embarked on a very much more gradual advance northwards in the direction of Karlovac and, ultimately, Zagreb. Reed marvelled at how American and British equipment had transformed the ragged mountain fighters he had encountered in Croatia in 1943. 'The Partisans are now', he observed:

> doing tremendous things with tanks and guns which we have presented to them and which we've trained them to use. Side by side with the crack British-trained spearhead are black masses of old-fashioned guerrilla types who come swarming down from the mountains to join in the fun. The result is one of the oddest armies ever seen...half-way between the old fashioned free-for-all Partisan of a year ago who fights with his teeth if need be, and a well equipped, well dressed modern army, with black berets with stars on, Spitfires roaring over head.[30]

As soon as territory was liberated the Partisans established their own administrative machinery. By the end of April their wartime government of Croatia, Zavnoh, was being replaced by a more permanent body which was founded at the coastal town of Sibenik, in preparation for the move to Zagreb when enemy forces withdrew.[31] Since Reed's departure from Croatia at the end of June 1944 the nationalist sentiments of the former Croat leader, Hebrang, had incurred Tito's displeasure and he had been replaced by Bakaric.[32] Instead of remaining at Sibenik, Bakaric preferred to accompany GSH during their advance on the capital, and he proved happy to discuss with Reed the new government's plans, which were no doubt subsequently passed to ISLD.[33]

By the end of April the Partisans were preparing for their final offensive against Karlovac, which would open a route up the Una valley into southern Zagreb. 'Our hosts are having a good clean out of their weapons tonight in honour of tomorrow (1 May) when they'll really let fly with everything they've got', Reed recorded on the 30th.[34] But the situation in Croatia was by now completely overshadowed by events further to the north-west in Venezia Giulia, where both the Partisan Fourth Army and the British Eighth Army were converging from opposite directions on Trieste in what Reed described as 'a most enthralling race'. The impending confrontation loomed far larger in his dealings with GSH than Germany's imminent surrender, and he was forced to consider the implications for his mission and for the other Allied outposts in Yugoslavia if overt hostilities broke out between the two forces.[35] On 1 May, with the Eighth Army's New

Zealand Second Division still 20 miles to the west at Monfalcone, the leading units of the Fourth Army entered Trieste and made contact with Slovene Partisan groups within the city.[36] That day Reed discussed the crisis with his superior officer in the Military Mission, Colonel John Clark, who was on his way to Istria over land, but it was evidently agreed that the principal British missions should remain in place for the time being.[37]

During the next few days the two forces occupied Trieste, the Partisans set up a makeshift government there, and a tense stand-off began, which was to last for a month, while negotiations proceeded between Tito and the Western Allies to determine the city's future. With Clark's agreement, Reed now travelled by jeep to the other missions to appraise them of the situation, and to finalize plans for their withdrawal as soon as Germany surrendered.[38] His journey ultimately led him as far north as Fiume, where he found the Allied mission jointly located with a Partisan command post in a large hotel. There he spent a miserable evening listening to a veritable barrage of hysterical allegations and complaints: that the British had broken an agreement not to cross the Isonzo river, that they were already fighting communism and were ignoring residual German resistance, and that they were tolerating the activities of anti-communist resistance groups in Trieste.[39] 'They solve all their problems by a sort of two-foot rule', Reed observed with disgust:

> Anyone who has different notions from the official line is labelled 'reactionary' and anyone who tells them how wonderful they are (or Russia is) is labelled 'progressive'. Thus they group the whole world into friends or foes ... You can't criticize their motives [but] you often must criticize their intellectual honesty. If two and two have hitherto made four and the world has hitherto been a miserable failure, all right – in future two and two shall make five and the world will be a fit place to live in ... When I tell them that these are the mental processes of Goebbels and that the world will get nowhere till it can face hearing the truth, a pitying look comes over their faces – Ah these reactionary Britons! When will they learn?[40]

Like so many others, he was deeply troubled by a mounting suspicion that the innumerable hardships and sacrifices of the last six years had merely contributed to the victory of a political system that was barely less oppressive than national socialism. 'We've beaten the Germans', he wrote, 'but only to find the laborious gains of British civilization as isolated and threatened as they were at the time of Munich'.[41] It was thus with feelings of the most acute futility that he made his way back down the coast on the very final day of the Second World War in Europe.[42]

By the time he reached Otocac the war with Germany was effectively over. During the first week of May the remaining enemy units in the

Karlovac area had been routed, leaving southern Zagreb open. Although expected to mount a last-ditch defence of the city, the Ustase had no stomach left for fighting and fled north-west with the intention of surrendering to the Western Allies; on 7 May Pavelic ordered the Croatian capital to be declared an open city and then made his escape.[43] With many other members of his bloodthirsty regime he would in time find his way to relative safety in South America.[44] The German garrison withdrew to the hills north of Zagreb and then laid down their arms. Zagreb was duly liberated on 8 May by units of the Partisan Third Army and 10 Corps operating from the north of the city, and by the First and Second Armies advancing from the south and south-west.[45] That day Reed's mission moved from Otocac to Karlovac. 'We have been streaming along in the wake of the Partisan Army in our jeeps', he wrote.[46] The inhabitants of the area seemed divided in their response to the Partisans' victory, 'dazed and scowling [Croat] peasants contrasting with rapturous Serbs'. On his arrival he found a much-reduced populace and life everywhere at a standstill. 'The VE fervour misses Karlovac', he noted laconically.[47]

He received permission to proceed to Zagreb two days later, on 10 May, and arrived in the city at midday, just behind one of the other British missions. Temporary accommodation was found for him at the Hotel Dubrovnik, which until recently had been occupied by the Gestapo, but he promptly embarked on a search for more permanent quarters.[48] 'Our liberty of movement and private contacts is surprising', Reed signalled to ISLD. 'We have however had many warnings privately [that] members of staff [ought] to be careful as we are watched.'[49] By 14 May, four years after James Millar and Bill Stuart fled from Zagreb to evade the Germans, he had established a new British consulate in a suitably luxurious villa on a suburban hilltop, and a Union Jack had been hoisted up outside.[50] Most of the other British missions formerly located at Partisan corps headquarters in Croatia were now closed and withdrawn, but Reed inherited some of their staff. Hence a certain Captain Rowe, of the British mission with 10 Corps, became Reed's second-in-command.[51] From the consulate, with the assistance of the ever-faithful Ryan, Reed relayed any military and political intelligence he could acquire to ISLD. Many of his signals were also summarized into more general reports to the British ambassador in Belgrade.[52]

Anyone with the slightest reason to fear the Partisans made a beeline for him.[53] 'I am', he wrote:

> bearded and waylaid wherever I go by well-dressed civilian types who sweep off their hats with a grand gesture and tell me they have been protecting the interests of Great Britain here at immense personal risk for the last five years.

Particularly striking was the extraordinary atmosphere of prosperity left over from 1939. 'These people haven't had a war at all', Reed decided after a few days:

> The place has never been bombed or starving or hit by anything at all. To see the populace in fashioned stockings and Paris summer models watching the dusty sweating Partisans march around is a picture. Their faces are the most baffled study in snobbery, guilt, incredulity, resentment and pride that you could possibly imagine. None of them know what's coming to them in the next few days. You couldn't live here without collaborating to a certain extent, and you could [not] collaborate without someone else knowing it, so everyone's waiting to see if everyone else has told on them or not.[54]

As well as meeting many ordinary citizens of Zagreb, Reed made contact with other consular representatives there. The most remarkable was his French counterpart, André Gaillard, who had lived in the city since 1939, and who possessed a unique knowledge of the recently departed Ustase regime. Reed was baffled by the disappearance of Pavelic and his followers, and managed to obtain only 'an unbelievably vague and feeble' account of the liberation from General Gosnjak.[55] It was Gaillard who described how the Ustase government and military leadership had decided to abandon Zagreb without a fight. In fact he maintained that he himself had persuaded them to do so, urging them to surrender to the Western Allies, and his claims were in time corroborated by several other sources.[56]

As soon as Zagreb had been liberated, the communist propaganda machine swung into action. Massive portraits of Tito and Stalin appeared in all the main streets, and the city's newspapers were crammed with sickening adulation for Yugoslavia's new rulers.[57] The Partisans organized a series of enormous military parades and demonstrations, and largely ignored the city's civil administration. The reason, almost certainly, lay in Tito's desire to present a show of strength in a city where many inhabitants had collaborated with the Germans, and had displayed a marked preference for particularism rather than the federalism that separated the Partisans from all other political movements in wartime Yugoslavia. Zagreb's expansive squares amassed huge and enthusiastic crowds to order for these events, but Reed doubted the sincerity of their support for the new regime, suggesting that the proportion of citizens who welcomed the liberation was about equal to the proportion who felt uneasy about the Partisans' arrival.[58] Despite Tito's Croatian origins, many Croats clearly suspected that federalism was merely a front for Serb domination of the post-war Yugoslavia. The Partisans' uncertainty over their position in Zagreb was reflected in the arrangements they made for Tito to address the city's population. Reed recorded how Zagreb Radio summoned the populace to the huge Jelacic Square for the speech, only for Tito to deliver it from a window in Markov Square, which was much smaller and less accessible. 'This may have been a security measure or may have been designed to exclude all but a selected audience', he suggested.[59]

Representatives of the Western Allies were treated with open disdain on such occasions. At a demonstration on 11 May the platform was reserved for the most senior members of the Partisan hierarchy and for Russian liaison officers. 'Beside them', Reed noted, 'we are very much the poor relations and are quite obviously in a lower classification'. On the 13th he and his American colleagues were summoned at only ten minutes' notice to Pavelic's former mansion to attend a reception and a march past by the First Army. They arrived breathless in their battered uniforms and worn-out jeeps while their hosts and their Russian associates, immaculately attired in full-dress uniform, were triumphantly conveyed in gleaming Mercedes-Benz roadsters abandoned by the Germans only a few days before.[60] 'Triumphal procession to rostrum and two hours of misery at the salute', Reed noted in his diary. 'Slogans "Istria ours forever" [and] "The might of our army is the guarantee of the freedom of our fatherland." Rampant fascism.'[61]

Reed was always careful to report such intelligence as he could obtain about Partisan troop dispositions in and around Zagreb, although reliable information was scarce. It is clear that ISLD was greatly interested in the strength of Partisan formations there, not least because of the possibility that they might shortly be transferred to Venezia Giulia.[62] At least one specific deployment, involving the 4th Corps' 'departure from the Zagreb front to the Trieste area' is described in Reed's first report from the city.[63] But that day, while standing at the salute in full view of every senior Partisan officer in Zagreb, he committed to memory all the important details of the troops parading before him; his recollections were duly relayed to the British embassy in Belgrade, and doubtless also to ISLD:

> At the First Army march past a most formidable array of infantry, probably about one British Division in number, led the parade, consisting entirely of infantry companies armed with Russian tommy guns with an anti-tank rifle section (eight men, four rifles) with each company. Artillery consisted of two batteries of small anti-tank guns, 24 in number (about 37 mm) towed by semi-tracked lorries, 12 6-inch howitzers with similar traction, 12 75-mm anti-tank guns (all above Russian and all brand new), 12 American self-propelled guns on Sherman chassis and about 24 Russian medium tanks with 76-mm guns. However, as the personnel and material had obviously been specially chosen and armed for the occasion this standard should not be taken as representative of the army as a whole.[64]

While he was attending the parade a signal arrived via Military Mission headquarters declaring that all British military personnel were to be withdrawn immediately from Yugoslavia on the order of SACMED himself; only a few exceptions were listed, including the consul at Zagreb and his staff.[65] The British embassy was said to be seeking permission from Tito's government for him to be granted diplomatic status, which he would retain until his replacement by a permanent consul.[66] The cessation of hostilities with Germany naturally helps to explain the decision to withdraw the other mission personnel, but the continuing confrontation in Trieste was probably of equal significance. On the 16th, Britain and the USA issued a joint statement demanding from Tito the withdrawal of Yugoslav forces from the areas they had occupied in western Venezia Giulia, including Trieste. The American mission in Zagreb was closed on the direct order of the State Department in Washington the very same day, when a number of British officers and ORs were also evacuated from the nearby airstrip at Stupnik.[67] The crisis culminated in the orchestration of a deliberate Allied show of force. Facing the prospect of open hostilities with the vastly superior Western armies and lacking Soviet support, Tito finally capitulated and with the very greatest reluctance agreed to the creation of an Allied Military Government in the disputed territory.[68] For the few remaining British liaison officers this was a period of extreme tension.[69] The threat of all-out war over Trieste left them particularly vulnerable to retribution; all the principal Partisan authorities now became unco-operative and openly antagonistic towards Britain and the USA with the sole and very important exception of Dr Bakaric. Somehow, throughout the Trieste crisis, Reed maintained relatively cordial relations with the new Prime Minister of Croatia (whom he had known since October 1943), and even secured private audiences with him on at least two occasions.[70]

Reed found a range of consular duties awaiting him in Zagreb. About 50 American airmen,[71] a small number of British POWs, a steady trickle of Jews and a very few British citizens with Croatian connections were immediately brought to his attention. He was also compelled to represent the interests of about 150 French citizens after the Partisans initially refused to recognize Gaillard's consular status. Among the more extraordinary characters to emerge at this time was an elderly British subject, Herbert Tilstone Harrison, who had spent two years as a prisoner of the Gestapo and another two as the guest of the Swiss consul. There was also an escaped Indian POW, Ahmed, who had walked all the way from Berlin to Zagreb in four months with seven different permits, all in different names.[72] With the diminutive resources at Reed's disposal there was little that he could do for them except arrange for their evacuation by air. Certain Partisan officials deliberately impeded his efforts to obtain the necessary exit permits but after cultivating the friendship of the commandant at Stupnik airfield he usually managed to overcome their obstruction. On occasion, too, he persuaded Bakaric to intercede on his behalf. Otherwise he helped with the provision of food, clothing and accommodation for those who were compelled, for whatever reason, to remain in Zagreb.[73]

On 23 May the American mission was evacuated from Stupnik together with two former POWs and seven Jewish refugees. The British consulate was now left alone with the unenviable task of representing the interests of both Western Allies. Reed returned from the airfield that day 'to find Zagreb very lonely and hostile'.[74] Worse was to follow. On 26 May the decision was finally taken to evacuate all remaining British Military Mission personnel: the Military Mission to Yugoslavia itself was to close forthwith.[75] Reed arrived at the consulate to find the news awaiting him and immediately sought guidance on his own position. He was instructed that five of his staff were to be evacuated the very next day, but he himself was to remain in post for the time being with Paddy Ryan and just one other NCO. 'With such a skeleton staff we can clearly attempt only the bare necessities of efficiency', he reported.[76] But a second and more important problem now confronted him: the closure of the Military Mission blew his cover. Despite the best efforts of the British Embassy, Reed was never granted formal consular status. He retained his authority to operate purely from his position as a representative of the Military Mission and following its closure the Partisans immediately began asking him when he intended to leave. 'This is', he remarked dryly, 'a fair reflection of our welcome in Zagreb'.[77]

The closure of the Military Mission also unexpectedly denied him the supply and support infrastructure on which much of his consular work depended. After promising Gaillard on 28 May that he would evacuate the French POWs by air, Reed was informed by ISLD that the transport aircraft formerly at the disposal of the Military Mission were no longer available. This issue was all the more pressing because the number of refugees in Zagreb and the surrounding area was increasing steadily. Reed found that he had only to motor 50 miles in any direction to meet Poles, Czechs, French and even British and Americans who had been pressed into labour gangs by the Germans and were drifting without help of any kind from one place to another. 'We have not yet touched the fringe of the problem', he informed the ambassador on 4 June.[78] Fortunately, over the next few days, more formal bureaucratic machinery for the repatriation of POWs and displaced civilians was set up in Zagreb. Reed himself assisted in the establishment there of an office for the United Nations Relief and Rehabilitation Administration (UNRRA). Duane Wilson, the senior UNRRA representative at Zagreb, later described Reed as 'one of the cream of the British crop'.[79]

By this time the extreme delicacy of Reed's position was preventing him from openly seeking information on Partisan troop dispositions, and he could only guess at the rough whereabouts of the principal formations involved in the liberation of Zagreb. His continuing presence in the city nevertheless allowed him to obtain some valuable intelligence on their military potential. Hence regular visits to Stupnik airfield to organize air evacuations allowed him to witness the arrival of some 79 Yugoslav-manned Russian aircraft – 45 Stormoviks and 34 Yak fighters – and even to talk to their crews.[80] He was also on hand to describe the activities of the Partisan security service, OZNA, who conducted mass arrests and interrogations during the early weeks of the liberation in an effort to identify Ustase members and those who had collaborated with Pavelic's regime or the German forces of occupation. He personally found little evidence that detainees were physically mistreated, and most were apparently released after interrogation. But the experience was clearly intimidating. 'In general', he wrote, 'the psychological effect is the same as that created by the Gestapo and Ustase Secret Police'.[81]

More worrying were the indications that OZNA was rounding up citizens with British connections, a strategy which Reed immediately reported to ISLD and to the ambassador:

> Among Anglophiles arrested are Babic, Counsellor at the Jugoslav Embassy in London in 1939, Bozidar Strizic and Salik . . . Independent reports from two sources state they were arrested on denunciation by a previous Gestapo agent, now working for OZNA, by name Cuca Smokvina, wife of a radiologist at the Zagreb University Clinic. Details in my tel. Nr 12 of June 2nd to ISLD.[82]

OZNA also helped the new regime to establish itself more firmly in Zagreb by exploiting the inevitable cycle of denunciation and counter-denunciation that followed the liberation. In one instance Reed described how a certain Gustav Elmer, manager of the Swedish-owned Société Monopole des Allumettes and Swedish consular representative in Zagreb, was arrested after he was denounced by a former employee who had been dismissed and imprisoned by the Ustase for embezzlement. The denunciation alleged that Elmer had collaborated with the German authorities and the Ustase, and accused his enterprise of false accounting. All the allegations were, according to Reed's sources, entirely fictitious. Nevertheless, taking a favourable view of anyone incarcerated by the Ustase, the Partisans appointed Elmer's accuser commissar of the Monopole. 'The Partisan authorities are making all possible use of his information to obtain adequate pretext for putting the Monopole under Government control', Reed observed. 'For this they are very anxious to secure evidence of "bad management" and the denunciation of Elmer therefore suits their purpose.'[83]

Finally, he supplied information on OZNA's efforts to suppress political movements that had flourished in Croatia before the War, such as the Croat Peasants Party, who potentially represented a serious threat to the Partisans' consolidation of power. Another of their targets was the Catholic Church. Many prominent priests, including the Archbishop of Zagreb, Dr

Stepinac, had been openly supportive of the Ustase, and were promptly apprehended and interrogated. Reed subsequently managed to interview Abbot Marcone, the Apostolic Delegate of the Holy See at Zagreb, to obtain the Church's view of both the departed Ustase regime and the communist take-over. From the evidence available it appeared that Tito was not at first inclined to attack the Church head-on. In his report, Reed referred to Tito's 'respect for the Church's political power, which he is anxious to mobilize as a national (Yugoslav) force'.[84]

In summary, despite the innumerable obstacles arrayed against him, Reed managed to provide ISLD with a vivid description of many different aspects of the Partisan revolution in Croatia. His reports offered a remarkably detailed insight into their military capabilities and political strategies, and chronicled at length their efforts to manipulate Croatia's economic and cultural institutions to their own advantage. But, by the first week of June, his days in Zagreb were numbered. Since the closure of the Military Mission he could no longer claim the status of a military liaison officer and in any case his links with British intelligence were well known to the Partisans, who were apparently becoming increasingly suspicious of his activities, not without justification. Any residual goodwill he had enjoyed among Gosnjak's staff evaporated as the Trieste crisis reached its climax. On 2 June he was formally asked to leave by the Chief of Staff, Pavlovic.[85] He hung on for another four days, trying desperately to finalize arrangements for the evacuation of Gaillard's French POWs, but a peremptory order from Tito himself on 6 June decided the issue once and for all.[86] That night Reed and his NCOs loaded all essential equipment and supplies into two jeeps, bequeathing the remainder to UNRRA.[87] The next morning they duly set off for Belgrade leaving the Union Jack flying defiantly outside the consulate.[88]

Reed reached the British embassy in Belgrade the following day, and spent the next week briefing the ambassador and former senior officers from the now defunct Military Mission, such as John Clarke and Bill Deakin. On the 17th he left Yugoslavia for the last time and flew to Bari, before continuing over land to ISLD's Italian headquarters at Naples to brief his own senior officers on the Partisan take-over. They in turn sent him as 'the only up-to-date authority on Europe's darkest corner' to appraise military and intelligence staff in Trieste, Klagenfurt, Venice and Rome. 'I've got to pass judgement on things which are beyond me', he wrote on the 20th with typical modesty, 'and it keeps me awake at night wondering if my blundering attempts at honest analysis will be used to pave the way for the next war'.[89] In July he finally returned to Britain, where he spent a brief period describing his second and third missions in Yugoslavia to the SIS hierarchy. Among those who listened attentively to his story was an officer named Kim Philby, the notorious Soviet spy, who had recently been appointed head of SIS's new Soviet department.[90] SIS offered Reed a permanent position but he wisely declined, and was promptly posted to the Foreign Office, who seconded him to the BBC at Bush House. There, appropriately enough, he became temporary head of the Balkan Service. His subsequent move back into permanent employment with the BBC was little more than a formality.[91] A remarkable period in the life of a very straightforward and unassuming man was at an end. 'That chapter's closed', he concluded. 'It was interesting but it leaves very few illusions.'[92]

NOTES

1. RP, OR to PR, undated, postmarked 3 March 1945.
2. RP, OR to PR, 12 March 1945.
3. RP, OR to PR, undated, postmarked 3 March 1945.
4. West, *MI6*, p. 386.
5. AHB file IIJ1/130, The History of the Balkan Air Force, pp. 66–7.
6. RP, Reed diary, 17 March 1945; RP, OR to PR, 20 March 1945.
7. AHB file IIJ1/130, The History of the Balkan Air Force, pp. 67–8.
8. RP, OR to PR, undated, postmarked 3 March 1945.
9. RP, OR to PR, 8 April 1945.
10. RP, Reed diary, 16 March 1945.
11. RP, Reed diary, 17, 18 and 21 March 1945; RP, OR to PR, 20 March 1945.
12. RP, Reed diary, 22 March 1945.
13. RP, Reed diary, 24 March 1945.
14. *Ibid.*
15. RP, Reed diary, 1 April 1945.
16. RP, OR to PR, 20 March 1945.
17. RP, Reed diary, 18 and 19 March 1945.
18. RP, OR to PR, 20 March 1945.
19. RP, Reed diary, 18 and 19 March 1945.
20. RP, Reed diary, 11 April 1945; RP, OR to PR, 15 April 1945.
21. WO 204/9673, report by Captain Byrd, 15 April 1945.
22. Hinsley *et al.*, *British Intelligence in the Second World War*, vol. 3, pt 2 (London: HMSO, 1988), p. 740; Lindsay, *Beacons in the Night*, p. 296.
23. RP, OR to PR, 30 April 1945.
24. WO 202/445, signal to Fungus, 12 April 1945.
25. RP, Reed diary, 12–16 April 1945; WO 202/308, Rear Macmis to Outlaw, undated; WO 202/445, signal to Fungus, 17 April 1945.
26. RP, OR to PR, 15 April 1945.
27. RP, Reed diary, 17 April 1945; WO 202/446, signal to Fungus, 17 April 1945.
28. RP, OR to PR, 15 April 1945.
29. RP, Reed diary, 23 April 1945.
30. RP, OR to PR, 22 April 1945.
31. RP, Reed diary, 24 April 1945; WO 202/301, report by Reed, 14 May 1945.
32. Tanner, *Croatia*, pp. 164–5. Hebrang was summoned to Belgrade and appointed to a position in the Yugoslav government. In 1948 he was demoted and placed under house arrest; he died in custody.

33. RP, Reed diary, 27–8 April 1945.
34. RP, OR to PR, 30 April 1945.
35. *Ibid.*; RP, Reed diary, 30 April 1945.
36. Lindsay, *Beacons in the Night*, p. 298.
37. RP, Reed diary, 1 May 1945.
38. RP, Reed diary, 3, 5 and 6 May 1945.
39. RP, Reed diary, 6 May 1945.
40. OR to Esther Reed, undated, postmarked 6 May 1945.
41. RP, OR to PR, 20 June 1945.
42. RP, Reed diary, 7 May 1945.
43. WO 202/315, telegrams from Outlaw addressed to Major Magill, 37 Military Mission, 12 May 1945.
44. The true story of Pavelic's escape may be impossible to reconstruct on the basis of the surviving documents. According to some accounts, he and many of his followers left Croatia with millions of dollars in gold coin, which they used to bribe Allied forces and to meet the other costs of their escape. The Vatican has been accused of aiding and abetting their subsequent passage to South America. Pavelic lived for some years in Argentina but fled to Paraguay after an attempt on his life in 1957. He died in Spain two years later.
45. WO 202/315, telegrams from Outlaw addressed to Major Magill, 37 Military Mission, 12 May 1945; WO 202/301, report by Reed, 14 May 1945.
46. RP, OR to PR, 14 May 1945.
47. RP, Reed diary, 8 May 1945.
48. RP, Reed diary, 10 May 1945.
49. WO 202/315, telegrams from Outlaw addressed to Major Magill, 37 Military Mission, 12 May 1945.
50. RP, Reed diary, 14 May 1945; RP, OR to PR, 14 May 1945.
51. RP, report by Reed to the ambassador, Belgrade, 29 May. Other 10 Corps mission personnel were evacuated.
52. Only a few of Reed's ISLD signals from this period have found their way into the National Archives; see WO 202/315, summary of telegrams from Outlaw addressed to Major Magill, 37 Military Mission, 12 May 1945. However, others are referred to in Reed's reports to the British ambassador in Belgrade, one of which may be consulted in WO 202/301. The other four reports have been preserved among Reed's private papers.
53. RP, Reed diary, 10 May 1945.
54. RP, OR to PR, 14 May 1945.
55. WO 202/301, report by Reed, 14 May 1945; RP, Reed diary, 10–11 May 1945.
56. RP, report by Reed to the ambassador, Belgrade, 29 May 1945.
57. RP, OR to PR, 20 June 1945.
58. RP, Reed diary, 11 May 1945; WO 202/301, report by Reed, 14 May 1945.
59. RP, report by Reed to the ambassador, Belgrade, 29 May 1945.
60. WO 202/301, report by Reed, 14 May 1945; RP, OR to PR, 14 May 1945.
61. RP, Reed diary, 13 May 1945.
62. Interview with Reed, 4 November 1989.
63. WO 202/301, report by Reed, 14 May 1945.
64. *Ibid.*

65. WO 202/445, signal to Fungus, 13 May 1945.
66. AIR 23/8138, signal to Freedom, 13 May 1945.
67. RP, Reed diary, 16 May 1945; RP, report by Reed to the ambassador, Belgrade, 29 May 1945.
68. Whittam, *Drawing the Line*, pp. 368–70; Lindsay, *Beacons in the Night*, pp. 309–11.
69. RP, Reed diary, 19–22 May 1945.
70. WO 202/301, report by Reed, 14 May 1945; RP, report by Reed to the ambassador, Belgrade, 29 May 1945; RP, Reed diary, 14 and 21 May 1945.
71. Until his withdrawal, the American liaison officer in Zagreb was responsible for all American citizens there, but it had been agreed that Reed should handle all air transport matters, and he therefore arranged for their evacuation.
72. RP, report by Reed to the ambassador, Belgrade, 29 May 1945; RP, Reed diary, 24 May 1945.
73. WO 202/301, report by Reed, 14 May 1945; RP, report by Reed to the ambassador, Belgrade, 29 May 1945.
74. RP, Reed diary, 23 May 1945.
75. RP, Reed diary, 26 May 1945.
76. RP, report by Reed to the ambassador, Belgrade, 29 May 1945.
77. *Ibid.*
78. RP, supplementary report, 4 June 1945.
79. *Ibid.*; RP, report by Reed to the ambassador, Belgrade, 29 May 1945; Duane Wilson to Reed, undated, but sent from the UNRRA office in Zagreb to the British Military Mission, Belgrade, June 1945.
80. RP, Reed diary, 27 May 1945; RP, report by Reed to the ambassador, Belgrade, 29 May 1945.
81. RP, supplementary report, 4 June 1945.
82. *Ibid.*
83. RP, report on the arrest of consular representative of Sweden, 4 June 1945.
84. RP, supplementary report, 4 June 1945; report on interview with Abbot Marcone, Apostolic Delegate of the Holy See at Zagreb, 2 June 1945. Stepinac was in fact tried for war crimes in Yugoslavia in 1946 and sentenced to life imprisonment.
85. RP, Reed diary, 2 June 1945.
86. RP, Reed diary, 6 June 1945; RP, OR to PR, 17 June 1945; RP, supplementary report, 4 June 1945.
87. RP, Reed diary, 6–7 June 1945; RP, Duane Wilson to Reed, undated, sent from the UNRRA office in Zagreb to the British Military Mission, Belgrade, June 1945.
88. RP, Reed diary, 7 June 1945.
89. RP, OR to PR, 20 June 1945.
90. Interview with Reed, 4 November 1989; the appointment with Philby is recorded in Reed's diary.
91. RP, Reed interviewed by J. Lane, 'Oral History of the BBC'.
92. RP, OR to PR, 17 June 1945.

10

Conclusion:
From Judge to Outlaw

Interviewed many years later for the BBC's 'Oral History', Owen Reed was asked for details of his wartime service in Yugoslavia. In response he rather guardedly described how he found himself working for one of the various Allied organizations that were penetrating occupied Europe. 'SOE was the best known', he went on. 'This was a less well known but more classic organization.'[1] It was in fact SIS. At the beginning of this book I referred to the absence of serious research on SIS operations in the Second World War. The few general histories of the Service have largely concerned its higher direction and top-level interaction with other organizations – notably SOE – and research on field agents working in enemy-occupied territory has almost exclusively been confined to SOE. Approaching SIS from the field officer's perspective, this account has thus sought to map territory that has hitherto been largely unexplored in an effort to reappraise their wartime history in general, and their activities in Yugoslavia in particular. Such broader historical questions as emerge from Owen Reed's experiences must now be considered. But first it is necessary to summarize the salient features of his story.

Owen Reed was an actor and broadcaster, who joined the Army in 1940 with the intention of serving in the Royal Armoured Corps. He was quickly recommended for a commission and then received such standard training as the RAC offered to their subalterns. But thereafter his war obstinately refused to follow what might be termed a conventional course. Immediately after his embarkation for the Middle East his appointment as ship's broadcaster unexpectedly returned him to his peacetime profession and in the process brought him to the attention of his brigade's commanding officer, Brigadier Kenchington. Soon afterwards Kenchington attached Reed to his staff. In Egypt Reed remained with the brigadier's staff as a liaison officer, an assignment which may well have saved him from death or injury at El Alamein. But having emerged from the battle unscathed, he fell victim to jaundice, and more than six months passed before he was declared fully fit again. Promoted captain, he worked for the BBC in Cairo for much of the intervening period, juggling news broadcasts with Arabic programmes and office administration, and becoming ever more frustrated about his growing separation from the War. By the time he had fully recovered, hostilities in north Africa had ceased, and there seemed little prospect of returning to regular military service. But repeated visits to GHQ finally opened the door to SIS (masquerading under the name of 'Inter-Services Liaison Department'), who were recruiting field officers for infiltration into Yugoslavia.

SIS operations in Yugoslavia during the Second World War may conveniently be divided into three phases. During the first phase – from the outbreak of war to the German occupation in April 1941 – SIS worked through the British Embassy in Belgrade and through consulates in Zagreb, Split and elsewhere. James Millar, Bill Stuart and their colleagues operated under diplomatic cover, and recruited agents among British Council lecturers and members of the British and Commonwealth business community. In the second phase – from April 1941 to early 1943 – SIS collaborated with the Yugoslav government-in-exile and worked through royalist Yugoslav officers who had escaped at the time of the occupation. They also enlarged their intelligence picture by exploiting their privileged access to signals intelligence. Finally – from the spring of 1943 – they began to deploy British officers like Stuart, Syers, Cooke and Reed, and Yugoslav émigrés like Leonard into the field. Field operatives were thereafter central to SIS's wartime intelligence-gathering activities in Yugoslavia.

In July 1943 Reed had little knowledge of Yugoslavia and spoke no Serbo-Croat, but he could offer SIS his experience in the collection of information, a proven ability to work alone in remote territory, a basic knowledge of military staff work, and at least some evidence of linguistic aptitude. Apparently this was enough. Following his recruitment he received a training that can only have been rudimentary – a broad introduction to intelligence gathering, assessment and presentation, Allied strategy, languages and codes, and aircraft pick-ups – and was then despatched to Croatia with a radio operator and an interpreter. He spent his first month with the Partisans under virtual house arrest and was then abandoned by the head of the British mission, Anthony Hunter; in January his interpreter joined the Partisans. But despite this inauspicious beginning, his first mission to Croatia was unquestionably the most successful of his three SIS assignments.

Promoted local major, Reed headed the British mission in Croatia until the end of June 1944, representing both SIS as Judge and SOE as Fungus, often working in close proximity to the enemy and regularly enduring bombing and strafing attacks by the Luftwaffe. Through his Partisan hosts he obtained a steady supply of intelligence, which he passed to SIS. While the value of this information no doubt varied, the surviving documents do at least demonstrate a direct link between specific signals and subsequent Allied military actions, particularly in the days that followed the German attack on Tito's headquarters at Drvar. At the same time he arranged for the delivery of increasing quantities of supplies to the Partisans and eventually succeeded in organizing landing grounds where Dakotas could both deposit stores and evacuate vulnerable personnel – wounded, orphans, escaped POWs and downed airmen – to the safety of Allied-occupied territory. His mission also acted as a vital staging post for SOE, SIS and other Allied officers transiting through Croatia. These officers afterwards returned to friendly territory with their own intelligence appreciations, some of which were scrutinized at the uppermost levels of British government.

Reed was flown back to London in July 1944 to report on the Partisans' territorial ambitions in Venezia Giulia, and was duly debriefed by SIS. It was decided that he should next be despatched to Istria but when he arrived there at the beginning of September he found operational conditions very different from those he had known in Croatia. Numerous Allied covert organizations – the British Military Mission, LRDG, SBS and OSS – were working without proper co-ordination on or near the peninsula, and relations with the Partisans had deteriorated sharply. With the end of the War very obviously approaching, political differences between Tito and the Western Allies were assuming a more prominent role in their association than any common interest in Germany's defeat. Within two weeks Reed's mission had effectively been closed down; his two Slovene radio operators then disappeared in deeply suspicious circumstances. He remained in Istria until October in the hope of regaining the Partisans' confidence, but his efforts came to nothing and SIS eventually transferred him to Slovenia.

In Slovenia Reed was at least able to resume his task of intelligence gathering, but continuing difficulties with the Partisans severely inhibited his activities. His sources of information were largely confined to their intelligence handouts, which were only sometimes of value and which were difficult, if not impossible, to verify. His movements were closely monitored, and he was denied direct contact with ordinary Slovenes. In dealings with the vehemently anti-Western Partisan leadership he found himself engaged in an almost constant struggle against suspicion, prevarication and outright obstruction. At best his repeated protests achieved but a slight improvement in the performance of the Partisan intelligence staff. Early in 1945 he became embroiled in a futile attempt to secure the evacuation of two German prisoners to Italy: although they both possessed information that might have been of considerable value to the Western Allies, the Partisans obdurately refused to release them. Their unwillingness to co-operate persuaded SIS that his presence in Slovenia was pointless and, as important work had still to be done elsewhere, he was withdrawn to Italy.

Reed's last assignment brought him back to Croatia under the codename Outlaw. After an unexpected struggle with some of the other British officers there, he was once again appointed to represent both SIS and the Military Mission. During the closing weeks of the war he followed the Partisans' triumphant final march on Zagreb, entering the city only shortly after it was liberated and establishing himself on the Foreign Office's behalf as the British Consul. In this capacity he combined his consular activities with intelligence gathering, providing SIS with a remarkably vivid insight into the communist take-over in Croatia. But his freedom of action was progressively reduced, as the Trieste confrontation came to dominate the already troubled relationship between the Western Allies and the Partisans, and he was finally ordered out of Yugoslavia at the beginning of June. Having been one of the first SIS officers to arrive in Yugoslavia, he was also one of the very last British officers to leave. He never went back.

One fundamental fact emerges from Reed's story. Notwithstanding the somewhat negative judgements of the official historians,[2] SIS *did* play a part in British intelligence-gathering activities in wartime Yugoslavia. Indeed, they assumed quite an aggressive posture there. Before the German occupation they were extremely active in both the capital and other key cities; from Zagreb they extended their influence from Croatia into Slovenia and Austria. And they showed considerable ingenuity in re-establishing their presence in the following year. By the summer of 1943 SIS had contacts in parts of Yugoslavia where SOE was barely represented. It is true that SOE reached the Croatian Partisans before SIS; but SIS had other contacts in Croatia. And in November 1943 SOE effectively relinquished their position at Partisan headquarters Croatia when Anthony Hunter was withdrawn, leaving Reed to run the British mission until July 1944.

The tendency to underestimate SIS's role in Yugoslavia, which is not confined to the official history, stems partly from their steadfast refusal to release any records into the public domain, and partly from a widespread misunderstanding of the manner in which they operated. Hence it is assumed that they were not active in Yugoslavia because of their failure to despatch British officers into the field after the German occupation. In fact, with signals intelligence and a varied network of Yugoslav agents at their disposal in this period, there was no obvious reason for SIS to infiltrate British officers as well. That need only arose at the beginning of 1943 because British field agents were required to lend additional authority to SIS intelligence reports in London. Thereafter, SIS attached British officers to most of the main Partisan formations with the exception of Slovene headquarters, where Leonard's Yugoslav team appears to have functioned very successfully until Reed relieved them in October 1944. SIS operatives like Dan Gatoni, Mervyn Whitfield and Edward Parks, also operated on Slovenia's frontier with Austria. And shortly before VE Day, as we have seen, SIS took over liaison posts from the British Military Mission in provincial capitals like Zagreb and Ljubljana. In short, SIS were deeply involved in events in Yugoslavia for the duration of the Second World War.

Beyond the official history SIS's association with Yugoslavia has been acknowledged by a small group of authors whose principal aim has been to challenge the entire basis of British policy towards the resistance movements of Tito and Mihailovic. Their view is essentially that Britain should have continued its early support for Mihailovic instead of abandoning him in favour of the Partisans. They argue that the British secret organizations – SIS and SOE – had been extensively penetrated by left-wingers, who manipulated intelligence from the field to exaggerate the Partisans' military achievements and falsely accuse Mihailovic of inactivity or outright collaboration with the enemy. British backing was duly transferred to Tito, ensuring the communist take-over at the end of the War.[3]

Does Owen Reed's story lend any substance to these allegations? Clearly, SIS were penetrated by communists like Kim Philby during the 1930s and 1940s, but there is no obvious indication in the surviving documents to suggest that communist agents influenced SIS policy in Yugoslavia. SIS did not favour the Partisans from the outset and worked closely with the Chetniks and other Yugoslav political organizations in 1942 and early 1943. And, despite growing doubts about Britain's support for the Chetniks, they did not suppress intelligence that was critical of the Partisans. Their conviction that the Partisans represented by far the most active resistance movement in Yugoslavia was based not on political prejudice but on their reading of what they termed 'most secret' sources – that is, Enigma and other decrypts. The contents of many of these decrypts have been published in the official history of British wartime intelligence, and they disclose abundant evidence from German sources to sustain SIS's assessments of the two Yugoslav resistance movements. By the beginning of 1943 the Partisans were more numerous, more active, and geographically more widespread than the Chetniks, and were holding down more enemy troops. The Chetniks were largely confined to Old Serbia and Montenegro and were collaborating with the Italians against the Partisans.

Reed's personal experiences shed some light on SIS's politics. He was not himself a political man, and politics played no part in his recruitment into the Service or in such training as he received before his infiltration into Croatia. He found SIS divided in their political affiliations. But the more overtly left-wing staff, such as James Millar, did not attempt to influence his reports in a manner favourable to the Partisans; on the contrary, they were often sceptical about the accuracy of Partisan intelligence. The story of Stump Gibbon's evacuation must also cast doubt on the accusations of political bias that have been levelled against Millar and his team. As soon as Gibbon reached Bari, and despite his strident denunciation of the Slovene Partisans, Millar arranged for his return to London where, as a direct result, his critique of Tito's movement reached a number of senior officials in SIS, SOE and the Foreign Office.

The accusation of political bias is thus unproven. But there are grounds for questioning whether SIS were in any case sufficiently powerful to exercise undue influence on British policy towards wartime Yugoslavia. Their intelligence failed to persuade Churchill's government to reconsider Britain's sponsorship of Mihailovic at the beginning of 1943, and the debate only slowly began to favour the Partisans thereafter. SIS's most important intervention came neither in the field nor in Cairo, but in London, where Menzies passed an increasing number of Enigma decrypts on Yugoslavia to Churchill in the spring and summer of 1943. Otherwise, the documents demonstrate with the utmost clarity that the Allies' growing interest in Tito and the Partisans resulted directly from their decision to invade Italy; it is therefore legitimate to argue that considerations of grand strategy played a more important part in reorienting British policy than intelligence assessments of the strength of either Yugoslav resistance movement. Nor do the surviving records suggest that SIS played more than a partial role in the events which culminated in Churchill's final decision to abandon Mihailovic; they were clearly involved, but their contribution was not of fundamental significance. The field agents deployed to Slovenia, Bosnia and Croatia during the second half of 1943 could inevitably do little more than confirm the conclusions that SIS had already drawn from signals intelligence. Moreover, their reports feature far less prominently in the available files than the powerful and persuasive memoranda prepared by SOE officers like Churchill's former research assistant, Bill Deakin, and his personal envoy, Fitzroy Maclean.[4] It was Maclean who recommended decisively that support for Mihailovic should be discontinued, and that the trickle of Allied aid then reaching Yugoslavia should be concentrated exclusively on the Partisans.[5]

One consistent theme in the broader historiography of British covert operations during the Second World War is the rivalry that existed between SIS and SOE, and the friction that punctuated their co-existence was in abundant evidence in the Yugoslav theatre. The Special Operations Executive was primarily created as a separate department from SIS for political rather than military reasons.[6] In theory, the responsibilities of the two organizations were separate and quite clearly defined; in reality, SOE agents inevitably found themselves in a position to acquire valuable intelligence, which they quite properly relayed to their senior officers. This inevitably brought SOE into conflict with SIS, who were formally charged with the intelligence-gathering role.[7] There is no need to dwell further on the fundamental disagreements that emerged between them in the evaluation and interpretation of intelligence on Yugoslavia's resistance movements, or on their various disputes over the allocation of vital resources, notably air transport.

Yet there was clearly more to the SIS–SOE relationship than incessant inter-departmental strife. Indeed, their disagreements over Yugoslavia seem largely to have been confined to headquarters staff and were inextricably linked to the determination of certain SOE executives in Cairo to maintain

British support for Mihailovic. Following Maclean's arrival, however, these officers were replaced, SOE's Middle East organization was subordinated to GHQ Cairo, and British support was transferred to the Partisans.[8] The surviving records contain far less evidence of friction between SIS and SOE thereafter. In marked contrast, SIS and SOE operatives in the field enjoyed an association that was for the most part harmonious, co-operative and productive. Almost as soon as the two organizations established a presence in the Mediterranean theatre they began to deploy joint missions into enemy territory, SIS dealing with the intelligence responsibilities of these missions and SOE concentrating on operational matters. By the summer of 1942 the British mission with Mihailovic and the Chetniks was functioning in this way, although SOE also submitted their own intelligence reports. And the first British mission despatched to Tito's headquarters was, of course, a joint SIS–SOE mission. Reed was sent to Croatia purely to assist with intelligence duties, under the local command of an SOE officer. Soon afterwards he found himself representing both organizations, and working closely with SOE agents passing through his mission. As SOE's operation in Yugoslavia was transformed into the more orthodox Military Mission, the majority of Allied units with the Partisans were organized in collaboration with SIS along joint lines.

This study has demonstrated that from the very beginning of the Second World War SIS made a considerable commitment to intelligence gathering in Yugoslavia. It is difficult to measure the precise impact or value of the information they obtained there, but some such assessment must nevertheless be attempted. One official account, a history of the Balkan Air Force, records:

> The section of ISLD that dealt with Yugoslavia (No. 1 Intelligence Unit) came to Bari towards the end of 1943 and immediately started to furnish reports from their representatives in Yugoslavia. They supplied much useful intelligence, especially in such matters as road and rail communications, enemy supply problems, results of air attacks etc.[9]

In general, it would appear that the information obtained by SIS field operatives did make a valuable contribution to the construction of a broader Allied intelligence picture assembled from a variety of sources, including signals intelligence, SOE reports and aerial reconnaissance.[10] More specifically, the targeting and battle damage assessment information they supplied helped to sustain Allied air support for the Partisans, enabling them to withstand repeated attacks by the Germans, who were thus compelled to garrison Yugoslavia with forces that were desperately needed elsewhere. For the Western Allies, the *raison d'être* for backing the Partisans lay in their capacity to tie down very large numbers of enemy troops.

It nevertheless seems that SIS conceived their task far more broadly than this, and the Service's performance as an intelligence agency must be considered accordingly. Reed was despatched in October 1943 with a remit to supply intelligence on both the Germans *and* the Partisans. This did not necessarily mean that SIS was spying on Tito's followers. Initially their thirst for knowledge merely reflected the paucity of reliable information on domestic conditions in Yugoslavia. What SIS wanted more than anything in 1943 was a presence at the main Partisan headquarters – 'our man in Yugoslavia' – capable of confirming or denying existing preconceptions of the Partisan movement and of assisting in the evaluation of intelligence supplied from other sources. However it was achieved, the collection of such information was a legitimate part of the British war effort against Germany, especially given Churchill's interest in staging a landing on the Adriatic coast, and his government's decision to support the Partisans with weapons, ammunition and other supplies.

But in time, and in the context of Europe's impending division into rival communist and capitalist blocs, SIS began to see communist organizations as intelligence targets in their own right. The establishment of a communist government in Yugoslavia appeared to represent a dangerous expansion of Soviet influence into south-eastern Europe, and the Partisans' desire to annex Venezia Giulia suggested that the threat might even spill over into northern Italy, where there was also a strong communist guerrilla movement. By mid-1944 SIS were thus, in a sense, enjoying the best of both worlds. By attaching their officers to left-wing resistance movements in both Yugoslavia and Italy they could acquire valuable military intelligence on German dispositions and simultaneously monitor the development of European communism. Within the space of a few weeks in May–June Reed had helped to guide Allied bombers on to German targets in Croatia and Bosnia *and* submitted a detailed report to SIS on Partisan territorial claims on the Italian frontier.

This happy situation was never likely to endure for very long. SIS had of course been penetrated by Soviet agents, and it may well be that communist leaders like Tito were warned from Moscow that the SIS officers attached to their units held a dual brief. Or the Partisans may have grown suspicious of their own accord. Whatever the truth is, SIS began to encounter mounting difficulties in their dealings with Tito and his followers in the later months of 1944. They were prevented from operating at all in particularly sensitive locations, such as Vis and Istria, and elsewhere the activities of their operatives were closely monitored, obstructed, or frustrated altogether. Similar problems arose in other eastern European countries, such as Bulgaria and Romania.[11] This turn of events gave SIS every reason to anticipate that under Soviet direction the Partisans' antagonism towards the West might ultimately assume the proportions of outright hostility. In such circumstances it appeared all the more important to maintain their presence in Yugoslavia, and to observe the communist take-over there.

By the time of Reed's final mission, SIS were already on a Cold War footing, a reorientation reflected in the establishment of the new Soviet department at their London headquarters. The transition was not difficult to effect, for SIS had directed their activities towards the Soviet Union for much of the 1920s and 1930s; in 1945 they merely sought to resume their inter-war posture. Reed was personally less enthusiastic about the prospect of his reports being used, in his words, 'to pave the way for the next war', but he did as he was told. There was still, in fact, a limited amount of operational information to be acquired on German and Ustase dispositions in Croatia when he arrived there in March, but not enough to justify his deployment. The truth is that he was primarily sent to gather intelligence about the new political regime, operating under the cover of the British Military Mission, whom he represented as a liaison officer. And in this capacity his contribution to Western intelligence was unique. In May 1945 he represented virtually the only official British source of information on the triumph of communism in Croatia.

The operational lessons that might be gleaned from SIS's experiences in wartime Yugoslavia are indeed myriad. In planning their Yugoslav operations, SIS failed to establish a rational command and control structure incorporating a clear demarcation of responsibilities between London and Cairo. Before the German occupation, SIS activities in Yugoslavia were directed from London and, in its aftermath, the Broadway headquarters proved reluctant to cede full jurisdiction to Cuthbert Bowlby at ISLD. The strength of Broadway's position was enhanced by the presence in Britain of the Yugoslav government-in-exile, which maintained many useful contacts inside occupied territory. Consequently, on occasion, both Broadway and ISLD dealt directly and independently with James Millar's Yugoslav operations section; new initiatives were launched from both London and Cairo, and the two headquarters periodically found themselves at loggerheads over operational policy. On Yugoslavia SIS spoke with two voices and periodically delivered very different messages.

The availability of thoroughly trained and highly motivated personnel is central to the success of any military enterprise, but fundamental to the specialized and unconventional activities of clandestine organizations such as SIS. Before the Second World War SIS rarely took the risk of deploying British agents into hostile territory.[12] After the disintegration of their European networks during the first ten months of the War, the loss of Section D deprived them of the few agents who they had prepared for infiltration into occupied countries and most of those with the requisite skills or inclinations were subsequently recruited into SOE. The consequences for SIS were particularly well reflected in their Yugoslav operations section. While Bill Hudson, formerly of Section D, was spearheading SOE's efforts to re-establish a presence inside Yugoslavia, the SIS Yugoslav desk in Cairo was being staffed by junior and middle-ranking diplomats or former English lecturers – the 'very unmilitary and unregimental' contingent described by Reed in the summer of 1943. Quite apart from their manifest unsuitability for covert military work, they were also largely devoid of essential linguistic expertise; there were no British Slovene speakers at all, despite Slovenia's location on the southern frontier of the Third Reich.

Lacking British officers with appropriate experience or qualifications, SIS were left with no option but to rely heavily on their access to signals intelligence. However, in competition with SOE, who deployed British officers into the field, they found themselves at a distinct disadvantage, and their experience with foreign personnel was far from entirely satisfactory. Yugoslav émigrés may not necessarily have been predisposed to favour one resistance movement or the other in their intelligence reports, but there must always have been a suspicion that they lacked objectivity. And the recruits from the Jewish Agency very obviously pursued their own agenda in Yugoslavia, although fortunately they shared some of SIS's basic objectives.[13] The same cannot be said for the former Austrian POW known as 'Black', who betrayed SIS, SOE and the Partisans in Slovenia at the first available opportunity.

Apart from personnel, the two most important components in SIS's Yugoslav missions were air transport and communications. A chronic shortage of long-range transport aircraft in Egypt during 1941 and 1942 severely restricted the scope for infiltrating agents into southern Europe, while competition between SIS and SOE for the few available transport sorties exacerbated their mutual antipathy. The only practicable alternative was to locate radio sets with resistance organizations and political groups inside occupied territory. The position improved gradually during 1943; but in October SIS could still reason that it was preferable to send Reed's party to Croatia without the required Partisan authorization than to sacrifice a valuable Liberator sortie.

With agents deployed in the field, the role of air and radio communications became even more vital. Any expectations SIS harboured of maintaining contact with their field officers by sea evaporated after the Germans occupied the Dalmatian coast at the end of 1943, but for many months the prospects for using air transport instead were limited by poor weather: there were very few supply drops or aircraft pick-ups between October 1943 and March 1944. Reed found himself confronted by the daunting task of encoding all his intelligence reports so that they could be despatched by radio. As the weather cleared in the spring the number of supply drops increased steadily, so that SIS could at least despatch material to their agents more easily. But the field officers themselves remained critically dependent on radio until June, when the first regular Dakota landings began. From then on, air transport was central to all Allied activities in Yugoslavia until the end of the war in Europe, only partially being displaced by shipping in the early months of 1945.

A more effective command and control, recruitment and training, and transport and communications infrastructure might thus have facilitated SIS's task. But one other factor also exerted a fundamental influence on the success or failure of their missions – the field officer's ability to establish cordial working arrangements with his hosts. Throughout the War SIS displayed an aversion to despatching agents 'blind' into enemy territory. In the absence of diplomatic or commercial cover for their operatives, they had no option but to work through indigenous resistance groups like the Partisans, so that nothing was more important than the maintenance of their whole-hearted and enthusiastic co-operation. After a bad start, for which he was not to blame, Reed forged an amicable and lasting bond with the Croatian Partisans based on consummate tact and diplomacy and an acute awareness of local sensitivities; he was scrupulous in his observance of protocol and seized every available opportunity to generate goodwill. In so doing he secured numerous tangible operational advantages – more information, verification – and also accumulated a reserve of genuine friendship, which proved enormously valuable when he returned to Croatia in 1945. Conversely, in the absence of Partisan goodwill, the task of intelligence gathering was virtually impossible, as Reed's experiences in Istria and Slovenia demonstrated all too clearly. In neither region was there any scope for him to improve working relations, for the Partisan formations to which he was attached had almost certainly been ordered to reduce their collaboration with British and American intelligence to an absolute minimum.

In the abrupt collapse of Britain's alliance with the Partisans may be identified one concluding lesson, which remains relevant today. When powerful countries involve themselves in the internal affairs of weaker ones there must always be a tendency for different factions in the weaker countries to exploit foreign intervention to further their particular ambitions. And it will always be extremely difficult for foreign powers to prevent them from doing so. The territory which became Yugoslavia after the First World War has been contested by rival empires for centuries. For countless generations of southern Slavs, survival itself has often rested on their capacity to manipulate the foreign armies which have so frequently marched across their soil. In recent years, resurgent nationalist movements in Slovenia, Croatia, Bosnia and Kosovo revived this honourable tradition by seeking Western support for their objectives, while Serb nationalists looked to their old ally, Russia, to represent their interests in the international arena.

During the Second World War both the Partisans and the Chetniks sought to exploit Allied intervention for their own benefit, while the Ustase used the Axis occupation to further the cause of Croat nationalism. In the competition for Western patronage, Tito ultimately triumphed over Mihailovic because the location of his movement in north-western Yugoslavia and his policy of active resistance accorded with British and

American strategic objectives in the Mediterranean. This ostensible confluence of interests caused the British, SIS included, to assume that they could ally themselves with the Partisans in the pursuit of one common goal – the defeat of Hitler's Germany – and this simplistic belief lay behind the naïve enthusiasm, optimism and idealism displayed by some SIS officers in 1943, and in the first half of 1944. Hence they were deeply disillusioned when the Partisans turned against the Western powers in the closing months of the War, apparently espousing an authoritarian communist creed under Moscow's direction.

It is entirely understandable that SIS should then have concluded that Tito's movement represented the vanguard of European communism and Soviet expansionism, and that officers like Reed, sharing this mistaken view, returned to Britain in 1945 with feelings of disappointment and futility. They were by no means alone in their assumption that Tito's Yugoslavia was merely a Soviet satellite. Yet, in the light of Tito's break with Stalin only three years later, it may be suggested that such negative reflections were somewhat premature. Certainly, the close bond established between the West and the Partisans during the War – a bond created first and foremost by Allied officers in the field – facilitated the post-war rapprochement.[14] As one leading Yugoslav official said in 1949:

> During the War the Partisan leaders had come to know the British and Americans who had parachuted to them and who had shared in their fighting against the Axis... They had learnt from these Allied officers for the first time about the West, its people, and its institutions... These wartime discussions with British and American officers, he said, had also been a factor in their decision to resist Moscow.[15]

Yugoslavia remained subject to authoritarian government, but was at least given the confidence to cast off the Soviet yoke.

At the end of the War Owen Reed returned to the family life he loved and missed so much, and to the BBC. In one sense his broadcasting career followed a similar pattern to his wartime work in Yugoslavia, in that his achievements were always exceptional when he was given sufficient scope and opportunity to achieve. He rose rapidly to the top of Children's Television, and became a very successful departmental head. Adapting to the advent of mass television broadcasting in the 1960s was difficult for anyone schooled in the philosophies of Lord Reith, and Reed was no exception. But he successfully weathered a storm which drove many of his contemporaries out of the Corporation altogether. His saviour was Frank Gillard, for whom he had worked in Cairo early in 1943.[16]

For many years Reed spoke little of the War, nor did he write his own account of the events described in this book; the man remembered by Sir

William Deakin as 'one of the very best officers we had in the field'[17] was far too modest to believe that anyone would be interested in reading his story. But in later life he returned to the subject more often, particularly after the discovery in the National Archives of documents relating to his service with SIS, and he came to take a more positive view of his achievements in support of the Allied and Partisan causes than he had held in 1945. During the War he had of course lacked both the power and the remit to exert any influence on Yugoslavia's post-war government, but his later intelligence reports repeatedly insisted that many Croats did not favour a communist or federal system. So he was immensely saddened but not surprised by Yugoslavia's descent into civil war in the early 1990s. 'They are such marvellous people', he once said of the Yugoslavs:

> but they are consumed by a ferocious hatred of one another. My greatest hope was that one day, if they got the government they wanted instead of one that was imposed on them, they might be able to live together in peace. They certainly deserve it.[18]

It was a laudable hope, and a sincere one – the considered reflection of a man who once earnestly believed he was assisting them in their struggle for freedom, but who had later to endure the anguish of seeing their country pass from one form of dictatorship to another. It can only be hoped that current aspirations for stability, democracy and peace in the region are built on firmer foundations.

NOTES

1. RP, Reed interviewed by J. Lane, 'Oral History of the BBC'.
2. Hinsley *et al.*, *British Intelligence in the Second World War*, vol. 1, pp. 369–71; Hinsley *et al.*, *British Intelligence in the Second World War*, vol. 3, pt 1, p. 144.
3. This is the central thesis in both Lees, *The Rape of Serbia*, and Martin, *The Web of Disinformation*. See also Vukevich, *Diverse Forces in Yugoslavia, 1941–1945*.
4. Lindsay, *Beacons in the Night*, p. 341; Hinsley *et al.*, *British Intelligence in the Second World War*, vol. 3, pt 1, pp. 149–50, 153–6.
5. *Ibid.*
6. West, *MI6*, pp. 158–61.
7. Hinsley, *et al.*, *British Intelligence in the Second World War*, vol. 1, p. 278; Hinsley *et al.*, *British Intelligence in the Second World War*, vol. 3, pt 1, pp. 462–3.
8. Hinsley *et al.*, *British Intelligence in the Second World War*, vol. 3, pt 1, pp. 462–3; Wilkinson, *Foreign Fields*, pp. 132–7. On Maclean's difficulties with SOE in Cairo see FO 371/37612, record by Maclean of a meeting with Lord

Glenconner on 2 August 1943; FO 371/37611, Minister of State Cairo to Foreign Office, 31 August 1943.

9. AHB file IIJ1/130, History of the Balkan Air Force, p. 76.

10. The documents disclose clearly how reports from the field were continuously fused with both signals intelligence and aerial reconnaissance imagery before their incorporation into broader Allied intelligence appraisals. See WO 202/513, Military Report on Slovenia and Western Croatia by Lieutenant-Colonel P.N.M. Moore, RE, compiled at HQ Croatia on 23 January 1944; AIR 51/263 contains numerous comments on SIS reports by HQ Mediterranean Allied Photographic Reconnaissance Wing.

11. West, *MI6*, p. 384.

12. *Ibid.*, pp. 80–1. According to West, SIS did not maintain a station in Moscow between the wars; to collect intelligence on the Soviet Union they relied on stations in adjacent countries. It is said to have been customary for individual stations to gather information on their neighbours to avoid incurring the displeasure of their hosts.

13. Lindsay, *Beacons in the Night*, pp. 49, 361.

14. *Ibid.*, pp. 331–2, 336–9; Wilkinson, *Foreign Fields*, pp. 210–11. In the American case, Franklin Lindsay, who had been parachuted into Slovenia in the Second World War, was made responsible for strengthening Yugoslavia's ability to remain independent of Moscow after 1948. Over the next ten years the USA provided more than one billion dollars of military and economic assistance to Yugoslavia, while Britain also supplied considerable quantities of aid.

15. Franc Primozic, Yugoslav minister in Washington, quoted in Lindsay, *Beacons in the Night*, p. 339.

16. RP, Reed interviewed by J. Lane, 'Oral History of the BBC'. Gillard helped to engineer Reed's transfer from children's television to training.

17. In conversation with the author, August 1998.

18. In conversation with the author, July 1995.

Bibliography

MANUSCRIPT AND ORIGINAL SOURCES

Records held in public depositories

National Archives, Kew (class numbers only; piece numbers are cited in the endnotes)

AIR 20: Air Ministry, and Ministry of Defence: Air Historical Branch: Unregistered Papers.

AIR 23: Air Ministry and Ministry of Defence: Royal Air Force Overseas Commands: Reports and Correspondence.

AIR 27: Air Ministry and successors: Operations Record Books, Squadrons.

AIR 40: Air Ministry, Directorate of Intelligence and related bodies: Intelligence Reports and Papers.

AIR 51: Mediterranean Allied Air Forces: Microfilmed Files.

BW 66: British Council: Registered Files, Yugoslavia.

CAB 101: War Cabinet and Cabinet Office: Historical Section: War Histories (Second World War), Military.

CAB 121. Cabinet Office: Special Secret Information Centre.

FO 366. Foreign Office and Diplomatic Service Administration Office: Chief Clerk's Department and successors: Records.

FO 369. Foreign Office: Consular Department: General Correspondence from 1906.

FO 371. Foreign Office: Political Departments: General Correspondence from 1906.

FO 536. Foreign Office: Embassy and Legation, Yugoslavia (Formerly Croatia, Serbia and Slovenia): General Correspondence.

HS 3. Special Operations Executive: Africa and Middle East Group: Registered Files.

HS 4. Special Operations Executive: Eastern Europe: Registered Files.

HS 5. Special Operations Executive: Balkans: Registered Files.

HS 6. Special Operations Executive: Western Europe: Registered Files.

HW 1. General records of the Government Code and Cypher School and Government Communications Headquarters.

PREM 3. Prime Minister's Office: Operational Correspondence and Papers.

WO 106. War Office: Directorate of Military Operations and Military Intelligence, and predecessors: Correspondence and Papers.

WO 169. War Office: British Forces, Middle East: War Diaries, Second World War.

WO 201. War Office: Middle East Forces; Military Headquarters Papers, Second World War.

WO 202. War Office: British Military Missions in Liaison with Allied Forces; Military Headquarters Papers, Second World War.

WO 204. War Office: Allied Forces, Mediterranean Theatre: Military Headquarters Papers, Second World War.

WO 208. War Office: Directorate of Military Operations and Intelligence, and Directorate of Military Intelligence; Ministry of Defence, Defence Intelligence Staff: Files.

Commonwealth War Graves Commission
Commonwealth War Graves Commission Debt of Honour Register.

Imperial War Museum
The papers of Kenneth Syers.
Photographic archive.

Other depositories

Air Historical Branch (RAF), Ministry of Defence
Class II (official narratives).
MAAF Weekly Summaries.
Photographic archive.
Squadron histories.
Yugoslavia basic handbook, 1943.

BBC Written Archives Centre, Caversham
File R13: records of the BBC's Cairo office, 1939-45.

Private sources

Author's correspondence with Michael Gold, Paul Stichman's grandson.
Author's interview with Owen Reed, 4 November 1989.
The private papers of Owen Reed.

Books and Articles

Auty, P. and Clogg, R. (eds), *British Policy towards Wartime Resistance in Yugoslavia and Greece* (New York: Macmillan, 1975).

Barker, E., *British Policy in South-East Europe in the Second World War* (London: Victor Gollancz, 1980).

Boyle, A., *The Fourth Man* (New York: Dial Press, 1979).

Cave Brown, A., *'C': The Secret Life of Sir Stewart Menzies, Spymaster to Winston Churchill* (New York: Macmillan, 1987).

Cooper, A., *Cairo in the War, 1939–1945* (London: Penguin, 1994).

Cox, G., *The Race for Trieste* (London: William Kimber, 1977).

Deakin, F.W.D., *The Embattled Mountain* (Oxford: Oxford University Press, 1971).

Deakin, F.W.D., Barker, E. and Chadwick, J., *British Political and Military Strategy in Central, Eastern and Southern Europe in 1944* (New York: St Martin's Press, 1988).

Deroc, M., *British Special Operations Explored: Yugoslavia in Turmoil 1941–1943 and the British Response* (Boulder, CO: East European Monographs/distributed by New York: Columbia University Press, 1988).

Ehrman, J., *Grand Strategy*, vol. 5, *August 1943–September 1944* (London: HMSO, 1956).

—, *Grand Strategy*, vol. 6, *October 1944–August 1945* (London: HMSO, 1956).

Foot, M.R.D., *SOE – The Special Operations Executive, 1940–46* (London: BBC, 1984).

Ford, K., Jr, *OSS and the Yugoslav Resistance, 1943–1945* (College Station, TX: Texas A&M University Press, 1992).

Gilbert, M., *Winston S. Churchill*, vol. 7, *Road to Victory, 1941–1945* (London: Heinemann, 1986).

Hinsley, F.H., and Simkins, C.A.G., *British Intelligence in the Second World War*, vol. 4 (London: HMSO, 1990).

Hinsley, F.H., with Thomas, E.E., Ransom, C.F.G. and Knight, R.C., *British Intelligence in the Second World War*, vol. 1 (London: HMSO, 1979).

—, *British Intelligence in the Second World War*, vol. 2 (London: HMSO, 1981).

—, *British Intelligence in the Second World War*, vol. 3, pt 1 (London: HMSO, 1985).

Howard, M., *British Intelligence in the Second World War*, vol. 5 (London: HMSO, 1990).

Lane, A., *Britain, the Cold War and Yugoslav Unity: 1941–1949* (Brighton: Sussex Academic Press, 1996).

Lees, M., *The Rape of Serbia: The British Role in Tito's Grab for Power 1943–1944* (San Diego/New York/London: Harcourt Brace Jovanovich, 1990).

Lindsay, F., *Beacons in the Night: With the OSS and Tito's Partisans in Wartime Yugoslavia* (Stanford, CA: Stanford University Press, 1993).

Maclean, F. *Eastern Approaches* (London: Reprint Society, 1949).

Martin, D., *The Web of Disinformation: Churchill's Yugoslav Blunder* (San Diego/New York/London: Harcourt Brace Jovanovich, 1990).

McConville, M., *A Small War in the Balkans: British Military Involvement in Wartime Yugoslavia, 1941–1945* (London: Macmillan, 1987).

Millar, G., *Horned Pigeon* (London: Pan, 1970).

—, *Road to Resistance: An Autobiography* (London: The Bodley Head, 1979).

Pitt, B., *The Crucible of War: Year of Alamein, 1942* (London: Jonathan Cape, 1982).

Roberts, W., *Tito, Mihailovic, and the Allies, 1941–1945* (New Brunswick, NJ: Rutgers University Press, 1973).

Rogers, L., *Guerilla Surgeon* (London: Collins, 1957).

Smith M. and Erskine, R. (eds.), *Action This Day: Bletchley Park from the breaking of the Enigma Code to the Birth of the Modern Computer* (London: Bantam Press, 2001).

Stafford, D., *Britain and European Resistance 1940-1945* (London: Macmillan, 1980).

—, *Churchill and Secret Service* (Woodstock/New York: Overlook Press, 1999).

Sweet-Escott, B., *Baker Street Irregular* (London: Methuen, 1965).

Tanner, M., *Croatia: A Nation Forged in War* (New Haven, CT/London: Yale University Press, 1997).

Trew, S., *Britain, Mihailovic and the Chetniks, 1941-42* (London: Macmillan, 1998).

Vukervich, *Diverse Forces in Yugoslavia 1941–1945* (Los Angeles, CA: Author Unlimited, 1990).

West, N., *MI6: British Secret Intelligence Service Operations, 1909–1945,* (London: Grafton, 1985).

Wheeler, M. C., *Britain and the War for Yugoslavia, 1940–1943* (Boulder, CO: East European Monographs/distributed by New York: Columbia University Press, 1980).

Whittam, J.R., 'Drawing the Line: Britain and the Emergence of the Trieste Question, January 1941–May 1945', *English Historical Review* (April 1991), pp. 360–2.

Wilkinson, P., *Foreign Fields: The Story of an SOE Operative* (London: I.B. Taurus, 1997).

Index

Made in the USA
Middletown, DE
06 April 2021